A Practical Guide to

Information Systems Strategic Planning

Second Edition

OTHER AUERBACH PUBLICATIONS

Agent-Based Manufacturing and Control Systems: New Agile Manufacturing Solutions for Achieving Peak Performance
Massimo Paolucci and Roberto Sacile
ISBN: 1574443364

Curing the Patch Management Headache
Felicia M. Nicastro
ISBN: 0849328543

Cyber Crime Investigator's Field Guide, Second Edition
Bruce Middleton
ISBN: 0849327687

Disassembly Modeling for Assembly, Maintenance, Reuse and Recycling
A. J. D. Lambert and Surendra M. Gupta
ISBN: 1574443348

The Ethical Hack: A Framework for Business Value Penetration Testing
James S. Tiller
ISBN: 084931609X

Fundamentals of DSL Technology
Philip Golden, Herve Dedieu,
and Krista Jacobsen
ISBN: 0849319137

The HIPAA Program Reference Handbook
Ross Leo
ISBN: 0849322111

Implementing the IT Balanced Scorecard: Aligning IT with Corporate Strategy
Jessica Keyes
ISBN: 0849326214

Information Security Fundamentals
Thomas R. Peltier, Justin Peltier,
and John A. Blackley
ISBN: 0849319579

Information Security Management Handbook, Fifth Edition, Volume 2
Harold F. Tipton and Micki Krause
ISBN: 0849332109

Introduction to Management of Reverse Logistics and Closed Loop Supply Chain Processes
Donald F. Blumberg
ISBN: 1574443607

Maximizing ROI on Software Development
Vijay Sikka
ISBN: 0849323126

Mobile Computing Handbook
Imad Mahgoub and Mohammad Ilyas
ISBN: 0849319714

MPLS for Metropolitan Area Networks
Nam-Kee Tan
ISBN: 084932212X

Multimedia Security Handbook
Borko Furht and Darko Kirovski
ISBN: 0849327733

Network Design: Management and Technical Perspectives, Second Edition
Teresa C. Piliouras
ISBN: 0849316081

Network Security Technologies, Second Edition
Kwok T. Fung
ISBN: 0849330270

Outsourcing Software Development Offshore: Making It Work
Tandy Gold
ISBN: 0849319439

Quality Management Systems: A Handbook for Product Development Organizations
Vivek Nanda
ISBN: 1574443526

A Practical Guide to Security Assessments
Sudhanshu Kairab
ISBN: 0849317061

The Real-Time Enterprise
Dimitris N. Chorafas
ISBN: 0849327776

Software Testing and Continuous Quality Improvement, Second Edition
William E. Lewis
ISBN: 0849325242

Supply Chain Architecture: A Blueprint for Networking the Flow of Material, Information, and Cash
William T. Walker
ISBN: 1574443577

The Windows Serial Port Programming Handbook
Ying Bai
ISBN: 0849322138

AUERBACH PUBLICATIONS

www.auerbach-publications.com
To Order Call: 1-800-272-7737 • Fax: 1-800-374-3401
E-mail: orders@crcpress.com

A Practical Guide to

Information Systems Strategic Planning

Second Edition

By
Anita Cassidy

Auerbach Publications
Taylor & Francis Group
Boca Raton   New York

Published in 2006 by
Auerbach Publications
Taylor & Francis Group
6000 Broken Sound Parkway NW, Suite 300
Boca Raton, FL 33487-2742

© 2006 by Taylor & Francis Group, LLC
Auerbach is an imprint of Taylor & Francis Group

No claim to original U.S. Government works
Printed in the United States of America on acid-free paper
10 9 8 7 6 5 4 3 2

International Standard Book Number-10: 0-8493-5073-5 (Hardcover)
International Standard Book Number-13: 978-0-8493-5073-3 (Hardcover)
Library of Congress Card Number 2005050533

Library of Congress Cataloging-in-Publication Data

Cassidy, Anita.
    A practical guide to information systems strategic planning / Anita Cassidy.-- 2nd ed.
        p. cm.
    Includes bibliographical references and index.
    ISBN 0-8493-5073-5 (alk. paper)
    1. Information technology--Management--Planning. 2. Strategic planning. I. Title.

HD30.2.C395 2005
658.4'038--dc22
                                    2005050533

Taylor & Francis Group
is the Academic Division of T&F Informa plc.

**Visit the Taylor & Francis Web site at
http://www.taylorandfrancis.com**

**and the Auerbach Publications Web site at
http://www.auerbach-publications.com**

Contents

Preface

The second revision of this book reflects the continual changes and advances in technology, and provides improvements and additional detail in the planning methodology. The process outlined in this book has been enhanced from lessons learned by using the methodology in various companies, cultures, and environments. Additional details, examples, and templates are included to help guide your planning process.

Many organizations today continue to experience increasing information systems (IS) costs. In addition to increasing costs, organizations are finding their IS to be a bottleneck to business improvements and growth. These organizations are assessing their IS and asking basic yet tough questions, such as:

- Are we obtaining true value from the investments in IS?
- Are the current IS applications meeting the business needs?
- Are we working on the right IS projects to provide the most value to the business?
- Will our current applications meet business requirements in the future?
- What IS mission, objectives, strategies and computing architectures are necessary to meet the business challenges of the future?

Old business application software is hampering many companies' ability to implement new technology. Many organizations are ready to invest in new technology to gain a competitive edge in the marketplace, or may even find improvements necessary to stay in business. Organizations will continue to invest more in new IS hardware and software than they have in the past. Today, there are more options, packages, and directions available to choose from than in the past, making a planned direction more important than ever. Many industry examples show that companies that have gained a competitive edge have effectively invested in IS initiatives. A properly planned IS direction is a critical component for an organization's success.

Following the process outlined in this book will improve communication between business management and the IS function. Often, business management does not have a good understanding of the IS function and might have questions such as:

- What is our current IS environment? What computers and software do we use to manage the business? What is the condition of our IS environment? What are the strengths, weaknesses, and areas of vulnerability of our IS environment? Do the IS and associated processes help us facilitate the delivery of services and products to our customers in the most cost-efficient and effective manner?
- How can we make the best decisions about our IS investments? What should be our investment priorities?
- What is our IS resources currently working on? How do the IS employees spend their time? How does the size of our IS organization compare with the industry?
- How much money is the company spending on IS? How does our IS spending compare to the industry? How much has the spending grown over the past few years? We have been doing well without substantially increasing spending, so why do we need to spend more now? How can we decrease our spending on IS, or spend our money more wisely?
- What are the industry technology trends, and how do the industry trends affect us?
- What is the status of our competitors' IS? Is our company behind or ahead of our competitors?
- Do we have the internal skills necessary to take the environment where it needs to be? How much can we do with internal resources, and how much should we utilize external resources? Why does it take so long to get things done?

Similarly, IS management may not have a thorough understanding of the business direction and might have questions such as:

- What are the business mission, objectives, and strategies?
- What type of business will the company be in during the next few years?
- How does the business want to function in the future?
- What are the true business requirements and priorities?

- What are the key information needs?
- What are our customers and suppliers demanding of us?
- Are there any IS issues constraining the business?

An effective IS strategic planning process can answer all these questions and provide a communication vehicle between the IS function and business management.

The foundation of the process outlined in this book is that the business direction and business requirements must drive the IS direction and computing architecture. Although this sounds like a basic concept, many organizations will actually reverse the concept and let the attractive new technology drive their direction. In actuality, these organizations end up looking for a business problem to solve with the technology they want to utilize. This book will outline a systematic approach to guide you through the process of developing a solid IS plan that is formulated from the business plan. Even if your organization lacks a defined business plan, the approach in this book steps you through a fact-gathering process to obtain the necessary information regarding the business direction.

Although IS planning is critical, many organizations spend too much time and money in the planning process, complete the plan in isolation, or skip the planning process altogether. This can result in overanalysis, an inability to obtain approval of the plan, or the spending of millions of dollars solving the wrong problem. Many companies mistake a proper IS strategic planning process as something that must take many months (or even years) and thousands (or even millions) of dollars. However, with a solid process and methodology in place, you can complete the planning process with your own internal resources in a matter of weeks or a few months.

This book will outline a quick and easy approach to completing a thorough plan. It will also provide a set of concepts, techniques, and templates for analyzing, organizing, and communicating the information in the IS strategic plan. The process described will assist the organization with a collaborative effort that will result in a solid direction that has the support of the entire organization. Through the process, you will have a plan that will sell itself to management and others who need to approve the necessary investment.

The book provides a step-by-step process for developing a strategic plan. Modify the process to fit your particular needs, organization, and culture. The following explains the organization of the book:

- The first chapter of the book provides background to the purpose of an IS strategic plan.
- Chapter 2 discusses a framework for the governance process that must be the foundation of the strategic planning process.

- The third chapter provides an overview of the four phases of the planning process.
- Chapter 4 through 7 review each of the four phases of the planning process, including visioning, analysis, direction, and recommendation.
- Chapter 8 outlines what to do next and how to make planning an ongoing process.

This book is intended for both IS executives and consultants as well as business executives interested in improving their IS environment and utilizing IS as a competitive advantage. If your IS function is an integral part of the business and well connected with the business plans and direction, portions of this planning process will go quickly. For companies without a solid business plan or companies without aligned IS, the process will outline a systematic approach to determining and documenting the business direction so that it can be the foundation for the IS direction. Although this book presents developing an IS strategy as a formal project, CIOs may choose to handle much of what is included as part of their everyday organizational listening and ongoing planning process.

This book references information systems (IS) as the name of the function that provides computer-based business applications and technology for the organization as well as the technology itself. In some companies, this organization may be referred to as information technology (IT), information services (IS), information resources (IR), or similar names.

I sincerely hope this book helps you in your journey to world-class IS. Good luck on your planning process!

Acknowledgments

Without the support of my family and friends, this book would not have been possible.

First, I would like to thank my husband Dan for his assistance on this book. With Dan's 28 years of experience in IS, his insight and comments have been of tremendous value in writing this book. His continual support, understanding, patience, and encouragement are astounding. I would also like to thank my sons, Mike and Ryan, for giving me something to worry about, think about, and focus on besides this book. As they enter college and choose a profession, I hope that they are fortunate enough to land in a career that is their true passion. Of course, my mother, Randie Ekenberg, continues to be an inspiration, providing love and support. Thanks also goes to my friend Stephanie Renslow for keeping me on target by periodically asking "Are you done yet?"

I would also like to thank all those with whom I have worked during the years from both the business and IS areas. They have given me continuous support and ideas as I have developed the strategic planning process presented in this book. In particular, I would like to thank several colleagues who have spent countless hours reviewing and providing input into this book, including Ruth Dessel, Barb Zimmerman, Bob Lewis, Dan Christian, and Keith Guggenberger. This book would not have been possible without their expert insight and input. I would also like to thank my clients the past eight years, because they have allowed me to do what I really love doing.

About the Author

Anita Cassidy has over 27 years of experience in IS. She has served as director, vice president, and CIO at worldwide manufacturing companies. For the past seven years, Cassidy has been founder and CEO of a consulting organization, Strategic Computing Directions Inc., in Minneapolis, Minnesota. Strategic Computing Directions (http:// www.strategiccomputing.com) specializes in executive IS management consulting in the areas of:

- Strategic planning
- IS assessment
- E-business strategy
- Interim and advisory CIO
- IS process improvement
- Software selection

Cassidy has personally completed over 40 IS strategic plans and assessments for companies of all sizes and in a variety of industries. She has published articles in national magazines, is a writer for a technology research company, and is a national speaker on IS strategic planning. In addition to *A Practical Guide to Information Systems Strategic Planning*, Cassidy has authored the following books, published by St. Lucie Press:

- *A Practical Guide to Information Systems Process Improvement* (2000), with Keith Guggenberger
- *A Practical Guide to Planning for E-Business Success* (2002)

Cassidy has a BS degree from the University of Minnesota and also attended St. Cloud State University. She can be reached at: acassidy@strategiccomputing.com.

Chapter 1

Purpose of Information Systems Strategic Planning

He who is outside his door already has a hard part of his journey behind him.

— Dutch proverb

The word "strategy" is often misused. In some circles, it is synonymous with "important." In this book, "strategy" refers to a global level of thinking about the information systems (IS) organization and its integration with the rest of the enterprise. A strategy must be coherent, consistent, and directional. *Coherent* means it is clear to both the business and IS organization. *Consistent* means that it is constructed to fit together. *Directional* means it directs changes of some kind. Strategies do not merely endorse the status quo.

A strategic plan is more than a statement of strategy. Although it might seem obvious that merely stating strategy is not enough, many strategies stop with a statement of intent. This book is about the strategic planning process, about defining strategic intent and then developing a plan of action for achieving the envisioned changes. Often, the strategic planning effort results in a book on the shelf. To be effective, implement strategic planning as an ongoing process to ensure it keeps current as business and technology changes.

Why do we need to complete strategic planning for the IS function? What is the purpose of the planning process? The planning process enables IS to help the organization meet its business objectives. The IS strategic planning process may be initiated in an organization for a variety of reasons. Some examples include:

- A recently acquired company initiated the planning process to determine how to meld the systems and processes of two previously separate organizations. Business management viewed the application systems and processes as critical vehicles for providing customers with a common face for the new organization. In addition, executive management wanted to obtain consistent information to manage the newly merged company as one organization. The new business also saw an opportunity to leverage synergies and reduce overhead costs of the previously separate organizations.

- A small and growing company was experiencing severe quality problems and found that the company was losing its competitive edge in the marketplace. In the past, the company had very favorable statistics and key indicators (such as sales, inventory turns, days sales outstanding, and profits) relative to the competition. The company was gradually falling behind the industry as sales and profits were on a downward trend. Management viewed IS applications as a major roadblock to improving the quality, business processes, and key measurements. Executive management initiated the planning process to review the business application systems available on the market to determine the best direction.

- A newly hired vice president of IS in a government agency initiated a strategic planning process to assess the current IS situation. The planning process gave the new leader an opportunity to provide input into the direction and create a vision of IS for the future.

- In another company, the business departments were frustrated with the response of IS. The departments did not feel that the IS department was responsive to the business. Response for any changes requested by the business was extremely slow. The business applications simply could not keep pace with the changes in the business. Management initiated the strategic planning process to determine the cause of the problems, to link IS closer to the business direction, and to determine the proper solution.

- A manufacturing division of a large worldwide organization was under pressure to implement a particular vendor-supplied application package selected by the corporate division of the company. The manufacturing division was not directly involved in the selection of the software and felt the package would probably not be the best fit for the unique business requirements of the division. Divisional executive management initiated the IS strategic planning process to determine the best solution rather than simply following the desired corporate direction.

- One company faced the common problem of a growing and endless backlog of IS projects. This company began the IS strategic planning process to prioritize the projects and align the IS priorities with the business priorities. The IS department also wanted to determine if it should continue to build upon and invest in the current systems or start over with a new set of business applications.

- A company faced the unpleasant task of downsizing. Executive management initiated the IS strategic planning process to determine ways to reduce costs and gain efficiencies. Management wanted to evaluate the possibility of leveraging or consolidating multiple data centers and differing business applications to reduce costs while still meeting the business needs.

- A high-growth company restructured its business to operate on a worldwide basis. Previously, the company functioned on a geographic basis from both a business accountability standpoint as well as having unique IS in each geographic area. Management began the IS planning process to determine how to bring the information together so that it could manage the new worldwide business.

- An organization had completed a business planning process to determine and document its business vision, mission, and objectives. Management began the IS strategic planning process to develop an IS strategy and direction aligned with the organization's newly stated business direction.

- A company let its IS grow over time without a plan in place. After many years, the firm had high IS costs, redundant systems, and systems that were very slow and costly to change. It initiated the strategic planning process to obtain a complete inventory and understand its current environment. The company used the planning process to identify redundant systems, identify opportunities to reduce its total cost of ownership, and identify opportunities to improve its ability to respond to business changes in a timely manner.

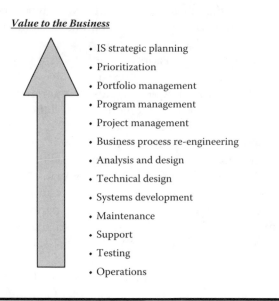

Value to the Business

- IS strategic planning
- Prioritization
- Portfolio management
- Program management
- Project management
- Business process re-engineering
- Analysis and design
- Technical design
- Systems development
- Maintenance
- Support
- Testing
- Operations

Figure 1.1   IS responsibilities

Benefits of IS Planning

Although the reasons driving the development of an IS strategic plan may be different, there are similarities in the benefits of a plan. There is more value and benefit in the strategic planning function than many other IS responsibilities, as shown in Figure 1.1. The benefits of IS strategic plans include:

- Effective management of an expensive and critical asset of the organization
- Improving communication and the relationship between the business and IS organization
- Aligning the IS direction and priorities to the business direction and priorities
- Identifying opportunities to use technology for a competitive advantage and increase the value to the business
- Planning the flow of information and processes
- Efficiently and effectively allocating IS resources
- Reducing the effort and money required throughout the life cycle of systems

Each of these benefits is discussed in more detail below.

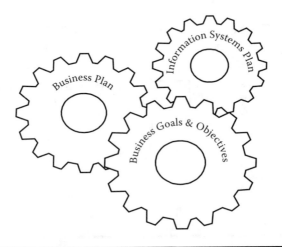

Figure 1.2   IS plan critical for the business

Effective Management of an Expensive and Critical Asset to the Organization

A strategic plan is a key component to the success of any IS function and an important factor in assisting a company in meeting its business objectives, as shown in Figure 1.2. However, business management may view IS as a necessary evil rather than as a critical business function. Many times this is because business management does not understand the function and there is a lack of communication. IS may be slow to change, hampering the business, or out of line with the business direction. If this is happening in an organization, it may even be difficult for the IS department to schedule time with executive management for a presentation. Why should management take the time to understand IS if it is not in touch with the business? Management may not even realize the potential benefits and opportunities that IS can offer to help meet business objectives.

For any company, IS are an expensive asset. If the company invested the same amount of money in a building, each member of management would know the location, age, and purpose of the building. Many companies spend more money on their IS, yet business management may not know as much about their systems as they do about their building! Similarly, a manufacturing company always knows the unit cost of the products manufactured and the drivers of the costs, and understands how to manage the costs.

Does management know how much money the company is spending on IS? Do managers realize how much each business application is costing

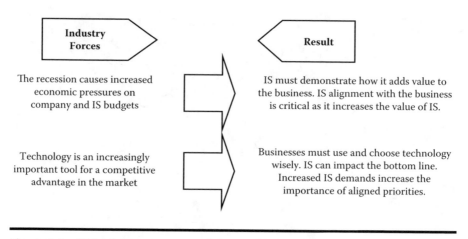

Figure 1.3 IS budget pressures and demand increases

and if they are worth maintaining? Do they know the cost per e-mail, the cost per help desk call, and the cost per server? What is the company really getting for its investment, and will the systems meet the company's needs in the future? Do managers know the level of service quality and responsiveness that IS delivers? Do they know how to manage IS costs through demand planning, capacity and resource planning, and monitoring as they would any other asset? Management must have a clear understanding of the IS environment to manage this asset as effectively as it would any other business asset.

Budget pressures are common in many companies. Continually doing more with less money is a common challenge faced by IS management. However, as the IS budget is squeezed, the business appetite for new technology and improved business processes increases, as shown in Figure 1.3. The IS planning process is a tool to balance these conflicting forces.

Through the planning process, the organization can proactively balance conflicting forces and manage the direction of IS rather than continually building upon the current IS investment in a reactionary mode. As a result, IS will be in a position to support the growing requirements and strategic direction of the business in the most cost-effective manner.

Improving Communication and the Relationship between the Business and IS Organization

Following this IS planning process will significantly improve communication between business management and the IS department. Business management will obtain an excellent understanding of current IS, as well as learn how to identify risks and opportunities. The IS organization will gain a greater understanding of the business direction and be able to identify how technology can assist with the company's objectives. The mutual understanding that business management and IS will gain working through this process will help establish a solid direction for IS that is in alignment with the business goals, and it will assist in the approval process necessary to get the new direction sold throughout the organization. By improving communication and aligning IS, the environment can significantly improve so that the business perceives IS as a critical component to achieving company objectives.

Aligning the IS Direction and Priorities to the Business Direction and Priorities

Over the past few years, companies have felt increasing pressure to improve efficiency and effectiveness, decrease costs, and enhance competitive position. Companies can attain these goals through aligning the IS direction with the business direction. Proper alignment can have a considerable impact on a company's financial performance. Although much is written about aligning IS with the business, companies still struggle to achieve effective alignment. In fact, in many surveys, alignment is often cited as the top management concern. What is alignment? How do you achieve alignment?

When all IS activities provide optimal support for the business goals, objectives, and strategies, then IS and the business are in alignment. True alignment implies that the IS strategy and the business strategy are developed concurrently rather than sequentially so that technology enables the business strategy. It is important to embed the IS strategy within the business strategy, rather than developing it as an afterthought. Alignment is not just "lip service." Companies should integrate IS with the business in a symbiotic relationship. As shown in Figure 1.4 and Figure 1.5, the IS strategy, organization, processes, infrastructure, applications, projects, budget, and metrics should reflect alignment with the business. As Figure 1.6 indicates, alignment and distinct correlations should be visible when reviewing each section of a company's business plan and IS plan. All of the IS components should have the same objectives and direction as the business.

It is easy to identify organizations that have not achieved alignment. Symptoms of poor alignment include:

- Canceled projects
- Redundant projects

Figure 1.4   Alignment components

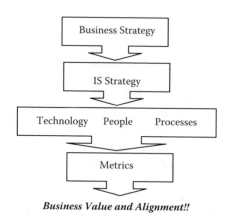

Figure 1.5   Business value and alignment

- Projects that do not deliver the intended value
- Lack of coordination between the business and IS
- Systems that do not meet the needs of the business
- Systems that cannot respond quickly to the demands of the business
- Business users unsatisfied with IS services

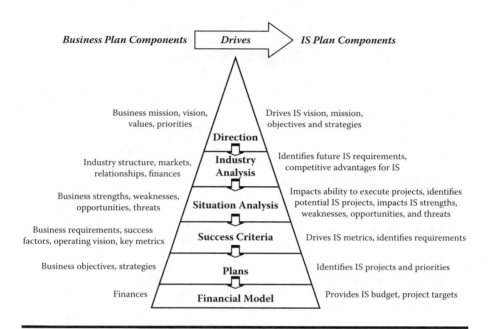

Figure 1.6   Business and IS plan alignment

- Reactive, constant fire fighting
- Never enough resources; fighting for resources
- Churning of priorities; slow progress
- Uninvolved business management
- High IS costs with a sense of low value
- Systems and tools not fully utilized
- Lack of integration of systems
- IS decisions made as a result of emotion or opinions

As shown in Figure 1.7, planning can align these organizations and totally transform them.

In organizations where IS align with the business, different business strategies result in unique IS strategies and priorities, as shown by the examples in Figure 1.8. With alignment, IS can strengthen the business value proposition. In their book *The Discipline of Market Leaders* (Addison-Wesley, 1995),[1] Tracey and Wiersema outlined three alternative business value propositions. As shown in Figure 1.9, they contend that successful market leaders focus on one of the following value propositions: operational excellence, customer intimacy, or product leadership. Each of these value propositions results in very different IS focus and priorities, as outlined below.

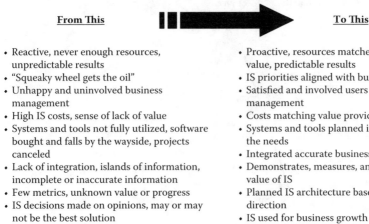

With Planning, Companies Transform IS

From This		To This

- Reactive, never enough resources, unpredictable results
- "Squeaky wheel gets the oil"
- Unhappy and uninvolved business management
- High IS costs, sense of lack of value
- Systems and tools not fully utilized, software bought and falls by the wayside, projects canceled
- Lack of integration, islands of information, incomplete or inaccurate information
- Few metrics, unknown value or progress
- IS decisions made on opinions, may or may not be the best solution
- IS used for efficiency
- IS separate from the business
- IS viewed as an expense to control
- IS viewed as technical resources

- Proactive, resources matched to business value, predictable results
- IS priorities aligned with business priorities
- Satisfied and involved users and business management
- Costs matching value provided
- Systems and tools planned in advance to meet the needs
- Integrated accurate business information
- Demonstrates, measures, and increases the value of IS
- Planned IS architecture based on the business direction
- IS used for business growth
- IS inseparable from the business
- IS viewed as an asset to manage
- IS viewed as business problem solvers

Figure 1.7   Planning transformation

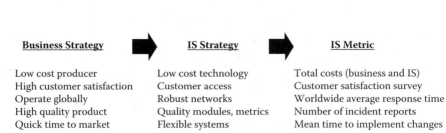

Business Strategy	IS Strategy	IS Metric
Low cost producer	Low cost technology	Total costs (business and IS)
High customer satisfaction	Customer access	Customer satisfaction survey
Operate globally	Robust networks	Worldwide average response time
High quality product	Quality modules, metrics	Number of incident reports
Quick time to market	Flexible systems	Mean time to implement changes

Figure 1.8   Different business and IS strategies

Operational Excellence

With a best total cost strategy, the business focus is on operating and business process efficiency, and on controlling costs. Companies with this strategy provide best price and overall value through standardized and automated processes. They focus on high quality, easy and quick customer service, quick delivery and purchasing, and products with limited choices. In operationally excellent companies, the IS strategy needs to focus on supporting business process improvement, increasing efficiencies, and

Product Leadership
"Best Product"
Product Differentiation

Operational Excellence
"Best Total Cost"
Operational Competence

Customer Intimacy
"Best Total Solution"
Customer responsive

"Successful market leaders must have one consistent driving
niche as the basis for all company priorities and decisions"

The Discipline of Market Leaders
By Michael Treacy & Fred Wiersema

Figure 1.9   Business strategies

controlling costs. IS projects that receive high priority in this environment include cost reductions, business process improvements, financial analysis and reporting systems, quality systems, supplier performance delivery systems, logistics systems, mobile technology, and automation of the supply chain. A strong enterprise requirements planning (ERP) system is important to facilitate operational efficiency, including a strong forecasting and production planning system, to ensure that manufacturing meets and does not exceed demands. Customer service applications may also be important for efficiency. In these companies, IS organizations are often centralized to control costs and take advantage of specialized technical skills. IS processes need to be efficient, with focus on the operational processes such as problem management, change management, software distribution, performance, and availability management. IS metrics important in this environment are availability, reliability, and costs. An operationally excellent environment is depicted in Figure 1.10.

Customer Intimacy

A *customer-intimate* company supplies the best total solution for the customer, builds a strong relationship with the customer, and provides custom solutions at a reasonable cost. The business strategy focuses on customer satisfaction and customer needs. Similarly, the IS strategy should focus on both customer and business satisfaction and provide technology to improve the customer relationship. Flexible business applications must accommodate individual customer needs. Strong customer relationship

Operationally Excellent Environment

Business Strategy	IS Organization
– Business process focus – Standardized and automated processes – Low prices – Focus on costs, removing waste	– Centralized – High technical skills

IS Strategy	IS Processes
– Reduce IS costs – Focus on processes and efficiency – Support business process management	– Performance and Availability Mgmt – Change Mgmt – Problem Mgmt – Software Distribution Mgmt

Technology	IS Metrics
– ERP, Costing, Pricing, Supply Chain – Mobile technology – In general, conservative deployment	– IS costs – Availability, reliability, service levels – IS process improvements

Figure 1.10   Operationally excellent environment

management (CRM), customer IS, and order management systems are critical to forge and maintain a strong connection with the customer and maintain detailed information about each customer. A strong Internet site, support for customer surveys, and obtaining and acting on customer input is important. The business analyst role is a key IS role in this company. The IS organization in this type of company is typically more decentralized and organized by customer segment, in alignment with the organization. IS processes that are important include service-level management, external and internal customer satisfaction management, business analysis, and understanding requirements. Figure 1.11 depicts a customer-intimate environment.

Product Leadership

A product leader continually improves products and product offerings. Creativity, research and development, efficient engineering, and time to market are critical. The business strategy is future driven and focused on solving problems and anticipating customer needs. The culture is usually flexible, decisive, and used to taking risks. The IS strategy would include flexibility, providing technology that enables cooperation and creativity, and supporting product management. Critical applications include product data management (PDM), engineering and CAD systems, and a CAD interface to engineering, configurator, and project management. Knowledge management, conferencing, and product life cycle management (PLM) would be useful. The most effective IS organization is flexible, with

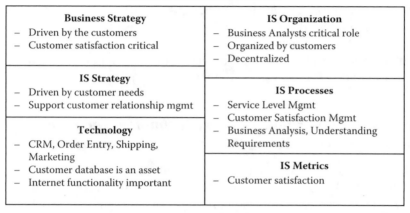

Customer Intimate Environment

Business Strategy	IS Organization
− Driven by the customers − Customer satisfaction critical	− Business Analysts critical role − Organized by customers − Decentralized
IS Strategy − Driven by customer needs − Support customer relationship mgmt	**IS Processes** − Service Level Mgmt − Customer Satisfaction Mgmt − Business Analysis, Understanding Requirements
Technology − CRM, Order Entry, Shipping, Marketing − Customer database is an asset − Internet functionality important	**IS Metrics** − Customer satisfaction

Figure 1.11   Customer-intimate environment

Product Leadership Environment

Business Strategy	IS Organization
− Future driven − Decisive − Risk taking − Flexible organization	− Loose organization, flexible
	IS Processes − System Development Process
IS Strategy − Technology enabling cooperation − Flexibility − Support product management	**IS Metrics** − Time to implement projects
Technology − Product Data Mgmt, Engineering systems, Document Mgmt, CAD to Mfg interface, Configurator, Project Mgmt − Knowledge mgmt, conferencing, PLM	

Figure 1.12   Product leadership environment

some resources researching new technologies. Important IS processes include the systems development process to be able to implement new products and projects quickly. Figure 1.12 depicts a product leadership environment.

Understanding the value proposition of the organization, be that of operational excellence, customer intimacy, or product leadership, helps align technology strategies. Through the planning process, IS can be a part of the solution to business challenges and can significantly assist the business. IS can work in partnership with the business, with the business actually having ownership in the direction of IS. With the proper infrastructure, tools, and technology in place, IS can be responsive and proactive to changing business requirements.

Identifying Opportunities to Use Technology for a Competitive Advantage and Increase the Value to the Business

In the article titled "IT Doesn't Matter,"[2] published by the *Harvard Business Review* in 2003, Nicholas G. Carr created quite a controversy in both IS and business circles. Carr compares corporate computing to electrical generation or the steam engine: it is necessary to the corporation, but insufficient, to consider information technology (IT) anything but a utility function. Discussions and arguments continue to ensue as to whether IS can provide a company with a competitive advantage. Although I agree with Carr that the technical infrastructure portion of IS may have become a commodity, technical infrastructure is not the critical point of the discussion. How a company uses technology (i.e., business applications and automated business processes) can provide, has provided, and for the foreseeable future will continue to provide businesses with a competitive advantage.

To ensure IS provides a competitive advantage, a robust planning process is required in which the IS department is a true business partner and identifies business opportunities using technology. Today, technology is integrated into every aspect of a business, business processes, and business interfaces. To obtain value and a competitive advantage, IS must partner with the business so they are one. Projects are not IS projects, but business projects. Technology by itself does not provide a competitive advantage, but redefining or aligning with the business strategy and optimizing business processes with the use of technology can provide a competitive advantage. As eloquently stated by Jim Collins in *Good to Great*, technology does not drive success, but it is an accelerator, or key enabler, of business success.[3] As shown by Figure 1.13, the role of IS increases as the business increases the business process goals.

To identify opportunities to utilize technology for a competitive advantage, it is important to understand the business strategy, because the technical opportunities are different depending on the business strategy. For example, an operationally excellent company achieves a competitive advantage by using technology to cut costs from its processes, improving profit margins, and allowing the company to reduce prices. As technology,

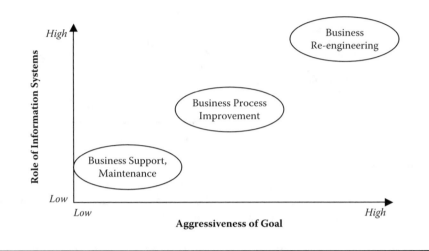

Figure 1.13 Role of IS in business process improvement

systems, and improved business processes are implemented, business costs will decrease. For example, an insurance company found that the cost of a transaction handled in person by an agent could cost $5 to $13, and a fully automated transaction on the Web costs only three to six cents, which can provide a tremendous competitive advantage.[4] Customer-intimate organizations may be able to achieve a competitive advantage by using technology for improved relationships with customers, proactively anticipating and addressing customers' unique needs. Product leadership companies could use technology that accelerates the development cycle for a competitive advantage.

With today's economic and competitive landscape, all companies are looking for ways to execute more effectively, efficiently, and at a lower cost. IS are a very important lever that businesses can use to affect their profitability. IS can be used to improve business processes. As shown in Figure 1.14, companies that simplify, standardize, automate, integrate, leverage, and eliminate waste of both processes and technology realize an increased value and decreased cost to the business. The bottom line is that the IS plan can affect a company's return on investment and profitability.

Planning the Flow of Information and Processes

Information is a valuable resource, and it is important to maximize its value for the corporation. Planning and managing the flow of information

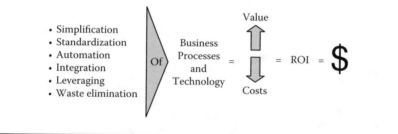

Figure 1.14 Increasing the value of the business

throughout the organization can minimize labor, data redundancy, and inconsistency, in addition to increasing the quality and accuracy of the information. When systems grow haphazardly over time, islands of information can develop, resulting in additional labor to maintain the disparate systems.

To improve the process flow, it is important to expand the IS planning process to look externally at the customer and all stakeholders that use the technology. The planning process will obtain input from all stakeholders, including customers, vendors, and partners. For each stakeholder, a company must identify and improve the process used to become aware of the business, engage in business, and complete business. Then, the company should review each step in its process to identify opportunities for technology to improve the process. Finally, a company should design systems and business processes so it is easy to do business with from the external customer perspective.

Efficiently and Effectively Allocating Information Systems Resources

In many businesses, IS allocates resources based on how much political influence different requestors have in the company, or even which executives become most vocal or angry when disappointed. Instead, the focus must be to develop systems that provide the largest business benefit and provide a competitive advantage. Planning will direct the effective allocation of IS resources and minimize the costs of redesign, rework, or correction of errors.

The IS department must manage both tangible and intangible resources, design flexibility and sourcing skills into the plans, and become business-focused consultants who help the company optimize all resources, not just computing resources. IS must utilize both computing and human resources to obtain the most value for the corporation. Figure 1.15 outlines the expectations of IS.

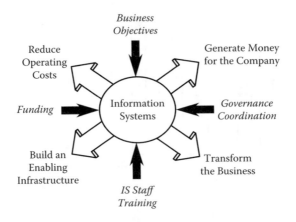

Figure 1.15 Expectations of IS

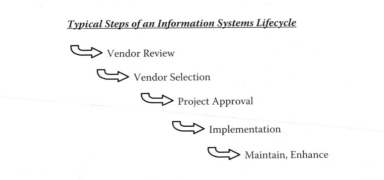

Figure 1.16 Typical steps in IS life cycle

Reducing the Effort and Money Required Throughout the Life Cycle of Systems

When a company has decided one of its systems no longer serves its needs and needs to be replaced, the company may jump right into a vendor review of business application packages. Typically, organizations will follow the steps outlined in Figure 1.16.

Without proper planning, several steps of the traditional life cycle are inefficient and waste significant time and money. The vendor review and selection process takes a long time because it may be unclear exactly what the company is looking for, what is important, or what problems the company is trying to solve. The company may utilize manual methods of developing requirements and reviewing vendor packages on the market.

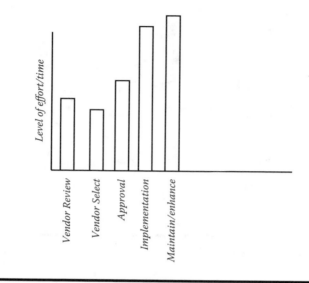

Figure 1.17 Time spent on typical life cycle

The approval step also consumes a large amount of time, because costs are generally more than management anticipates. Management starts asking questions such as, "Do we really need it?" "Are there less expensive alternatives?" "What are the real benefits to be gained?" Implementation takes longer than anticipated because it is an inefficiently planned execution, business process changes, or priorities are not clear. Trying to make an incorrectly chosen package fit the business results in more effort expended in the maintenance years. Figure 1.17 shows the time and effort expended in the typical life cycle.

Figure 1.18 outlines a more efficient process, including additional steps for strategic planning, implementation planning, and post implementation audit and planning.

Adding time to the beginning of the process for strategic planning will significantly reduce the amount of time spent in vendor review, selection, and project approval. An automated vendor review process, tool, or methodology to identify the business objectives and issues will save a considerable amount of time and effort. The strategic planning step will also obtain management support throughout all levels of the organization, which significantly accelerates the approval process. Careful planning and prioritizing of the implementation can reduce the implementation time. Understanding and identifying the scope of business process reengineering can significantly improve the implementation time and success of the project. A post implementation audit and check against the strategic plan will align priorities for critical enhancements. Overall time expended on the process is significantly less, as depicted by Figure 1.19.

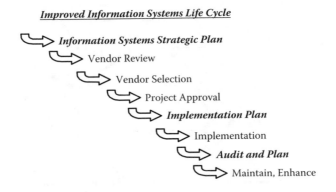

Figure 1.18 Improved IS life cycle

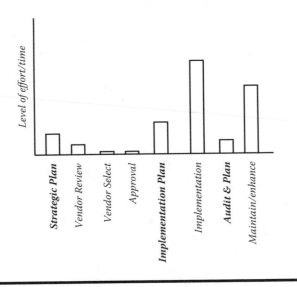

Figure 1.19 Time spent on improved life cycle

Planning Approach

The purpose of IS, like any other organization in the company, is to add value. The purpose of the planning process is to help the IS organization determine how to add optimum value to the company. How an IS organization adds value can be drastically different depending on the corporate or business unit strategies. The business unit strategy and

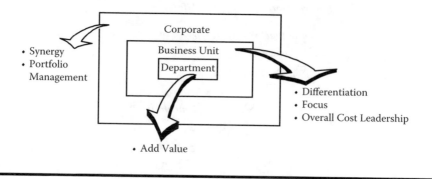

Figure 1.20   Corporate policy and business unit strategies

corporate policy establishes the boundaries for the IS direction, as shown in Figure 1.20.

A complex or large organization needs to consider the business direction and strategy of the corporation as well as the business unit strategy in its IS planning. For example, the corporation may have a stated strategy of synergy or a strategy of portfolio management. In a corporate environment of synergy, an IS planning process may be more closely aligned and bring business units together. The business units may even choose to leverage common systems across business units, where possible. A corporate environment of portfolio management would tend to drive the IS direction to be autonomous so that the business could be sold if necessary. Leveraging and sharing IS applications in a portfolio-managed company may not be easy or even encouraged.

The business unit (division, company) strategy could be one of differentiation, focus, or overall cost leadership. Again, each of these business unit strategies would have very different IS approaches. If a business unit has a strategy of differentiation, it will be important to utilize IS to provide the company with a competitive advantage. Utilizing new technologies to beat competitors to the market with added service or functionality is important. This approach would be drastically different from an environment of overall cost leadership, where cost containment is the number one goal.

Developing an IS strategic plan in a large corporate environment with multiple divisions or business units adds a level of complexity to consider before developing the approach and schedule for the IS planning process. Often, the planning effort may be constrained by politics, level of maturity, time, budget, or size of the various organizations involved. There are several different approaches to IS strategic planning in a large corporate environment with multiple divisions:

- Top-down approach: This is where the corporate unit completes the initial plan, establishes the areas of leverage, and recommends standards across business units. This planning approach works best in a company with a strong corporate entity with more autocratic power over the operating units.
- Bottom-up approach: In this approach, the business units complete their strategic plans first. The corporate entity then completes its plan by identifying areas common across the business units. This planning approach works best in a company with autonomous divisions.
- Combination: This is where the business unit plan is done jointly with a corporate entity, or initial high-level guidelines are developed as the basis for the business unit plans.

The IS planning approach should mirror the business planning approach. If the business planning approach is more central, so should the IS planning approach be centralized. The remainder of this book assumes a business unit plan, but the same principles and philosophies would apply to a corporate plan.

Conclusion

- Recognizing the need for an IS strategic plan and beginning the process is the most difficult step in the journey.
- Strategic planning will help establish IS as a key resource and enabler to meeting business goals.
- Completing an IS strategic plan adds value to the organization. The plan can improve the management of the IS asset, improve communication between the business and IS department, align the IS direction with the business, provide business opportunities and increase the value to the business, and plan the flow of information and processes. A plan can also result in the proper allocation of resources and reduce the cost of the life cycle of systems. A company should think through what it hopes to accomplish with its strategic planning project.
- The business strategies of operational excellence, customer intimacy, or product leadership require different IS strategies and priorities.
- For a large complex organization, think about your planning approach from a corporate or divisional scope.

Notes for My IS Strategic Planning Project

References

1. Treacy, Michael and Wiersema, Fred, *The Discipline of Market Leaders*, Perseus Books, New York, 1995.
2. Carr, Nicholas G., "IT Doesn't Matter," *Harvard Business Review*, Harvard Business School Publishing Corporation, Product Number 3566, 2003.
3. Collins, Jim, *Good to Great*, Harper Business, New York, 2001.
4. O'Rourke, Shawn, "More than a Handshake: Integrating IT Is Key to Corporate Success," DM Direct, October 2004, printed from DMReview.com.

Chapter 2

IS Governance

God grant me the serenity to accept the things I cannot change, the courage to change the things I can, and the wisdom to distinguish the one from the other.

— Reinhold Niebuhr (1892–1971)
American Theologian

Definition of Governance

Governance is a fundamental framework that must be in place for an information systems (IS) strategic plan and strategic planning process to be successful. Governance provides a decision-making and accountability framework for effective management of IS. There may be many components to IS governance, but the basic purpose of governance is to identify what decisions will be made, and by whom, and to define how activities will be monitored against the plan. The IS strategic plan is a very important component to effective governance. Conversely, a good IS strategic plan will include a clearly documented process for IS governance. Governance ensures that IS delivers value to the business and that risks are sufficiently managed.

Decisions may include areas such as the overall budget and allocation of resources; infrastructure; business applications, standards, policies, and priorities, IS guiding principles, and the IS strategic plan. Most often, the decisions are about time (schedule), money (budget), staffing levels, and allocations. However, other decisions also require governance, such as standards, policies, and desired behavior. One example of these decisions is setting a framework for when a company should utilize package software

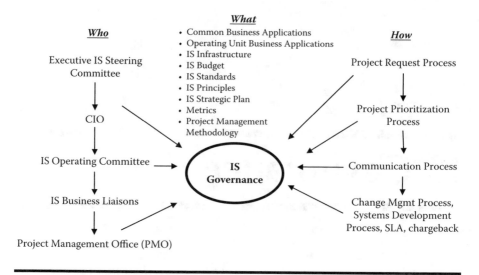

Figure 2.1   IS governance

and when custom software would be appropriate. The bottom line is that governance describes the process through which a company makes decisions.

A variety of individuals or groups may be involved in these decisions and processes, such as an IS steering committee, executive management, board of directors, the CIO, IS management, business line management, or business liaisons. Although these groups or individuals may be slightly different from organization to organization, this chapter discusses the general roles and responsibilities of each relative to the IS planning process. Activities may be monitored through various established IS processes, such as the budgeting process, project request process, project prioritization process, change management process, systems development process, and service-level management process. It is through effective governance that strategic planning becomes a process rather than a singular event. Governance ensures effective and efficient implementation of the strategic plan. IS management and processes deal with present issues of IS, and governance deals with future issues. Figure 2.1 shows an example of the different IS governance components in a company. Table 2.1 shows an example of how a company documented its governance by outlining who would be responsible for what decision.

Importance of Governance

Governance is a common principle used to manage other company assets. For example, for human assets, or employees, governance may include

Table 2.1 Decision-Making Matrix

	IS Infrastructure	Common Business Applications	Operating Unit Business Applications	IS Budget	IS Standards, Processes	IS Principles	IS Strategic Plan
Executive IS Steering Committee	Consulted	Responsible	Informed	Responsible	Consulted	Consulted	Responsible
IS Operating Committees	Consulted	Consulted	Responsible	Informed	Informed	Informed	Consulted
IS Business Liaison	Informed	Consulted	Consulted	Informed	Informed	Informed	Consulted
CIO	Responsible	Consulted	Consulted	Consulted	Responsible	Responsible	Consulted

a committee that does headcount planning, a human resources (HR) function that manages the performance review process, a committee that reviews the salary structures and determines increases, and a process to follow to hire an employee. Similarly, IS is a critical asset for a company and requires a set of committees or individuals and processes to manage the various aspects. The Sarbanes–Oxley Act of 2002 (SOX) requires diligent management of company assets, and governance helps with the management of IS assets.

If done properly, effective governance improves the efficiency of IS and simplifies life for the CIO as the function operates more smoothly on a day-to-day basis. If an organization is fighting about priorities, is slow in decision making, hears complaints about IS, feels that IS does not add value, or experiences disappointing returns on IS investments, there are probably opportunities to improve governance. Without governance, decision making may be slow and inconsistent because no one is sure who is responsible for the decision. In fact, IS governance issues are at the core of many reasons companies experience frustrations with their IS function. Some companies choose to outsource the IS function to relieve the frustrations. However, outsourcing requires even stronger governance and can actually make the problems more evident.

Good, defined, and clear governance contributes to the success of the IS organization and the company as a whole. A study documented in the book *IT Governance*, by Peter Weill and Jeanne W. Ross (2004), reviewed IT governance in over 250 companies worldwide. Their research revealed that firms with above-average IT governance had more than 20% higher profits than firms with poor governance.[1] The bottom line is that governance is a tool that implements the strategic planning process and improves IS efficiency, effectiveness, and overall success of the company. Through effective governance, a company can orchestrate its resources to execute a plan. Without clear and effective governance, a company will squander its efforts on a random assortment of unfocused actions. Individual strategies and projects may seem to make sense, but taken all together, they may not move the organization toward the overall strategic vision. Governance will manage the resources and initiatives at a cross-functional level. Governance provides a systematic approach for reviewing, evaluating, prioritizing, sequencing, communicating, and managing initiatives so the entire organization stays focused.

Clear IS governance is especially important because technology has become pervasive in companies. It is easy for any employee to go to his or her local technology store and purchase software or hardware to install. This software or hardware brought in through the "back door" can become critical to the functioning of the company. Without company agreement on processes and standards, it is difficult for the assets to be managed properly (i.e., data backed up, software that works properly in the environment, software that can be supported, protection against viruses). Standardizing technologies and processes whenever appropriate lowers a company's cost of ownership, allows some leveraging of economies of scale, and provides architectural integrity. Governance makes the standardization possible and encourages desired behaviors.

Governance is also critical because IS are expensive and limited by budgets. Any company has a limited bandwidth of resources and must manage how those resources are spent. More technologies and options are available today than ever in the past, and opportunities to utilize technology abound. Governance helps a company evaluate the opportunities and align projects with the business direction. Governance ensures that projects adding the most value to the business will be the projects initiated, therefore improving the ultimate value from IS. As business changes occur on a continuous basis, governance ensures that the IS plan and priorities change with the business.

Clear, defined governance improves the relationship between the business and the IS organization, because there is structure and definition to the relationship. Regular and consistent processes improve communication. Clear decision making and governance helps build trust; everyone understands how decisions are made. Even if everyone doesn't agree with every decision, people understand there was a defined process and reasons for a particular decision. Governance provides opportunities for IS and the CIO to consistently build credibility and trust with business management. Through governance, the IS organization can continually communicate how it is contributing business value. With proper governance, companies can transform into true business partners enabling new business opportunities.

Approaches to Governance

The following are examples of governance approaches that often occur without an intentional design:

> *IS dictator:* In this autocratic environment, the IS department makes all the decisions and keeps tight control over IS tools and assets. In this environment, the CIO and the IS organization are often criticized and disrespected. The business is often dissatisfied because it is not driving IS decisions.
>
> *People have the power:* In this environment, the individuals throughout the business may initially be satisfied because they can do what

they want, but dissatisfaction grows as pieces of the infrastructure do not work well together. This environment can be extremely wasteful and expensive, but the cost may not be visible — it may be hidden within individual department budgets.

Democratic: In this environment, everything is a vote. It can be a time-consuming and frustrating process. Often, the popular decision overrides the best decision. It can be political as opposing individuals vie for support.

Business management monarchy: In this environment, senior business executives make all the IS decisions affecting the entire corporation. This could be good or bad depending on the skill and knowledge of management.

Business unit power: It is common in a large company with unique divisions to have more power in the business units than centrally. Although this feudal method works well to achieve business unit objectives, it is difficult to leverage corporatewide strategic efforts across business units. This may also be more expensive because the business units may not use standards and common systems across business units.

Corporate power: In a highly centralized environment, a central corporate entity often makes the decisions. Although this may have some efficiencies because synergies can be leveraged, it often results in unsatisfied business units that do not feel in control of their destiny.

Indecisive: In this environment, no one makes decisions. There is a leadership void and unclear responsibilities on decision making.

As shown in Figure 2.2, governance design develops decision-making structures and organizations that balance all the above interests. No single approach to governance design works for every company. The IS governance model must fit the company and management culture, the maturity and size of the organization, and the business strategy. A more structured, mature organization may have a strict governance process, many defined processes and metrics, and very formal IS steering committee meetings. A large company with many divisions may have a much different governance structure and approach than a very centralized corporate environment. Often, IS governance mirrors the power and decision-making structure in the business. Rather than fighting the inherent power, it is important to recognize the business decision-making structure and work within it. No matter how immature, informal, or small, the IS function requires some form of governance and involvement of the organization to be successful. In any size company, governance can be designed to make decisions quickly and be responsive.

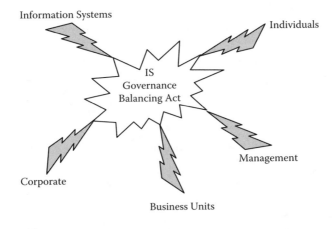

Figure 2.2   Governance balancing interests

Involvement of the Organization

How can a company ensure commitment to a strategic plan? Some IS organizations are very efficient in developing a strategic plan by taking their top computer technicians and outlining the technical architecture of the future. When these technicians complete their planning, they end up with a terrific technical plan, but one that business management hardly understands, let alone approves. These plans tend to accumulate dust on someone's bookshelf and never really influence the direction of IS or the business.

Where do these technical computing architecture plans go wrong? Their architects fail to involve the business and management throughout the process. It is through proper involvement of the business that a plan becomes executable and meaningful. Governance will monitor and provide ongoing management to the strategic plan. It is critical to have business management participation and ownership of the plan to ensure alignment with the business. The plan must reflect management ideas, styles, and objectives. To be successful, the entire organization must support the IS objectives. The single largest factor for a successful strategic plan that influences the organization is the involvement of the organization and ongoing governance. Communication and involvement are key aspects of the planning process. The planning process consists of 80% communicating and obtaining input, and 20% planning.

So, how can an organization start developing an IS strategic plan? How is it possible to get this involvement and commitment, even if it is difficult to get management's attention? How can an organization ensure ongoing

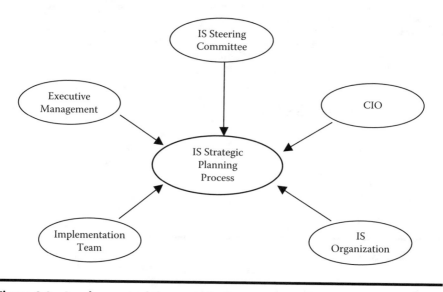

Figure 2.3 Involvement of the organization

management to the plan and governance? An organization should start the strategic planning process by involving all levels of the business organization in the planning and governance process.

There may be a need to form several planning groups to involve the various levels of the organization. The involvement of several groups and individuals in the initial plan development and ongoing governance is common in a typical organization, as shown in Figure 2.3:

1. Executive management
2. IS steering committee
3. CIO
4. IS organization
5. Implementation team

Executive Management

It is vital to involve executive management in the IS strategic planning process and the ongoing governance process. Ultimately, executive management will approve or reject the expenditure of funds. Managers' involvement at the beginning and throughout the process will make the approval process significantly easier. It is important that executive management have direct input and understand the challenges and opportunities.

The CIO, or top IS executive, typically reports to someone within the executive management level of the organization. Over the years, companies may have shifted the reporting relationship for the CIO to report to the CEO, the CFO, the COO, or other areas of executive management. Regardless of where the CIO reports, the CIO can be effective through leadership and by building strong relationships with the executive team. Although it is ideal if the CIO participates on the executive team and is at the table for business planning, a good IS planning process is still possible through interviews and informal relationships. Credibility and trust build influence, not organizational position. It is most helpful if the CIO has the commitment, involvement, and interest of the executive of the function and the CEO recognizes value in IS. If the CEO doesn't initially recognize the value in IS, he or she should by the end of the planning process with the proper involvement and business connection.

The role of the executive committee in the planning and governance process is to provide the IS organization with the strategic business direction and priorities. It is important to develop and maintain systems in accordance with the business objectives and direction. Typically, the executive committee addresses IS issues on an as-needed basis rather than having regularly scheduled meetings due to time constraints.

The CIO, or top IS executive, initiates the presentations. It is extremely helpful to have a businessperson supporting large investments and projects make presentations to the executive committee. This involvement demonstrates business management's ownership, support, and commitment to the recommendations because the projects are business projects, not IS projects. The business needs to sign up for and own the benefits that are anticipated from the investments.

In summary, the responsibilities of executive management relative to the IS planning and governance process are:

- To provide strategic business direction and priorities.
- To provide input to and approve the IS strategic direction and plans: The group will ensure the IS plans are in agreement with the strategic business plans of the organization.
- To approve all large project efforts and provide the final authority in the allocation of resources.
- To approve the IS budget.
- To provide direction relative to high-level business issues that affect IS.

IS Steering Committee

The IS steering committee is the most important group involved in the planning process and is instrumental in the success of the plan and ongoing governance. The steering committee provides the IS organization with a voice from all areas of the business. This group will formulate recommendations regarding project priorities and resources and provides input to the strategic direction of IS. The business must commit to delivering the business benefits of projects.

The committee typically consists of Directors, or individuals one level below the executive management. This level of the organization usually has a strong interest in IS and has a desire for changes because IS have an impact on their success as department leaders. Many companies have already formed IS steering committees. It is important to review the group to ensure it includes the correct composition of individuals to participate in the strategic planning process. The executive management team should select its representatives on the committee. It is in the best interests of these managers to ensure that they have the best person representing their interests and concerns.

If an IS steering committee has not been previously formed, a company should look at the organizational structure to see if there already is a business team functioning one level below executive management. In the most effective organizations, steering IS is just one of the many responsibilities of the business management team, rather than a separate IS steering committee. To help integrate IS governance with the business, it would be best to have the IS executive become a part of this business committee and dedicate a portion of the meetings to IS activities and plans. One company referred to this critical group of management as the "shadow" strategy committee, while the executive management team was referred to as the "business unit" strategy group. Another company referred to this group of management as the operating committee, while executive management was referred to as the policy committee. Whatever title this group of management has, IS should be an integral responsibility and focus of the group. Although this book refers to the group as the IS steering committee, it would be best to integrate with the business team and refer to the group however it has been previously defined.

It is important to include management from all the company's business areas, as well as the various geographic areas, on the IS steering committee. The members must understand the strategic business direction as well as the business issues. Although it is critical to have the major business areas represented, it is difficult to manage a group larger than 12 individuals. Companies should keep the size of the group small enough to efficiently conduct meetings and make decisions, and should consider using video or teleconferencing for individuals physically located around the world. At a minimum, a company should send out-of-town members material and notes from the meetings and have them attend critical meetings. Also, the company should post the minutes and presentations in an electronic mail bulletin board for all employees to see. Getting as much visibility to the information as possible is critical.

A company should not formally include individuals from the IS organization as voting members of the group. The top individual from IS (typically the CIO, Vice President, or Director) schedules, organizes, documents, and chairs the meetings. Additional members from IS can attend meetings as required to provide information or give presentations. The business representatives must see and feel they provide the direction to the committee, which is not the case if the committee includes many IS individuals.

The responsibilities of the IS steering committee are:

- To provide recommendations and input to the IS strategic direction and plans.
- To ensure the plans are in alignment with the business plans and direction.
- To communicate business issues and plans influencing IS activities or direction in technology.
- To provide input and assist in developing the vision for the deployment of technology to meet the business requirements of the future.
- To approve, sponsor, and support business requested project efforts and project plans through the ongoing governance process. This group will be the vehicle for users to propose and recommend IS projects.
- To prioritize all project efforts and review project plans. The group will provide recommendations in the allocation of resources and monitor project progress against the approved plan. Projects are efforts that meet one or more of the following criteria:
  - Estimated hours to complete the project exceed some predetermined amount of hours.
  - Departmental boundaries are crossed.
  - A capital expenditure or nonrecurring costs exceeds some predetermined amount.
  - Recurring costs exceed a predetermined amount per year.
- Prioritize all requests smaller than the above project definition through the normal IS work order process. The group determines the hours and cost limit thresholds for its specific environment. It establishes the approval level for projects so the committee is focused on major projects rather than work orders and small requests. Following the 80/20 rule, 20% of the projects will use 80% of the resources. It is this 20% that should be managed through the IS steering committee.

Table 2.2   IS Steering Committee Agenda

Agenda
IS Steering Committee Purpose
IS Strategic Planning Process
Current Business Situation
Current IS Situation
IS Industry
Assessment of Current Situation
Recommendations
Next Steps

- To provide communication to other members within the organization regarding IS activities.
- To sponsor and initiate business process reengineering projects.
- To commit to delivering the business benefits identified in projects.
- To communicate and discuss functional business issues arising from IS activities — for example, if the manufacturing department wants to structure the bill-of-material or product number one way and the engineering department wants it another way, and the groups cannot come to agreement.
- To review IS standards and procedures that have an impact on other business functions.
- To approve the allocation of the IS budget.

The IS steering committee meets on a regular basis, typically monthly. Usually the top IS executive (CIO, Vice President, or Director) schedules, organizes, and documents the meetings. Steering committee meetings should follow a formal agenda to guide the meeting. Table 2.2 shows a typical agenda for one of the first IS steering committee meetings. On an ongoing basis, a company should structure meetings to dedicate time to planning tasks as well as providing an update on projects. The group should document meeting decisions, conversations, and topics with meeting minutes distributed to the IS steering committee members, executive management, and the IS organization. Meetings should move quickly, stay on the topic, and keep to strategic discussions rather than detailed tactical discussions.

CIO

As discussed in many articles and books, the role of the CIO (or top person responsible for IS) is evolving and changing, as is the role of the

IS organization. Rather than just technical knowledge, it is critical that the CIO have an interest and understanding of the business, be familiar with business acumen, and have good business and financial judgment. Business understanding is critical in the strategic planning process. The CIO must have enough technical knowledge to understand the consequences and risks of his or her decisions, to plan and coordinate implementations, to ask appropriate questions and understand the answers, and to determine if what he or she is hearing is accurate.

The CIO must be a true leader, and not just a manager. As my astute associate, Bob Lewis, states in his book, *Leading IT: The Toughest Job in the World*, someone is not a leader if no one is following.[2] The IS strategic planning process is a wonderful opportunity to demonstrate leadership by demonstrating an understanding of the business goals, establishing a compelling IS vision to utilize technology to support the business, and influencing the organization to change. A vision and a passion for the new direction is a requirement to inspire others to follow. It is difficult to go somewhere if you do not know where you are going. The vision and plan provides a path of how to get the organization to the next level. Through leadership, the CIO must often influence and persuade other individuals in the organization. Strong executive relationships are critical to the success of a CIO. The CIO is a conduit for change, and the strategic plan can be an excellent vehicle to assist with change.

The CIO is typically the individual who initiates and orchestrates the strategic planning process. The CIO coordinates and directs the involvement of the entire organization in the strategic planning process. The CIO must clearly communicate the plan so that the entire organization understands it. The CIO is responsible for establishing and adhering to the budget guidelines. The CIO must continually communicate to the organization the value of IS.

IS Organization

Although the business must commit to changing business processes and delivering the business benefits of projects, the IS organization must commit to delivering projects within the costs and dates budgeted while meeting the functionality requirements. It is also important to involve the IS organization in the planning, because any changes in the direction will significantly affect that group. The IS organization is a technical reference and takes more of a secondary role in the process. The business units should lead the process. If possible, a company should involve the entire IS organization in the process to some extent, and at a minimum communicate with them at each step in the process. The top IS individual in the organization leads the involvement from the IS organization.

After obtaining a thorough understanding of the business direction in the planning process, a company must communicate the business direction to the entire IS organization. The IS organization can then be effective in brainstorming potential IS goals, objectives, and technology-enabled business opportunities.

Implementation Team

In the event the planning process leads to the conclusion that major changes are necessary (e.g., a new ERP system is necessary), an additional group may need to be formed to look at the various options in detail and implement the changes. Often this is a time-consuming task, and the steering committee may not have the time or the detailed knowledge to work at this level. The implementation team must include representatives from areas of the business impacted by the change, as well as one or two individuals from IS. The IS steering committee should appoint or select the individuals, because this group will be providing recommendations to the IS steering committee. The members of the IS steering committee need to feel that their area of the business is sufficiently represented. It is important to involve these individuals in preparing the detailed requirements, reviewing and implementing options, and determining and implementing business process improvements.

The implementation team is also typically the group of individuals a company would select to implement the new system or improved business processes. It is best to have the group that selects the new system also be the group implementing the system when possible. It is critical that these people have an excellent understanding of the business and the business processes, and are open to change. These individuals would be responsible for doing the business process reengineering, establishing the parameters and procedures on how the company will use the system, testing the system, and training the users. The following are specific characteristics desirable in team members:

- Have a thorough knowledge of the business area they represent
- Be respected and influential among their peers
- Be detail-oriented
- Be a good listener

- Be a good communicator
- Have good writing and documentation skills
- Be creative, and able to look beyond how things are done today
- Have an interest in transforming the company

The team leader is a critical position for the success of the project. The following are characteristics desirable in the team leader:

- Is a true leader
- Has the respect of the organization
- Is good at organization and planning, and project management
- Is decisive
- Is a good people manager
- Can say "no" and lead business process change
- Is creative, and able to look beyond how things are done today
- Has an interest in transforming the company
- Typically delivers on time and on budget
- Can manage risks
- Can manage the budget
- Can manage and direct outside consulting resources
- Is an excellent communicator

Conclusion

- Determine and design the appropriate governance for your organization; do not just let it happen. This governance will provide the stage for the successful execution of the strategic planning process.
- Identify what groups to involve in the planning process and how they will be involved.
- Document the roles and responsibilities of the various groups involved in the governance process so the decision-making authority is clear. It is important to specify who will be responsible for providing input and making the decisions involved in the planning process even before initiating the planning process.

After establishing governance, you are ready to begin the strategic planning process.

Notes for My IS Strategic Planning Project

References

1. Weill, Peter, and Ross, Jeanne W., *IT Governance*, Harvard Business School Press, Boston, 2004.
2. Lewis, Bob, *Leading IT: The Toughest Job in the World*, IS Survivor Publishing, Eden Prairie, MN, 2004.

Chapter 3

The Planning Process

Behold the turtle. He makes progress only when he sticks his neck out.

— James Bryant Conant (1893–1978)
American chemist, diplomat, and educator

Planning Components

What are the basic components of a strategic plan? Although the IS strategic plan differs from a business plan in many ways, there are several similar concepts to keep in mind:

Identification of where you are today: Assess the environment to answer the question, "Where are we now?" In an IS strategic plan, this includes looking internally and externally from the perspective of both the business as well as IS. An external view will answer the questions "What is possible?" and "What are the best practices?" Because the business must drive IS, you must understand thoroughly the business objectives and challenges in addition to where IS are currently.

Identification of where you want to be in the future: Through the planning process, develop the vision and strategy to answer the question "Where do we want to be?" In an IS strategic plan, answer the question from both a business and an IS perspective. The future business direction must be the main determinant in setting the IS direction.

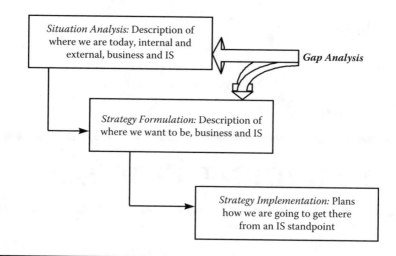

Figure 3.1 Plan components

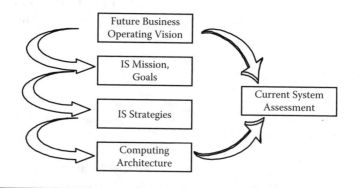

Figure 3.2 Plan development

Identification of the IS gap between where you are and where you
want to be in the future

Identification of how to get to where you want to be in the future:
Develop a plan to answer the question "How will we get there?"

Figure 3.1 depicts the components of planning.

The plan begins with understanding the future business operating
vision. The business operating vision becomes the basis for the IS mission,
objectives, strategies, and technical computing architecture. Assess the
current systems by comparing the systems to the future business operating
vision and the desired IS computing architecture, as depicted in Figure 3.2.

Planning Process

So, how do you actually develop an IS strategic plan?

As stated earlier, the foundation of the strategic planning process is that business direction and business requirements drive the IS direction and computing architecture. Although this sounds like a basic concept, it is amazing how many strategic plans do not have the business direction as the foundation of the IS direction.

Does this mean an IS strategic plan cannot be developed if the organization does not have a formal business plan in place? Absolutely not! It means a little more work and possibly a little more time, but it is possible and more necessary than ever. If a formal business plan does not exist, this process will outline how to develop the key components of a business plan that are necessary to establish a complete IS plan. Many companies may not have a complete business plan, but they may have important components, such as key objectives, vision, mission, values, key initiatives, budgets, and so forth. All of these key business-planning components can be used in the IS planning process.

In several companies, this IS planning process actually caused the business to begin a formal business planning process as management realized the lack of a clear and concise business direction. In one company, a very detailed financial plan was developed each year, but a formal business plan was never documented identifying how the business would actually achieve the financial forecasts. The president of the division claimed that the executive team had a shared vision of the future and was questioning why the business-understanding step of the IS planning process was necessary. However, when asked specific questions about the business direction, each vice president provided a slightly different perspective or set of priorities. When summarizing the findings and highlighting the inconsistencies, the president came to the realization that executive management had never formally agreed upon the business mission and goals, and a formal business planning process was initiated.

The planning process depicted in Figure 3.3 has four phases. Figure 3.4 outlines the next level of detail for each of the four phases. Chapters 4 through 7 of this book describe each phase in detail, providing samples and guidelines for each step of the process to assist with completing the IS strategic plan. The following is an overview of the four phases of strategic planning.

Phase 1: Visioning

In the first phase, visioning, establish and initiate the planning project and process. Treat the IS planning effort like any other project by developing

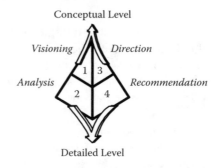

Conceptual Level

Visioning   Direction

Analysis   Recommendation

Detailed Level

Figure 3.3   Phases of the planning process

Visioning Phase
- Initiate and manage the project
- Understand business situation and vision
- Document and confirm the business analysis

Direction Phase
- Develop IS vision and direction
- Develop IS plan
- Identify IS projects

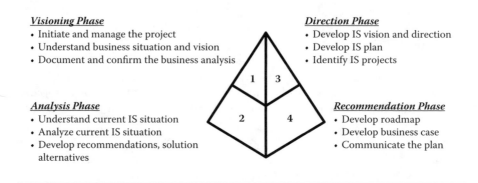

Analysis Phase
- Understand current IS situation
- Analyze current IS situation
- Develop recommendations, solution alternatives

Recommendation Phase
- Develop roadmap
- Develop business case
- Communicate the plan

Figure 3.4   Phases of the planning process

a project plan, schedule, tasks, and deliverables. Finalize and communicate the purpose of the strategic planning effort and outline what management hopes to accomplish with the effort. Establish, or define, the process that will be used to develop the plan, tailored for your organization's environment. Also, identify the individuals who will be involved in the planning process and define their roles and responsibilities. A key step is to identify the individuals from the business and IS group to interview as part of the planning process. Finally, establish the process and vehicle to communicate the status of the strategic planning effort on an ongoing basis. Last, formally announce the strategic planning effort to those involved in the process.

Also in the first phase, it is critical to understand, clarify, and document the business direction. This includes documenting the business mission, vision, values, goals, objectives, and business priorities. Obtain this information from business plans and documentation as well as through executive

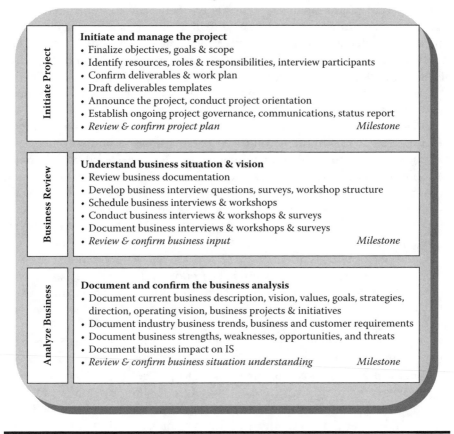

Visioning Phase

Initiate Project

Initiate and manage the project
- Finalize objectives, goals & scope
- Identify resources, roles & responsibilities, interview participants
- Confirm deliverables & work plan
- Draft deliverables templates
- Announce the project, conduct project orientation
- Establish ongoing project governance, communications, status report
- *Review & confirm project plan*   *Milestone*

Business Review

Understand business situation & vision
- Review business documentation
- Develop business interview questions, surveys, workshop structure
- Schedule business interviews & workshops
- Conduct business interviews & workshops & surveys
- Document business interviews & workshops & surveys
- *Review & confirm business input*   *Milestone*

Analyze Business

Document and confirm the business analysis
- Document current business description, vision, values, goals, strategies, direction, operating vision, business projects & initiatives
- Document industry business trends, business and customer requirements
- Document business strengths, weaknesses, opportunities, and threats
- Document business impact on IS
- *Review & confirm business situation understanding*   *Milestone*

Figure 3.5 Phase 1, visioning phase

interviews, workshops, and surveys or through a series of interactive conversations. Assess the environmental factors, including industry trends and external requirements. It is important to look externally and determine what customers, suppliers, or other external entities (for example, government, Food and Drug Administration [FDA], International Organization for Standardization [ISO]) are requiring from the company. The business operating vision will be statements or a vision of how management wants the business to function in the future. Analyze the strengths and weaknesses of the business. A key task of this phase is to analyze and document the impact the business situation has on IS.

Figure 3.5 outlines the details of the visioning phase, or phase 1. As you can see, the first phase of the planning process focuses on the business rather than on IS.

Phase 2: Analysis

In the second phase, analysis, thoroughly document and objectively analyze the IS environment. It is often enlightening to communicate the IS situation to executive management. Although managers may know that IS are critical to the company, they may not realize the complexity and all the various components until the documentation is presented. Obtain this information through a review of IS documentation, conducting interviews, workshops, or surveys of the IS organization.

Document all the various business applications used by the business. Begin by summarizing the technical infrastructure environment, including the personal computer (PC) environment, server environment, telecommunications environment, and network. Review the organizational structure, skills, roles, and responsibilities of the IS organization. With this base established, understand the IS processes and how work is completed. This phase also includes a review of the IS expenditures, identifies how the budget has changed, and analyzes where money is spent. Understanding the current workload is important. Identify the backlog, or all the various projects requested. Also, review the external IS trends and identify how industry trends may influence your environment and future. An interesting part of the planning process is to look at competitors and determine how they utilize IS. Compare your IS spending to that of the industry.

Objectively determine and document the gap of where the IS environment should be in the future compared to where it is today. It is important to "think outside the box" in this phase. Do not get locked into the trap of "We have always done it this way." Analyze the IS environment relative to the business requirements identified in the first phase. Objectively, identify the strengths, weaknesses, opportunities, and threats of your current IS situation in the areas of business applications, technical infrastructure, organization, and processes. Understand how the business threats and opportunities highlight system strengths and weaknesses. It is helpful to assess the situation utilizing surveys or scorecards to obtain a quantifiable measure in addition to qualitative comments. Identify key information requirements and business requirements. Using the list of requirements, identify what percent of the business requirements and information needs or key business indicators are met by the business applications in use. Finally, determine initial recommendations for all areas of IS to include in the IS direction.

Figure 3.6 outlines the second phase of the planning process.

Phase 3: Direction

It is in the direction phase where the mission and vision for IS is articulated using the business situation and direction as a basis. Formulate the strategic

Analysis Phase

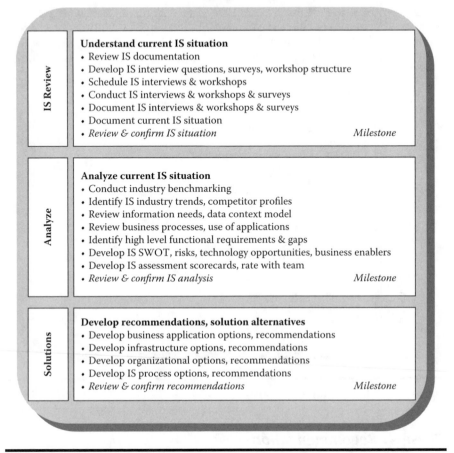

Figure 3.6 Phase 2, analysis phase

objectives that are necessary to assist the business in achieving its objectives. Review each business goal and determine ways in which IS can assist the business in achieving each goal. A key step is to determine how to measure the value or progress of IS on an ongoing basis. Determine the business application direction and specific projects required. Also, determine the technical computing architecture and projects that are necessary to reach the objectives, including changes in the area of PCs, servers, network, and telecommunications. Determine the desired IS service architecture, which includes the people and processes necessary in IS. Determine how to allocate resources and the role of outsourcing or alternative sourcing options. Finally, prioritize the various IS projects. Figure 3.7 shows the details of the third phase.

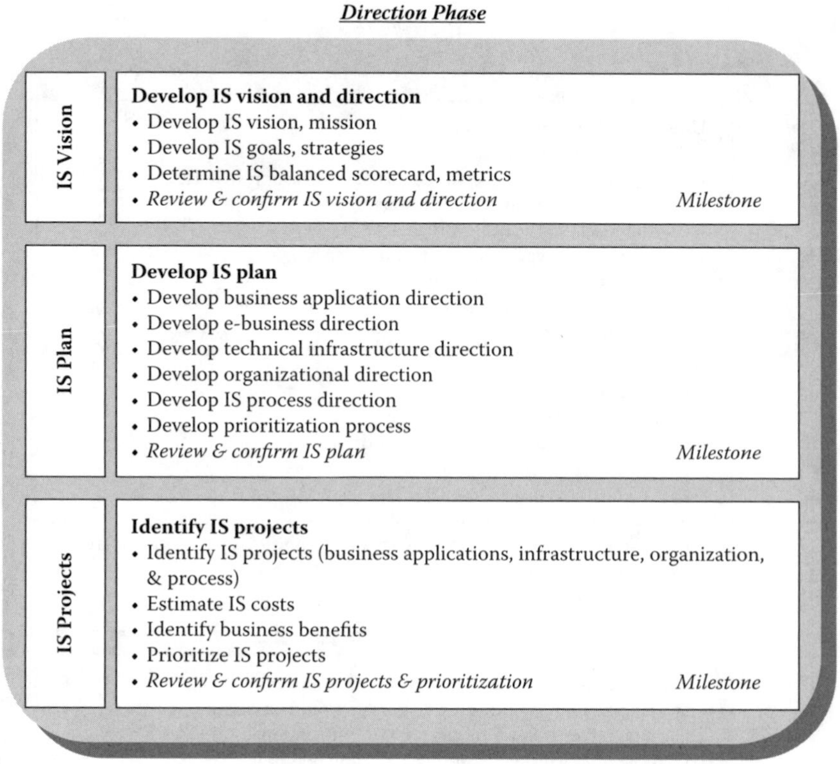
Direction Phase
IS Vision
Develop IS vision and direction
• Develop IS vision, mission
• Develop IS goals, strategies
• Determine IS balanced scorecard, metrics
• Review & confirm IS vision and direction
Milestone
IS Plan
Develop IS plan
• Develop business application direction
• Develop e-business direction
• Develop technical infrastructure direction
• Develop organizational direction
• Develop IS process direction
• Develop prioritization process
• Review & confirm IS plan
Milestone
IS Projects
Identify IS projects
• Identify IS projects (business applications, infrastructure, organization, & process)
• Estimate IS costs
• Identify business benefits
• Prioritize IS projects
• Review & confirm IS projects & prioritization
Milestone

Figure 3.7 Phase 3, direction phase

Phase 4: Recommendation

In this phase, document the detailed roadmap outlining projects for the next several years. Summarize the costs, time, and resources required. Benchmark data will be helpful to validate estimates. If there are multiple options, identify the various options, as well as the advantages and disadvantages of each option. Determine the proper recommendation with a return-on-investment analysis. Identify the organizational impact. Risk management is important; analyze the risks and determine how to mitigate them. A critical step is to develop the business case for action and business benefits so management can approve the plan and understand the business impact. Finally, develop the communication plan and an ongoing process to keep the plan up-to-date.

Figure 3.8 identifies the components of the fourth phase.

At the end of the planning process, you will have:

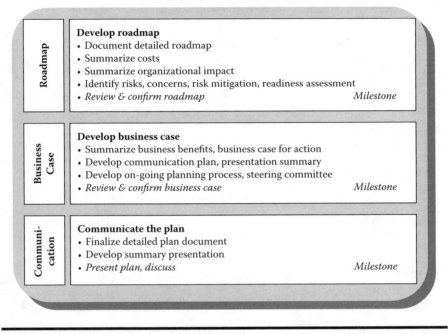

Recommendation Phase

Roadmap

Develop roadmap
- Document detailed roadmap
- Summarize costs
- Summarize organizational impact
- Identify risks, concerns, risk mitigation, readiness assessment
- *Review & confirm roadmap*   *Milestone*

Business Case

Develop business case
- Summarize business benefits, business case for action
- Develop communication plan, presentation summary
- Develop on-going planning process, steering committee
- *Review & confirm business case*   *Milestone*

Communication

Communicate the plan
- Finalize detailed plan document
- Develop summary presentation
- *Present plan, discuss*   *Milestone*

Figure 3.8   Phase 4, recommendation phase

- A well-documented IS strategic plan
- A business and IS situation that is understood by the entire organization
- A direction supported throughout the organization

Plan Contents

When completed, what will the plan look like? What can management expect to see and get from the plan document? It is helpful to have an understanding of where the planning process is headed and what the final deliverable will look like. Figure 3.9 depicts an example of an outline of the contents of a completed strategic plan document. Modify the plan document and process to fit the situation and requirements. Create a detailed document as well as a summary presentation while proceeding through the planning phases.

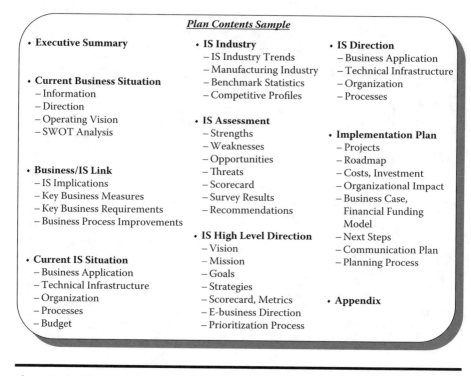

Plan Contents Sample

- **Executive Summary**

- **Current Business Situation**
  - Information
  - Direction
  - Operating Vision
  - SWOT Analysis

- **Business/IS Link**
  - IS Implications
  - Key Business Measures
  - Key Business Requirements
  - Business Process Improvements

- **Current IS Situation**
  - Business Application
  - Technical Infrastructure
  - Organization
  - Processes
  - Budget

- **IS Industry**
  - IS Industry Trends
  - Manufacturing Industry
  - Benchmark Statistics
  - Competitive Profiles

- **IS Assessment**
  - Strengths
  - Weaknesses
  - Opportunities
  - Threats
  - Scorecard
  - Survey Results
  - Recommendations

- **IS High Level Direction**
  - Vision
  - Mission
  - Goals
  - Strategies
  - Scorecard, Metrics
  - E-business Direction
  - Prioritization Process

- **IS Direction**
  - Business Application
  - Technical Infrastructure
  - Organization
  - Processes

- **Implementation Plan**
  - Projects
  - Roadmap
  - Costs, Investment
  - Organizational Impact
  - Business Case, Financial Funding Model
  - Next Steps
  - Communication Plan
  - Planning Process

- **Appendix**

Figure 3.9   Plan contents sample

Plan Development

When proceeding through the steps, it is extremely helpful to build the plan document and distribute it periodically to the IS steering committee, executive management, and the IS organization to obtain input. To obtain involvement from all areas of the organization, the planning groups outlined in Chapter 2 can develop and update the various sections of the plan document throughout the process. The plan is a living document and is best developed through iteration. The business should gain a sense of ownership for the plan and recommendations throughout the process. In each figure depicting the phase (Figures 3.5, 3.6, 3.7, and 3.8), several milestones are indicated. The milestones are points in the process that the plan deliverable should be updated with the information obtained, and confirmed with various individuals or groups involved in the planning review process. With this method, the plan is agreed upon throughout the process rather than waiting until the end. By reviewing the information at various points, there is also a more manageable amount of information for the group to absorb. Figure 3.10 shows the sample table of contents and identifies at which phase each section is completed.

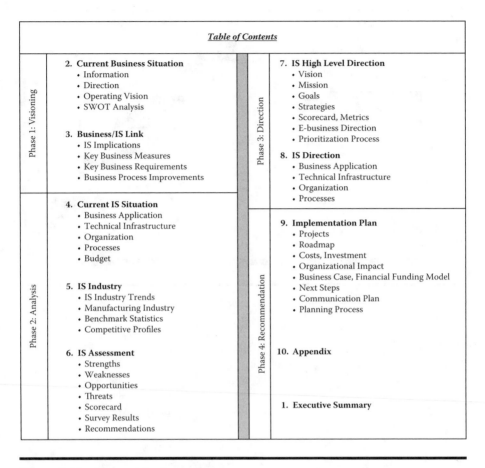

Figure 3.10   Plan contents by phase

The planning process does not need to be a time-consuming process. To be most effective, the process should proceed as quickly as possible. The length of time it takes to develop a strategic plan varies drastically with the size, complexity, and commitment of the organization. Figure 3.11 shows a sample schedule for each phase of the plan.

Several factors significantly affect the length of time of the planning process as shown in Figure 3.12:

Depth of plan: The level of detail and components included in the plan document impact the length of time to develop the plan. It is important to cover a minimum amount of detail, yet not become burdened with too much detail. The plan must be detailed enough to provide the necessary direction and rationale for the direction.

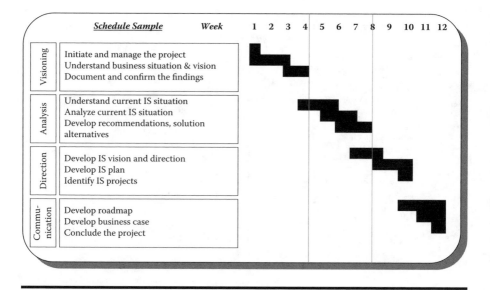

Figure 3.11   Schedule sample

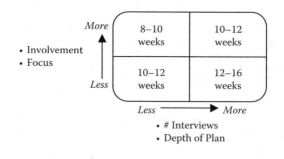

Figure 3.12   Factors impacting schedule

Number of individuals interviewed: The more individuals interviewed in the planning process, the greater the length of time needed. However, involving more individuals also increases the ownership of the plan, involvement of the organization, and visibility to issues. In a typical organization, plan to interview the executive management team, the level of management immediately below the executives, the members of the IS steering committee, the IS management team, and a few key individuals within the organization from both IS and the business organization structures. Typically, anticipate a minimum of 25 interviews.

Involvement of the organization: The more involved the organization is in the process, the less time the planning process takes as sections can be developed simultaneously. For example, obtain the assistance from several individuals in IS to document the current IS environment once the format of the deliverable is established.

Focus and priority of the effort: If the strategic planning process is not a priority for the organization, it will take significantly longer than if it is a key priority for the entire organization. Dedicate at least one full-time individual (consultant or employee) to the planning process to get it completed. Otherwise, it is too easy to let planning continually take the back seat and never complete the process. If the planning process takes too long, the plan will be out-of-date by the time it is complete.

Keep in mind that planning is a process. The first time through, the process may involve fewer individuals or be less detailed than what is preferred, but the planning process can be expanded the following year.

Conclusion

- Identify the planning process and steps you will use to complete the plan. Tailor the planning process so that it meets the needs of the organization and the purpose for completing the strategic plan.
- Give strategic planning the proper priority and attention so that it is completed in a timely fashion.
- Obtain involvement from the organization throughout the planning process.
- Communicate, communicate, communicate.

Notes for My IS Strategic Planning Project

_____

_____

_____

_____

_____

_____

_____

Chapter 4

The Visioning Phase

If you don't know where you are going, you might wind up someplace else.

— Yogi Berra (B. 1925)
American baseball player

As shown in Figure 4.1, the first phase of the planning process is the visioning phase. After organizing the planning project, the focus of this phase is to obtain a thorough understanding of the business situation, direction, and vision of how the business will operate in the future. As shown in Figure 4.2, the visioning phase has the following components:

- Initiate and manage the project
- Understand the business situation and vision
- Document and confirm the business analysis

Next, each of these components is discussed in more detail.

Initiate and Manage the Project

It is important to manage a strategic planning project just as any other business or IS project. Like any project manager, the CIO may not have authority over many of the individuals who need to participate in the planning effort. Therefore, be diligent about facilitating and obtaining

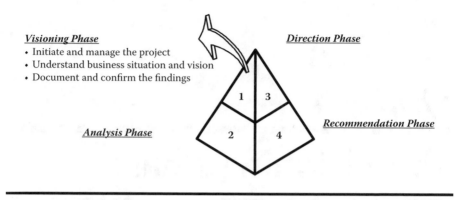

Visioning Phase
• Initiate and manage the project
• Understand business situation and vision
• Document and confirm the findings

Direction Phase

Analysis Phase

Recommendation Phase

Figure 4.1   Visioning phase

participant input. Begin by developing a project plan that outlines the planning effort, resources, and schedule. Establish a schedule with deliverables. Ensure the project team understands the priority of this effort and commits to the schedule. Without this communication and priority, the planning effort will be delayed as operational support responsibilities and other projects will take priority.

Finalize Objectives, Goals, and Scope

Determine and clearly document the objectives of the planning process. The purpose should include compelling, clear, and concise statements outlining the need for, or purpose of, completing an IS strategic plan. The objectives of a typical IS strategic plan include:

- Review the current business situation, business needs, business process improvements, and future business direction.
- Analyze the business situation and identify how the business affects the IS situation and direction as well as how IS affects the business.
- Review the current IS situation, including business applications, information repositories, technical infrastructure, organization, and processes.
- Assess the current IS environment relative to business needs, including its strengths, weaknesses, opportunities, and threats as it pertains to the opportunities and threats faced by the business.
- Compare the IS situation relative to the industry as a whole.
- Identify short-term recommendations or quick hits that can be implemented immediately.
- Determine the high-level IS direction, including the vision, mission, key objectives, and strategies.

Visioning Phase

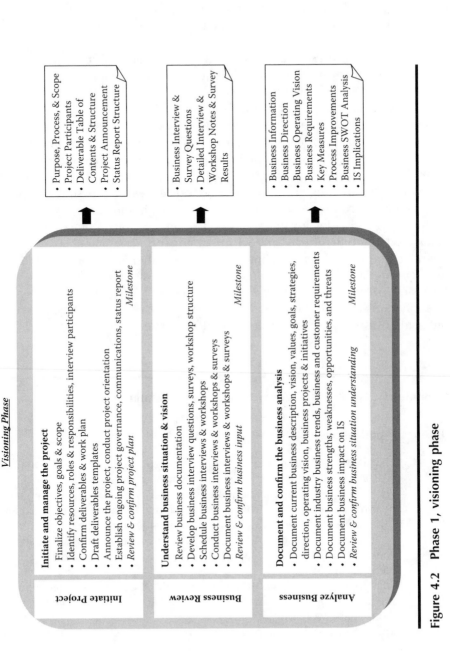

Initiate Project

Initiate and manage the project
- Finalize objectives, goals & scope
- Identify resources, roles & responsibilities, interview participants
- Confirm deliverables & work plan
- Draft deliverables templates
- Announce the project, conduct project orientation
- Establish ongoing project governance, communications, status report
- *Review & confirm project plan*   *Milestone*

- Purpose, Process, & Scope
- Project Participants
- Deliverable Table of Contents & Structure
- Project Announcement
- Status Report Structure

Business Review

Understand business situation & vision
- Review business documentation
- Develop business interview questions, surveys, workshop structure
- Schedule business interviews & workshops
- Conduct business interviews & workshops & surveys
- Document business interviews & workshops & surveys
- *Review & confirm business input*   *Milestone*

- Business Interview & Survey Questions
- Detailed Interview & Workshop Notes & Survey Results

Analyze Business

Document and confirm the business analysis
- Document current business description, vision, values, goals, strategies, direction, operating vision, business projects & initiatives
- Document industry business trends, business and customer requirements
- Document business strengths, weaknesses, opportunities, and threats
- Document business impact on IS
- *Review & confirm business situation understanding*   *Milestone*

- Business Information
- Business Direction
- Business Operating Vision
- Business Requirements
- Key Measures
- Process Improvements
- Business SWOT Analysis
- IS Implications

Figure 4.2   Phase 1, visioning phase

■ Develop the specific direction for the business applications portfolio and business process improvements.
■ Identify the required infrastructure necessary to support the business.
■ Identify the IS organizational impact and staff requirements.
■ Determine the IS processes requiring improvement.
■ Formulate the implementation plan, including specific projects, priorities, and the roadmap.
■ Identify an estimate of costs and business benefits.
■ Develop the communication plan, business liaisons, and governance necessary to implement planning as an ongoing process.

When determining the purpose and objectives of the strategic plan, document specific questions to answer through the planning process. Exhibit 4.1 provides examples of questions various companies have answered through the IS strategic planning process. This list does not identify questions to ask in interviews, but rather questions to address throughout the entire planning process. At the end of the planning process, go back to this list to ensure all the questions have been addressed. Identify questions to answer in the areas of business applications, technical infrastructure, people/organization, and processes.

▼

Exhibit 4.1   Questions to Answer During the Planning Process

Business Applications:

■ What is the current portfolio of business applications that the company uses? What percent are custom and what percent are vendor packages? What percent of the applications are supported by the business departments and what percent by IS? What is the age and viability of each component of the applications portfolio? What is the business purpose of each of the applications? How many individuals use each of the business applications? What are individual user applications, departmental applications, and enterprise applications?
■ What application projects are in progress? What projects are planned? Are these the proper projects for the business? What application projects should the company work on?
■ How fast are projects completed? Is delivery time meeting business requirements?
■ What are the strengths and weaknesses of the current business application environment? What are the areas of risk with the current business application environment?

- What is the business direction and what are the key business requirements for the future?
- What business process improvements are necessary?
- Will the current business applications meet the company's needs in the future?
- Will the current ERP system meet the needs of the future?
- From a global perspective, are the business applications meeting the needs?
- What technology and applications are the competitors or others in the industry utilizing?
- How do our business applications compare with competitors or the industry?
- How can the company utilize technology for a competitive advantage in the market?
- How can technology assist the business achieve the business goals? How can customer satisfaction be improved with technology?
- What is the e-business strategy? How can the company utilize Web technology more effectively?
- What are the strategies relative to business applications?
- What will be the business application portfolio that the company needs in three to five years?
- What is the business case for the investment required in business applications? Why should the company invest money in the business applications? What is the impact of not investing in the business applications? What is the next step?
- What are the risks to the business and are they properly managed?

Technical Infrastructure:

- What is the current technical infrastructure? What is the desktop, server, network, and telecommunication environment?
- Is the proper technical infrastructure in place to meet the business needs of the future?
- What are the service-level requirements for the technical infrastructure?
- What are the strengths and weaknesses of the current technical infrastructure?
- What are some of the risks with the current technical infrastructure?
- How does the technical infrastructure compare with the industry?
- What should be the long-term direction for the technical infrastructure? What are the vision and key principles that should guide infrastructure decisions and investments?
- What are critical technology trends and emerging technologies in the industry that the company should watch and potentially employ to assist the business?
- What technologies should be sunset (or eliminated)? What technologies should be strategic?
- How does the technical infrastructure need to change to meet the service-level requirements determined by the business?

- What is the business case for any technical infrastructure investments that are necessary?
- What are the risks to the business and are they properly managed?

People/Organization:

- How is IS organized? What are individuals working on? What are the roles and responsibilities of each area of the organization?
- What are the strengths and weaknesses of the current IS organization? What are the organizational risks?
- How should IS be organized?
- How satisfied or unsatisfied are the current IS employees?
- Do IS employees have the proper amount of resources? Do they have the right skill set and training to be effective in the future?
- Is the IS reporting structure proper for the company?
- How does IS fit into the overall company organization?
- What is the sourcing strategy for IS? Where, when, and why should the company utilize outsourcing?
- How does our IS budget and staffing compare with the industry? Should we have more IS resources or fewer? Do we have the right mix of resources?
- What should be the role of IS in the future in our organization?
- What are the risks to the business and are they properly managed?

Processes:

- What are the current IS processes?
- What are the strengths, weaknesses, and areas of risk with the current IS processes?
- How can IS increase its efficiency and effectiveness? What are ways to improve?
- How can IS better serve the needs of the organization?
- In what areas is IS doing a good job, and what areas require improvement?
- How should the company prioritize IS projects? What methodology or process should be used to balance the IS projects with the budget?
- How should the company develop and update an IS strategic plan on an ongoing basis?
- What are the expectations the business has of IS?
- What is the current level of IS satisfaction by the business departments?
- How should we measure the value of IS? What would be an appropriate balanced scorecard and metrics?
- How can the communication channels be improved between IS and the business?
- How can the system development, project management, and delivery process be improved?

- How can the alignment of IS to the business be improved? Does the proper governance process exist? What processes should be in place to obtain proper input from the business?
- How can IS implement a process improvement culture?
- How can the business support the IS process improvement culture?

Budget:

- What is the IS budget spent on?
- How does our IS spending compare with the industry?
- How can IS reduce costs and total cost of ownership?

▲

Meet with executive management team members to ask what they hope to accomplish from an IS strategic planning process. There may be a few hidden agendas. However, it is better to know these hidden agendas before beginning the process. Ask open-ended questions as to what they hope the planning process will accomplish, how success will be measured, and so forth. Document the purpose of the planning process and obtain agreement from executive management.

Scope

Define the scope of the IS strategic plan. Align the IS direction with business drivers and conform to boundary conditions imposed by the business environment. As shown in Figure 4.3:

- Business drivers identify what to do.
- Boundary conditions limit what can be done.
- The resulting plan describes how to do what can be done.

One company looked at three components in the strategic planning process:

Application architecture: business systems and business requirements
Technical architecture: client and server hardware, network, operating software
Service architecture: management information people and processes

The business strategic plan drove all three of these components. The business strategic plan identified business drivers that affect the business systems and the supporting architectures as key success factors and key strategic issues, as shown in Figure 4.4.

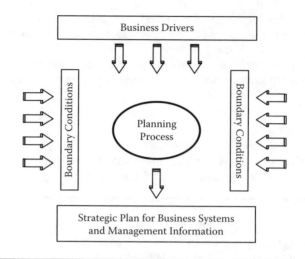

Figure 4.3   Business drivers and boundaries

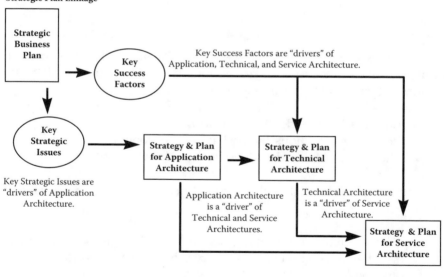

Figure 4.4   Drivers of IS plan

Include all aspects of IS in the scope of the plan, including the business applications, technical infrastructure (PC environment, network, telephone, and server environment), people or organization, and processes, as shown in Figure 4.5.

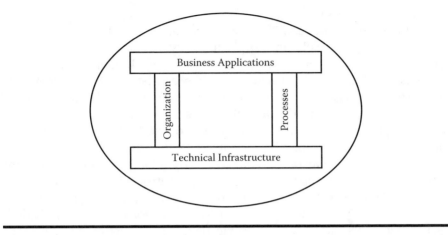

Figure 4.5 Scope of an IS plan

Management may also communicate some constraints or boundaries to deal with in the planning process. For example, executive management may have a constraint on the amount of expenditures or the timing of expenditures resulting from the plan. It is helpful to identify these constraints up front before beginning the process or you may waste a lot of time looking at alternatives that are not realistic. However, when possible do not set limits or constraints (such as "We have to keep the existing system," or "We cannot spend more than $x") and let the business requirements drive the solution as much as possible.

The scope will frame the planning boundaries. The following are some of the questions that the scope can address:

- What geographic locations are included and excluded?
- Does the scope include providing worldwide information or solutions? Do you have authority over the systems necessary to provide the information and systems, or does it require interfaces?
- What product lines or divisions are included and excluded?
- What functional departments are included and excluded?
- What business applications are included and excluded?
- Are there phases or timed expectations?
- Will the scope include business process reengineering? If so, to what extent will IS be involved in the business process reengineering exercise?
- Will the scope include interfaces to external entities (for example, customers, suppliers, and third parties)?
- Will the scope include paper files and manual processes?
- Will the scope include other hardware platforms (for example, engineering CAD/CAM environment)?

Many companies mistake the scope of the planning process to include only the business application systems that are under the control of IS. With the ease of developing applications with current PC software, a number of critical business applications are typically hidden from IS. These could be as simple as a Microsoft Excel spreadsheet, a Microsoft Access database, or even an Intranet application. Making sense of spreadsheets is especially tricky. The dividing line between simple, ad hoc financial models and significant applications built into Excel is blurry. Include too much and the process may be consumed by the trivial; ignore too much and critical components of the company's overall information architecture may be missed. If a department has a system it developed on a PC and it is critical to the operation of the business, include the system within the scope of the plan. Identify business applications that are individual user applications, departmental applications, as well as enterprise applications. The IS organization is responsible for protecting, auditing, and securing information and systems critical to the company, and for fostering innovation and the creativity of functional departments in solving their own business challenges. Establishing the right balance between these two competing objectives is difficult, and the solution for providing this balance is different in every company.

Use the following "acid tests" to determine the scope of business information that falls into the realm of IS procedures and plans. If any of these tests proves true, it is a good idea to include the system within the scope of the plan:

1. Information or a business process that is highly critical to the operation of the company
2. Information or a business process that is used, is accessed by, or involves more than one functional business department
3. Information that interfaces to any entity outside the company, whether a customer, supplier, representative, regulatory agency, or other related entity
4. Manual processes critical to the company that would benefit from IS automation

The scope should also identify the time frame of the planning horizon. The five-year planning horizon that used to be typical of traditional strategic plans is no longer feasible. The pace of changes in technology and changes in the business environment warrant no more than three years' planning horizon. Beyond that time frame, it is reasonable to assume that the business environment and available technology will be so different that a new strategy will be required. Even though the planning horizon may be two to three years, update the plan on an annual basis at a minimum to reflect changes. Companies must also increase the speed at which strategies are implemented to be able to keep pace with business and technology changes.

Identify Resources, Roles, and Responsibilities; Interview Participants

At the beginning of the planning effort, evaluate whether the organization has the proper resources to complete the IS strategic planning process successfully and in a timely manner. One of the greatest challenges in strategic planning is taking the time and committing the resources to finishing the plan. It may be desirable to augment the internal skills with external assistance in some or all of the phases. An external resource can be very useful in focusing on the planning effort to ensure it is completed in a timely manner. An external resource is also a neutral party that does not have the history of existing systems and may open thinking to solutions otherwise not considered. Be sure you are comfortable with the partner, because this consultant will be interfacing with executives, representing IS, and will have a key role in assisting to determine the IS future. When considering a partner to assist with strategic planning, keep in mind the following points:

- Is the partner focused solely on strategic planning, or also involved in implementation? If the partner is involved in implementation, ensure that the consultant will be objective and that the vendor's financial interests will not bias the direction. Many companies have learned, to their dismay, that a strategic planning partner is in an ideal position to come to conclusions that create outsourcing opportunities or major systems integration projects that may not be good business sense for the company. For example, if a firm that specializes in implementing Oracle applications assists with strategic planning, do not be surprised by a recommendation of Oracle applications as the key strategic direction.
- Review the partner's methodology and planning process. Ensure the process is a fit with the culture and desires. If possible, review other plans the consultant has developed. Ensure the level of detail aligns with your desires and expectations. Be sure the planning process used and plan deliverables are detailed enough rather than just a fluffy presentation with no true direction and without a solid basis for the decisions.
- Review the credentials of the specific consultants who will be assigned to the planning project and meet with them. Do they have the necessary experience and knowledge? How much IS experience do they have? Are you comfortable with them? Do you

trust them? The specific individual, not the company, will be doing the planning work, so focus attention on the specific individuals who will be doing the planning as well as their organization. How many strategic plans have they completed? Do they have significant experience in IS and are they up-to-date with technologies and directions? Do they have practical implementation experience?

■ Obtain customer references and talk with customers the specific consultant has assisted. Were they satisfied? Do they have a solid direction and plan? Was the planning process effective for their organization?

■ What is their approach to the planning project? How involved will the company be? Does the consultant take control of the planning effort, or do you retain control of the plan, the process, and the decisions? The role of the consultant is to guide the process and provide information, and leave the decision making to you, because it is your direction and plan. How will the consultant ensure knowledge transfer so you can continue the planning process on an ongoing basis?

■ How are changes to the project addressed? How will the status of the project be communicated?

■ What is the estimated cost and schedule? What are the assumptions in the estimates?

Document the specific roles and responsibilities of everyone involved in the planning effort. Identify the roles of the business and IS as well as the consultant. As Chapter 2 discussed, document the responsibilities of the various groups involved in the planning process, and identify their level of authority and decision-making responsibility.

Identify individuals to interview or converse with as part of the planning process. As mentioned in Chapter 3, the number of individuals to interview has an impact on the time required for the planning process and also affects the quality of the plan. As the number of individuals increase, ownership increases and there are more ideas and information, but the cost of this additional involvement is increased planning time. However, after a certain number of interviews, you may find that much of the information is repetitive. In a typical organization, plan to interview the following individuals:

■ The entire executive management team.
■ The level of management immediately below the executives.
■ A few key individuals in the business organization: This could be a master scheduler, someone in shipping or customer service. Typically, these are the "go to" people when there are questions in the business, and they have usually been with the organization for numerous years. It can also be helpful to interview a few

individuals new to the organization because they may have an interesting perspective.
- The members of the IS steering committee.
- The IS management team.
- A few key individuals within the IS organization.

Typically, a minimum of 25 total interviews are required from the business and IS organizations, but it could be significantly higher depending on the organization size and structure.

Confirm Deliverables and Work Plan

Review the planning methodology to develop the table of contents for your strategic plan. A sample table of contents was provided in Chapter 3. Review the table of contents with the list of initial questions identified in the purpose of the plan. Ensure there is a section to present information to answer each question. Review the deliverables and work plan with other participants in the planning process.

Draft Deliverable Templates

Right at the beginning of the planning process is an excellent time to draft the deliverable documents. The documents will become a repository for the planning information as it is developed. Then it can be reviewed by individuals at each milestone and can be updated through an iterative process. Develop the following deliverable documents:

- A document for detailed interview notes.
- A document for the detailed IS strategic plan. Begin with the table of contents that you have identified. In the Appendix, include the purpose, scope, and planning process. It is good to document this so that others can understand how the plan was developed and decisions were made.
- A document for the executive management presentation.

Announce the Project; Conduct Project Orientation

Next, announce the strategic planning project to those involved in the planning process and interviews. Exhibit 4.2 shows an example of an e-mail announcement that could be used.

If involving a team in the planning process, hold an orientation session outlining the project and each individual's responsibilities.

▼

Exhibit 4.2 Project Announcement Example

In an effort to continuously improve the information systems (IS) services that we provide, the company has initiated an effort to develop an IS strategic plan. The purpose of this plan is to align IS activities and projects with business goals and objectives. The roadmap will identify opportunities for IS to increase value to the business and move IS from being a reactive to a more proactive function. The planning process will involve many individuals throughout the company, and the process will be facilitated by *xxxxx*.

As part of the process, it is important that we meet one on one with key individuals throughout the company to understand the business needs and direction. We need your involvement and assistance in this process. The meetings will be held during the next two weeks. The IS strategic plan will be completed at the end of the month, with the complete plan posted on the intranet and presented to management.

Prior to the discussions, we will distribute a list of questions so you can see the type of information that will be discussed. In the next week, we will let you know the date and time of your discussion.

Thank you in advance for your participation on this very important effort. Your input and comments will be extremely critical in developing our IS plans for the future. In the meantime, if you have any questions or concerns about this effort, please call me.

▲

Establish Ongoing Project Governance, Communications, and Status Report

Communicating the progress of the planning effort is important because this is a key project for the organization. Determine who to keep abreast of the planning project and how often they should receive updates. Typically, the person to whom the CIO reports requires progress reports on a weekly or biweekly basis.

Review and Confirm Project Plan (Milestone)

It is also essential to keep the IS steering committee updated on a regular basis. The completion of a milestone is a great opportunity to provide this update. At this point, review the finalized project objectives, scope, project plan, roles and responsibilities, interview participants, and deliverable table of contents. Obtain feedback and modify the deliverables as necessary.

Understand the Business Situation and Vision

If the IS organization is closely integrated with the business, the business direction may be well known to the IS organization. In this case, the understanding of the business situation and vision may be completed very quickly. However, typically IS management does not fully understand all the business challenges and future direction of the business. This is not surprising because surveys have reported that many functional areas in the company do not fully understand the business goals and direction. Try a test: ask several executives, including IS management, to explain the top three objectives of the company. The company is an above-average company if all are able to recite the objectives!

It is difficult, if not impossible, to determine the proper direction of IS without a complete and thorough understanding of the business direction. Because business application systems are expensive and time consuming to implement, organizations often utilize their systems for ten years or more. With the frequent changes in the business environment, a company could often change products, customers, and channels of distribution, type of manufacturing, or even industry during the same time! Be aware of potential changes and account for them when planning the IS strategic direction.

As an example, one company selected and implemented a new manufacturing application system. At the time, the company was in the business of manufacturing reagents for blood testing, which is process manufacturing. When reviewing systems, the company looked mainly at the process manufacturing requirements. A few years after installing the system, the company began manufacturing instruments to automate the blood tests in addition to the liquid reagents. The instrument manufacturing was discrete manufacturing, which has different requirements than the original requirements. This resulted in having a system that did not meet the needs and had to be replaced after a few years. Had strategic planning been conducted effectively, the new requirements would have been identified and the organization would have selected a different application system to meet its current and future requirements.

A progressive organization will have a strategic business plan in place. An existing business plan makes this phase of the process proceed very quickly. However, many companies do not have an up-to-date strategic plan, or the plan may be missing many important components. Many businesses strategic plans focus mainly on the financial targets, and do not really address the key business questions as to how the organization will achieve the financial objectives. Whether or not a plan exists, it is a good idea to meet with executive management to review the goals of the business and ensure that you have a thorough understanding of the business direction and challenges.

Review Business Documentation

Begin understanding the business by reviewing business documentation. Here is an example of documentation that may exist:

- Business plan, planning material, and any departmental plans
- Brochures, sales and marketing literature, and product brochures
- Organization chart of the executives and individual departments
- Annual reports
- Monthly and annual status reports
- Quarterly financial updates; investor information
- Budgets and budget planning presentations
- All employee communications
- Mission, vision, and values
- Business objectives
- Business initiatives or key projects
- Internet site
- News releases and announcements
- All employee survey results
- Customer survey results

While reviewing the information, try to answer the questions in Exhibit 4.3.

You will be confirming the information during interviews, but it is helpful to gather and organize as much information as you can before the interviews. An understanding helps move the interview quicker and enables you to ask better questions.

──────────────────────── ▼ ────────────────────────

Exhibit 4.3   Business Situation

1. Charter, mission, vision, credo or values, goals, objectives:
   - What is the mission and vision of our business?
   - Are there any other high-level business direction statements, such as values, credo, brand, etc.?
   - What are the goals and objectives of our company?
   - What is our goal in terms of market position? Do we want to be number one in the industry for all markets or just for targeted markets?
2. Strategies, business priorities for the year, critical issues for the year:
   - What are the specific strategies or business priorities for this year, in priority order?
   - What are other prioritized business projects, issues, or objectives for this year?
   - What must our business accomplish this year to remain competitive?

- What critical issues face our organization today?
- What critical issues face our organization in the future?

3. Business information (history, description, financial summary):
   - What is a brief history of our company? When was it founded? Were there any acquisitions or changes of ownership? Are any acquisitions or divestitures anticipated in the future?
   - In what business markets does our company participate? Are there any changes in the business markets in the future? (For example, does our company design, manufacture, sell, distribute, service? Does our company plan to outsource service in the future? Is our company make-to-order, make-to-stock, engineer-to-order, process, discrete?)
   - Who are our customers? (For example, do we sell and lease, do we go through independent representatives, or sell to the government?)
   - What is our company's niche? Why do customers buy from us rather than from our competition?
   - Is our company global or local in nature? How is our company organized? Does management see this changing in the future?
   - Are there other divisions or related organizations? Do we need to bundle services or products with sister organizations, divisions, or buying groups?
   - What are our basic product lines?
   - What are our lead times?
   - What are our total sales for the past five years?
   - What has been the growth rate?
   - How many employees do we have on both a global and geographic basis? What is the planned number of employees in three years and in five years? What was the number of employees three years ago?
   - What is our capital budget?
   - What is our operating profit?
   - What are the inventory turns? How does it compare to the industry?
   - What are the days sales outstanding? How does it compare to the industry?
   - What is the cost of goods sold? Direct labor? Indirect labor?

4. Industry:
   - How large is the total industry? What market share does our company have? How many competitors are in the industry and what is their size? Who are their main competitors? Obtain a list of the competitors and their size. (For example, is it a highly polar industry with the top five companies sharing 60% of the market, while the next 200 share the remaining 40%?)
   - What is the global competitive situation?
   - Are there any industry associations or affiliations?
   - What are the trends, developments, or changes taking place in the industry at this time or predicted in the next few years? Is it a fast or slowly changing industry?
   - What change in the industry, if it could be made, would totally change the way we do business or serve our customers?

      – What are our customers requesting of us? Why do customers buy from us rather than our competitors?
      – What is our competitive advantage?
      – Do we plan on growth through acquisition?

5. External environmental factors:
      – What are our external environmental factors? What challenges do we face in the marketplace? What are our external opportunities and threats?

6. Internal strengths and weaknesses:
      – What are the internal strengths of our organization?
      – What are the internal weaknesses of our organization?
      – What are our internal environmental factors? What internal challenges, opportunities, and threats does our company have?

▲

Develop Business Interview Questions, Surveys, and Workshop Structure

Typically, the main vehicle to obtain information and input for the IS strategic plan is through business discussions or interviews. However, also consider other methods to obtain information, such as workshops or surveys. Workshops can prove helpful by involving a larger number of individuals and obtaining brainstorming across the group. Surveys can be helpful to get quantitative data. If you have properly established an internal network, most of this work is little more than a formality, making sure everyone knows what each has already explained informally.

Carefully develop the business interview questions to be sure you obtain all the information you need in the planning process. Structure the interviews so they are productive, and not just a complaining session. The discussions should be no longer than one and a half hours, so be sure questions are focused and direct. Formulate specific questions about areas of concern or vague areas in the business documentation and literature. Remember that the discussions are the main vehicle to obtain information, so ensure that they are complete. A separate list of questions may be necessary for the top executive of the company.

Structure the business discussions in three areas:

■ Learning about the interviewee's responsibilities and department
■ Understanding the interviewee's thoughts on the business as a whole
■ Understanding the interviewee's perspective on IS

Allocate approximately a third of the time of the discussion to each area. It is preferable to start with the individual's department, because that is the area the interviewee knows the best and is the most comfortable with. As can be seen, much of the interview discussion is focused on the business rather than on IS.

Exhibit 4.4 shows an example of interview questions.

▼

Exhibit 4.4   Business Interview Questions Example

1. Your business department, your job
   - What is your title, department, role, and area of responsibility?
   - What are the key functions or processes in your department? Walk through some of the key processes in which you are involved.
   - What are your departmental objectives for this year? Are there any goals beyond this year?
   - What are the strengths and weaknesses of your department?
   - What critical challenges do you face? What are your current areas of trouble?
   - What are some process improvements you would like to make? What are improvements or industry best practices that you would like to implement in your area? What key measures in your area are you going to improve to be more competitive?
   - What are your key information needs? What measures do you review on a regular basis? Are the measures readily available? Are there business decisions that are difficult to make given existing information?
2. The company as a whole
   - What is your understanding of the direction of the company as a whole? What are the goals, objectives, strategies, and priorities? Are there any potential changes in direction in the future that you are aware of? What are the specific growth plans for the company? How will the growth be achieved? What are key business initiatives in the next year?
   - What are the strengths of the company? What is the company's competitive advantage? Why do your customers buy from the company? Why do employees like working here?
   - What are the weaknesses of the company as a whole? Why do customers not buy from the company? Why do employees leave the company?
   - What are the opportunities and threats facing the company? What other critical issues does the company face?
   - What are some key trends and changes that are happening in the industry? What one thing, if it could be implemented, would change or impact the entire industry?
   - If you owned the company, what are some things you would change?
3. Information systems (IS)
   - What interface do you have today with IS? What services/systems do you or your department use? Do you have any key spreadsheets or systems that your department supports rather than IS?

- Overall, how well is IS today meeting your needs? How would you rate them on a scale of 1–5 (5 being the best, 1 not meeting your needs at all)?
- What is IS doing right that you would like them to continue doing?
- What could IS be doing better? How can IS be easier to do business with?
- Are you receiving communications from IS on what they are doing? Do you feel that you have input into the direction and priorities of IS?
- Are there specific projects or requests that you have of IS in the next 1–3 years? Is there any specific technology that you think would be useful to implement? Are there any additional ways that IS could assist you with your business goals for this year, perhaps things you have not formally requested of IS?
- Do you feel that IS is aligned well with the business? Why or why not?
- What are ways in which IS could assist the company in the future?
- Do you feel that IS provides a strategic advantage for the company? Why or why not? Do you think that IS is headed in the right direction?
- If IS could accomplish one thing next year, what would you like that to be?

▲

Surveys

Surveys are an important and useful tool for gathering quantitative data to compare progress from year to year. Surveys can be very short and general, or very long and specific. The more detailed the survey, the more specific information you have that will help lead to better decisions. However, detailed surveys require more time and patience from the business. Exhibit 4.5 is an example of a business survey.

▼

Exhibit 4.5   Business Survey Example

IS Services Survey
Response Key:
5—Strongly agree
4—Agree
3—Neither agree nor disagree
2—Disagree
1—Strongly disagree
N/A—Don't know or not applicable

- Please consider and rate the service and support you have received in the past year.
- Refer to the open questions at the end of the survey to supply additional information regarding any question.

	Question	Response
IS Help Desk	1. When I have trouble with my PC hardware and software, I most often turn to:	(Pull- down selection list) ■ Help desk ■ Individual IS employees ■ Other employees in my department or company ■ External individuals or companies ■ Other: _____
	2. I am aware of the process to follow and who to contact when I need IS-related assistance.	1 2 3 4 5 NA
	3. The hours of operation of the help desk are sufficient to meet my needs.	1 2 3 4 5 NA
	4. I have the ability to provide input into the priority of my requests.	1 2 3 4 5 NA
	5. In general, my expectation is to have requests acknowledged within this time frame.	(Pull-down selection list) ■ <1 hour ■ 1–3 hours ■ 3–8 hours ■ 8–24 hours ■ 24+ hours
	6. When I work with the IS help desk, the staff seeks to understand the problem I describe to them.	1 2 3 4 5 NA
	7. Help desk staff communicate with me in a nontechnical language and they are courteous and professional.	1 2 3 4 5 NA
	8. I receive the information I need regarding the status of my request.	1 2 3 4 5 NA
	9. The help desk follows through and resolves my request to successful completion.	1 2 3 4 5 NA

	Question	Response
IS Help Desk	10. The help desk staff is knowledgeable and capable.	1　2　3　4　5　NA
	11. My requests for assistance are resolved in a timely fashion.	1　2　3　4　5　NA
Tools	1. I have adequate PC hardware to do my job.	1　2　3　4　5　NA
	2. I have adequate software to do my job.	1　2　3　4　5　NA
	3. I am aware of the software and tools available.	1　2　3　4　5　NA
	4. The computer equipment I use (software, hardware, and network) is reliable enough to allow me to get my work done.	1　2　3　4　5　NA
	5. My hardware and software is generally fast enough to get my work done efficiently.	1　2　3　4　5　NA
	6. I am able to connect from external locations when necessary.	1　2　3　4　5　NA
	7. I have easy access to the business information and reporting I need to do my job.	1　2　3　4　5　NA
	8. The business information I get from systems is accurate.	1　2　3　4　5　NA
Training	1. I am comfortable using the software and tools I have.	1　2　3　4　5　NA
	2. I am aware of all the features and functions available to me in the tools I have.	1　2　3　4　5　NA

	Question	*Response*
Training	3. The training I receive on the PC and software I have meets my needs.	1　2　3　4　5　NA
	4. I would like to get advanced tips and techniques for software via (prioritize all that apply):	(Allow for 1–6) ■ A monthly newsletter ■ An IT web page ■ A lunch time forum ■ A training class ■ Self-help (i.e., frequently asked questions, online help capabilities) ■ Other (specify: _____)
	5. The documentation I have is sufficient.	1　2　3　4　5　NA
Application Projects	1. Within the past year, I have/have not worked with IS on a specific IS-related project.	(Pull-down) ■ Have ■ Have not (Questions 2–7 appear if the respondent answers 'have')
	2. I am aware of the process for submitting requests for an application project or enhancement.	1　2　3　4　5　NA
	3. When I have a request for an application project, I most often contact:	(Pull-down) ■ Help desk (xxxx) ■ Individual IS employee ■ Management ■ IS management ■ External individuals/ companies ■ Other: _____
	4. I have input into the prioritization of my project request.	1　2　3　4　5　NA
	5. IS seeks to understand my business goals and define my business requirements.	1　2　3　4　5　NA
	6. IS communicates in a nontechnical language and they are courteous and professional.	1　2　3　4　5　NA

	Question	Response
Application Projects	7. IS delivers quality solutions that meet the business goals.	1 2 3 4 5 NA
	8. I am satisfied with the way that projects are managed.	1 2 3 4 5 NA
	9. IS project resources follows through and resolves my project request to successful completion.	1 2 3 4 5 NA
	10. IS project resources are knowledgeable and capable.	1 2 3 4 5 NA
	11. IS completes projects in a timely fashion.	1 2 3 4 5 NA
Overall IS	1. IS has a strong customer service focus.	1 2 3 4 5 NA
	2. IS has a good strategic direction that is aligned with the business direction and priorities.	1 2 3 4 5 NA
	3. I know what IS is working on.	1 2 3 4 5 NA
	4. I am notified in advance of changes that impact me.	1 2 3 4 5 NA
	5. I am able to provide input into the IS direction as necessary.	1 2 3 4 5 NA
	6. IS provides a strategic advantage to the company.	1 2 3 4 5 NA
Overall IS	7. Overall, I am satisfied with the service I receive from IS.	1 2 3 4 5 NA
	8. In general, IS is responsive to my needs.	1 2 3 4 5 NA

Open Questions:

1. List two or three things that IS does best:

2. List two or three things that IS most needs to improve:

3. If IS could help you solve one problem, what would that be?

4. Are there any technology, tools, services, or training that would help you to do your job?

5. Other comments:

Respondent Information:

Building/country I work in: (Drop-down selection)

Department/function I work in: (Drop-down selection)

My job could best be described as: (Drop-down selection)

- Manager/supervisor
- Production employee
- Office employee

I have worked at the company: (Drop-down selection)

- Less than 1 year
- 1 to 3 years
- 3 to 7 years
- Over 7 years

Name (Optional):

--------------------▲--------------------

The following are tips to consider when using surveys:

- Use survey software to automate the survey process and the collection of data. It is well worth the price of the software. If the company does not have survey software, public Web sites are available for purchasing survey management, such as www.zoomerang.com. Distribute the survey via the Intranet. Send an e-mail message to all employees asking for their cooperation, with a link to the survey. An example of a notification is provided in Exhibit 4.6. In the notification, be sure to include a date when the survey is due, identify whom to contact for questions, and provide an idea of how long the survey will take and how they will obtain results back from the survey.

▼

Exhibit 4.6 Notification E-mail Example

WIN A $100 GIFT CERTIFICATE!!!!

In efforts to improve the services you receive from information systems (IS), we would like your input. You are our internal customer, and measuring your level of satisfaction is a way in which we can measure how we are doing as a service organization. Our focus is to meet the business objectives by providing you with the services and products that are necessary for you to do your job.

We are very interested in your input. Please complete the survey by clicking on this link: xxxxxxxxxxxxx and answering the questions by 9/1.

The survey has 25 questions and it will take less than five minutes of your time to respond. The survey is confidential and results will be reported in aggregate. Summary survey results and action items will be reported back to you after the results have been analyzed.

To thank you for your comments and to encourage participation in the survey, we will be randomly selecting five individuals who respond to the survey by 9/1 and they will each win a $100 gift certificate!

Thank you very much for your participation and comments as it will help us improve. Please contact me if you have any questions.

▲

- Distribute the survey to all employees, or at least all employees with a computer ID. A survey to a selective audience may slant the results.
- Think of ways to encourage involvement. For example, one company said that it would draw names from those who responded by a certain date to win money at the company store or a gift certificate. However, if you say you are going to do something, be sure to follow through and do it.
- Make sure that the average person in the business easily understands all questions. Do not use information systems acronyms, phrases, or systems that are not common knowledge.
- Keep the survey as short as possible, but ask specific questions about areas that may be a concern. Give advance thought to what might be some of the issues. Include questions relative to possible strengths and weaknesses.
- Obtain input on the survey questions and format from the IS management team.
- Test the survey, the link, and the reporting before releasing the survey to the general population. The IS group can be a good test group on the functioning of the survey, but sample the survey questions with a small group from the business. Obtain comments on the questions.

■ Give considerable thought to how to analyze the data and make sure those indicators are included on the survey in the respondent information area. For example: by division, by location, by level of the organization, or by length of time with the company.

■ Report survey results and actions planned. It is a huge mistake to not communicate what is planned as a result of obtaining the information. If not intending to follow through with the survey, do not do the survey at all because the business organization will expect actions once it provides input.

■ Take time to analyze the results. When done properly, the results can contain a lot of excellent information. Provide the results to the entire IS management team for further review.

■ Do not get defensive about the comments. Absolutely do not attack individuals about their comments or feedback will probably not be provided again. Do not, as one company did, treat responses you perceive to be negative as statistically irrelevant outliers that can safely be ignored. When presenting survey results to the IS group, emphasize the positive comments as well as the improvement areas.

■ Couple the survey input with objective interviews as the surveys may not tell the complete story.

■ Repeat the survey on a regular (annual) basis. Ask many of the same questions to report trends and improvements.

Schedule Business Interviews and Workshops

Next, schedule the business interviews and workshops. Scheduling can be an administrative challenge due to tight schedules and changes, so do not forget to ask for scheduling assistance. Exhibit 4.7 shows an example of an announcement for scheduling a business interview.

Exhibit 4.7   Interview Announcement Example

As announced in the earlier e-mail on *x/x/xx*, we would like to meet with you regarding the IS strategic plan.

Your discussion is scheduled for:

        March 1 at 10:00–11:30 in the conference room

Please let me know if you have any schedule conflicts with this date or time.

I have attached a list of questions. Because time is limited, we will not be asking each question of everyone. Although it would be helpful for you to look at the questions in advance and think through some key points, please do not feel as if you need to do a lot of preparation work. The meetings will be very informal discussions to obtain your honest opinions and thoughts. You can tell by the questions that we will spend a fair amount of time understanding your business area rather than just asking about technology.

If you have any questions or concerns about this effort, please call me. Thank you for your participation and candid comments on this important project.

▬▬▬▬▬▬▬▬▬▬▬▬▬▬▬▲▬▬▬▬▬▬▬▬▬▬▬▬▬▬

Conduct Business Interviews, Workshops, and Surveys

Begin discussions by emphasizing that it is critical for the planning team to have a good understanding of the business direction. This business understanding is necessary to ensure that the direction of IS is developed in a way that supports current and future requirements of the business. Interviews should be no longer than one and a half hours. It is extremely helpful to ask permission to record the discussion; recordings will help with taking notes and ensuring accurate facts. However, some individuals may be uncomfortable and not as willing to provide candid opinions while being recorded. Conduct the discussions in a flexible and casual manner. Be sure to listen closely and follow up with additional clarifying questions. Use the established questions as a guide, but probe into other areas as necessary. Do not get defensive during the interviews, or interviewees will tell you what you want to hear instead of what you need to hear. Even if you think their comments are inaccurate, suppress the urge to correct them. You are there to obtain information. You should hear something from several interviewees before considering it fact, so be sure to cross-check information you heard in previous interviews without saying where you heard the information. At the end of the discussion, ask if any other individuals in their area would be important to meet. After a few interviews, review the list of questions to ensure that you are obtaining all the information necessary or if additional questions are needed.

Document Business Interviews, Workshops, and Surveys

Document the detailed notes of the interviews. The notes will be helpful if you involve other individuals in the planning process as they will not have to repeat the interviews. Keep in mind confidentiality. If anyone was concerned about the information, do not document it; either protect the distribution of the information or provide anonymity. Some individuals may express a concern to see the notes to ensure they were quoted or understood correctly. It can be helpful to distribute the notes to individuals for their review and corrections. When having a workshop, it is often helpful to have an additional individual to act as a scribe and document the workshop findings and comments.

Also document the results of the survey. Summarize the results for each question. Document the results in the detailed plan document. Provide summary charts in the overview presentation.

Review and Confirm Business Input

This is a good milestone point to provide summary status information to the individual or group most involved in the planning process. Typically, the interviews are the most time-consuming step of the process, and it is helpful to provide an initial status or summary before analyzing the information. Identify how many individuals were interviewed and identify those individuals. Obtain feedback if any additional interviews are necessary to receive a complete picture. This is also an opportunity to confirm any unclear or inconsistent information.

Document and Confirm the Business Analysis

Document Current Business Description, Vision, Values, Goals, Strategies, Direction, Operating Vision, Business Projects, and Initiatives

In the IS strategic plan, document the following items regarding the business:

- Business situation
  - History: Outline who founded the company, when it was founded, and areas in which the company has grown.
  - Description: Document various divisions or business segments that comprise the company. Describe products, services, and sales by division. Outline the size of the organization, locations, headquarters, acquisitions, etc.
  - Financial summary: Summarize the size of the organization in revenue and other key financial metrics.
  - Customers: Identify how many customers you have and who the groups of customers are, identify if there is a small number of customers that generate the majority of revenue, identify if sales are made electronically, and identify where sales are coming from geographically.

- Vendors: Identify how many vendors you have, and list who they are.
- Industry information and competition: Identify whether business is seasonal, the type of competition, the main competitors, and trends happening in the industry, such as consolidation.
- Departmental specific areas of importance.

■ Business direction
  - Mission, charter.
  - Vision.
  - Values, credo.
  - Goals, objectives.
  - Strategies and business priorities for the year.
  - Financial targets.
  - Growth objectives: Identify how growth will occur, and if it is organic or via acquisition. Identify where growth will occur geographically. Identify what products or customer base will grow, as well as new channels. Identify key factors to achieve the growth. Identify growth constraints, such as capacity or facility constraints.

Business Operating Vision

Work with the IS steering committee to translate the high-level business direction to the next level of detail, the business operating vision. How is the company really going to look and function in the future? How does the company want to deliver services? The business operating vision has a direct impact on the IS strategic direction and requirements.

The members of the IS steering committee are in the best position to define the vision. Develop the business operating vision during several group meetings with the committee. Ask several high-level questions such as those stated below, obtain notes, and then meet again to report the summary. Then, present the updated results to the executive committee for confirmation and update of the business operating vision.

When working with the IS steering committee, tailor the following questions to your specific industry and business. Examples of questions or information to obtain include:

1. With the information obtained from executive management, read the mission and vision statements. Ask questions such as:
   - What businesses is the company in?
   - Is the company in any other markets? (For example: Do you develop, manufacture, sell, market, distribute, install, or service your product?)

- Is the product just one item, or several? (For example: In addition to a product, do you sell service and software?)
- Does the company need to be able to bundle services or products with sister organizations or divisions?
- Will the company change or expand businesses? Often, there can be other types of businesses found in certain corners of the organization. Although they are minor parts of the company initially, consider these other businesses, because the areas can expand significantly in the future.
- Who are the customers? With whom will the company need to interface? Who are the desired customers?
- What are the company goals in terms of market position? Does the company want to be number one in the industry for all markets or only certain markets?
- What are key industry trends? Is it a fast or slowly changing industry?
- Are acquisitions or divestitures likely?

2. How will the company operate the business in the future?
   - Will it operate locally or worldwide?
   - What business functions will be done locally and which worldwide?
   - How does the company want to deliver services in the future?
   - How will distribution be handled? Does the company need the ability to accept an order anywhere in the world and fill it anywhere depending on availability, inventory, etc.?
   - Will project teams be worldwide?
   - Will procurement be worldwide?
   - Will customer support and service be worldwide?
   - Are multi-languages and multi-currency required?
   - How does the company want the business processes to look in the future? How will the processes be different then today? (For example, e-mail, paperless, ease of obtaining information, no manual or redundant efforts, etc.)
   - What growth plans are in place? Do they plan growth through geographic expansion, product expansion, customer growth, or acquisitions?

3. What are the key factors for you to be successful in the market-place? (For example, does the company need to be fast, flexible, and service oriented?) Can the factors be weighted or prioritized?
   - How does the company want to look from a customer perspective? Does the company want to be doing business differently? (For example, electronic data interchange, electronic access, electronic payments, ability to bundle orders with sister organizations or divisions, use of the Internet, etc.)

It may take several meetings to get a complete business operating vision. When complete, the business operating vision is a list of items or high-level requirements on how the business wants to function in the future.

Executive management may be reluctant to prioritize the key factors of success in the marketplace. However, it can be very helpful to have a clear understanding of what is important to the business. Different priorities may drive very different IS approaches. As an example, one company identified the key factors in order of priority to be: limit customer risk, reduce cost to the customer, and increase speed of delivery. On a daily basis, as employees make decisions or make departmental plans, having clear priorities can help guide their decisions. To continue with the example above, if a change is requested in the company (with the priorities of risk, cost, speed) that will reduce the order time but will significantly increase costs to the customer, the change should be evaluated.

Global Requirements

One critical piece of information to determine is whether the company has global objectives now or in the future. If the company has intentions of a global presence, it may have significant implications on the IS strategic direction and scope. A company may make the mistake of determining the direction of IS domestically without recognizing the impact globalization can have. The way a company addresses the global market can have a tremendous impact on IS.

If a company states that it has global aspirations, there are several different ways to accomplish global business objectives. A business must decide if it wants to be more of an international enterprise or truly a global business with global business processes. There is a drastic difference in these business approaches, and it has a significant impact on the strategic direction of IS.

Many organizations are international. They run applications that autonomously support their international initiatives. They may loosely link application together, but lack the ability to function as a consolidated entity. To distance themselves from competition, to handle the tremendous cost and price pressures, and to meet the needs of global customers, a company may need to do more than support international locations; the company may need to operate globally. Customers who operate globally often demand global processes of their vendors. This may include the ability to place an order anywhere in the world and fill it anywhere in the world depending on inventory, availability, and capacity, ship to anywhere in the world, have consistent prices, consistent processes, consistent product, consistent quality, and consistent product numbers around the world. Many companies may need to have truly global operations with applications that have the power to streamline, consolidate, and maximize the capabilities of local uniqueness, and implement standard global business processes and procedures to ensure a single, unified, and global operation and access. Through this globalization and standardization of business processes, companies can realize substantial cost savings, better internal coordination, and a more comprehensive analysis. The bottom line is that they may be able to realize a competitive advantage in the market.

If the company operates on a global basis, executive management may choose to locate components of the business anywhere in the world. This means the design, development, procurement, and manufacturing functions can take place in different parts of the world. This issue prompts entirely different requirements on your IS strategy as your systems need to communicate, interface, share information, or even be the same system.

It is difficult for a company to go from an international strategy of loosely coupled international locations to a global business strategy with common global processes without rethinking and reimplementing IS. It is far better to determine the long-term business strategy and direction and then design systems in advance to handle a global business presence. Global applications do not automatically enable the organization to adopt global processes. However, the technology foundation of global applications provides the potential for global operation. Effective globalization is the result of strategically implementing and linking applications into seamless global business processes. It is far easier to establish a global strategy early in a firm's growth cycle rather than after having many international sites with differing processes and systems.

Globalization has several requirements for applications. Applications must support local language, currency, date and time formatting, accounting practices, labor reporting, tax regulations, and cultural attitudes of the local entities while adhering to global standards. Security must be designed with global requirements. Applications must be scalable to take into account the size and maturity of the local entity. The organization must understand the dynamics and impact of creating standardized processes across the entire organization while still accommodating the local practices. Consider local practices when designing processes, such as the sales process. The organization must be flexible to identify best practices and implement them across the organization, even if it involves changing business processes to fit software and corporate standards. The systems must also be able to consolidate local information to meet the global information needs. In summary, *global* and *international* are not synonymous. International denotes a worldwide presence, and global signifies an organization with worldwide operating capabilities and competitive advantage. Figure 4.6 shows how one company communicated the various global options for discussion and decision.

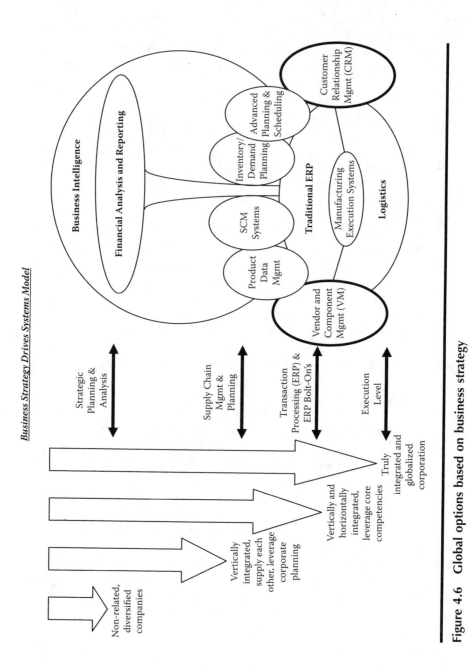

Figure 4.6 Global options based on business strategy

Document Industry Business Trends, Business, and Customer Requirements

Environmental Business Requirements

Environmental requirements are the high-level requirements the company has as a result of the product or type of business the company is in. Because different departments have varying types of business requirements, it can be valuable to have group discussions.

For example, an organization may find a few of the environmental requirements included in Exhibit 4.8.

▼

Exhibit 4.8   Environmental Requirements Example

- Make-to-order
- Make-to-stock
- Configure-to-order
- Process manufacturing
- Discrete manufacturing
- Repetitive manufacturing
- Job shop
- Discrete work orders
- Sell software
- Sell hardware
- Sell services
- Distributed processing
- Support of multiple divisions and locations
- Multiple plants, integrated
- Multiple locations in a warehouse
- Distribution
- Distribution network, multilevel
- Multiple currency: sell, invoice, buy, pay, report
- Purchase nonstock products for re-sale
- Configure products for sale
- Repair, recondition, or service our product
- Input to worldwide financial and sales reporting
- Sarbanes–Oxley requirements
- Blanket purchase orders
- Just-in-time manufacturing capabilities
- Decimal inventory/bill of material quantities
- Back-flush inventory and resources
- Finite capacity loading
- Computer-aided design and computer-aided manufacturing interface
- Electronic data interchange interface
- Web-enabled ordering
- Interface to automated plant equipment
- Shelf life sensitive materials
- Use potency and grade materials
- FDA and government reporting requirements (EPA, NRC, etc.)
- Free-stock capabilities
- Forecast demand
- Standard and actual costing
- Subcontract production
- Hazardous use and toxic materials
- Lot control
- Serial number control
- Radio Frequency Identification (RFID) control
- Engineering change control

▲

External Business Requirements

Identify all the stakeholders of the company. Stakeholders are any group that may have an interest in the company. The customer is the most important stakeholder, but there may be other stakeholders as well. There may be direct customers (such as distributors, agents, brokers, retailers, or dealers), but also the end customer, consumer, or influencer. For example, a hearing aid manufacturer identified the end customer as a stakeholder, but also identified customers' family members as an important stakeholder, because they are often the individuals involved in identifying a hearing loss. Stakeholders often include suppliers, strategic partners, or regulatory agencies.

Determine what external business requirements are requested of the company from the stakeholders. Typically, companies have customer and supplier surveys that have valuable information. It can be helpful to visit or talk directly to a customer or supplier, but companies typically like to control access to external entities so that may be difficult. The information can also be assembled from discussions with the IS steering committee.

Exhibit 4.9 includes examples of possible customer requirements.

Try doing business with your company as a customer and see how easy (or difficult) it is. Attempt to buy something, ask a question, return something, or complain. Customer requirements typically increase over time. Leaders in the industry continually raise the bar of expectations for an industry and force competitors to match or beat the requirements. The key to business success is to determine who the customers are and what they want. Identify how technology can strengthen or support the customer relationship. Following are questions to consider when analyzing customer requirements:

- Why do customers come to the organization?
- Why do customers leave the organization and go to competitors?
- Are customers satisfied? Why or why not?
- What other organizations do customers consider?
- What are potential customers and what would they want?
- What real-time information do customers want online?
- What makes customers successful or happy?
- How can existing customer business increase?
- What would customers change about the company if they could?
- What new advances would benefit customers?
- What steps or processes do customers go through to select and buy the product or service?
- What steps or processes are in place for unusual events such as returns, complaints, custom orders, or questions?

▼

Exhibit 4.9   Customer Requirements Example

- Web-enabled ordering
- Web customer service
- Get accurate price and delivery information online
- Interact seamlessly by phone, palm, Web, e-mail, voice response, in person, or mail
- Obtain invoices online
- Pay invoices online
- Secured information
- Electronic data interchange
- Electronic sales and compliance information via the Web
- Improved communication through the Internet
- Worldwide corporate combined information for buying agreements
- Ability to interface with distributors and affiliates
- Bar coding
- Radio Frequency Identification (RFID)
- Enhanced switchboard and telecommunications to more quickly get to the right person
- Credit card capabilities
- Powerful search capabilities on the Web to get information quickly
- Get quick personalized information and service
- Ability to speak to a real person if desired without going through lots of effort
- Ability to find answers online and help themselves
- Hassle-free returns
- Vendor-managed inventory (VMI)
- Proactive service
- Improved lead times
- Easy order entry
- Improved order information, availability, advise on late orders
- Ability to handle special or custom orders and requests
- Services subscriptions
- Better price and value
- High quality
- Easier to do business with
- Ability to provide electronic media and documentation (e.g., CD-ROM) via the Web
- Capabilities for providing data from bundling sales
- Warranty information

▲

- How can the customer process be streamlined or made more efficient for the customer?
- What are the various points of interaction the company has with the customer? How can each be improved?
- Does the company want to provide a single face to the customer, even from multiple divisions, product lines, or locations?
- How difficult is it to communicate with the company (i.e., e-mail addresses on a Web page)? How responsive is the company?

Exhibit 4.10 identifies examples of possible requirements from suppliers that the company utilizes.

▼

Exhibit 4.10 Supplier Requirements Example

- Ability to order via the Web
- Invoice electronically
- Pay electronically
- Electronic data interchange
- Supplier certification, preferred vendor information
- Ability to link and integrate with outside services for materials and dependent services
- Radio Frequency Identification (RFID)

- Electronic real-time forecast
- Collaborative forecasting and planning
- Supplier corrective action information
- Ability to interchange drawings and specifications electronically
- Joint product development
- Conformance history
- Product development information
- Supplier portal

▲

Value Chain Analysis

In addition to reviewing what customers and suppliers are requiring from the company, it is important to review the entire value chain for potential efficiencies and improvements. The value chain is the total combination of business processes that create value by delivering goods or services to the customer. These processes are from the beginning of the raw material, possibly passing through several companies, to the finished product in the customer's hands. Many companies have used technology to automate or change the value chain. Organizations within the value chain are collaborative partners, or an extended enterprise, and share information to achieve agility, speed, and reduced costs. When using technology to simplify the value chain, ensure you are not alienating an important piece of the value chain. For example, before offering customers ordering on the Web, consider the impact on the distribution channel and the impact of disintermediation. Following are questions to consider when reviewing the value chain:

- What are the various steps in the value chain?
- What are the weak links in the value chain?
- Can any of the steps be eliminated, simplified, or made more efficient?
- What technology or information, if shared throughout the value chain, would improve or significantly change the process?

- What best practices would improve the value chain?
- Is the customer willing to pay for each step in the value chain?

Business Measures

Identify the key information needs, or business measures that indicate the general health and direction of your business. This is typically the information that executive management requests immediately after having been out of the office for several weeks or months. Often, it is also this information that is reported to other branches, divisions, or a corporate entity to indicate the welfare of the business on an ongoing basis. A monthly or quarterly "President's Operating Report" or summary may include many of the key business measures. Each functional area has key business measures. Rather than identifying all the information needs, it is critical to focus only on the key business measures, which are different from company to company. Include not only the measures that they receive today, but also how management would like to measure the company. Identify what information is required on a real-time basis. Some of the measures may not be available today but should be identified as a business measure. Exhibit 4.11 is an example of key business measures found in various functions of a company.

▼

Exhibit 4.11 Key Business Measures Example

Financial:
- Sales (domestic, export, intercompany)
- Gross margin or profit (cost of sales), %
- Operating margin or profit
- Capital commitments and expenditures
- Days sales outstanding
- Cost reductions
- Incurred expenses
- Selling expenses, general and administration
- Other income and expenses
- Interest expense
- Net income
- Balance sheet
- Cash flow
- Budget
- Forecast
- Operating expenses
- Profits by customer or industry
- Backlog (units and dollars)
- Royalty income and expense

Human Resources:

- Employee information, including background, experience, demographic, personal
- Number of employees: Manufacturing, Product Support, Sales, Marketing, General and Administrative, R&D, by location
- Salary, increase, and pension data
- Training courses taken
- Employee survey data
- Turnover rate
- EEO measurements and government reporting
- Organizational reporting relationships
- Workers' comp incidents, costs
- Healthcare costs
- Benefit information
- Salary market data by geography, type

Manufacturing Operations:

- Variances (overhead spending, volume, manufacturing, purchases, work order, purchase price, other)
- Scrap (product changes, expiration)
- Overdue
- Throughput time
- Rework (percentage, hours)
- Scrap (dollars, units)
- Reserve for potentially obsolete material
- Shrinkage and inventory adjustments
- Scrap and obsolescence % to standard receipts
- Labor hours by system and operations (tracking run average of actual versus standard, labor tracking by part number)
- Variances (rework, work order, scrap, obsolescence) by product
- Inventory (turns, dollars, days inventory on hand)
- Allocation and backlog, average throughput time versus stated lead time by part number
- Direct material, direct labor cost, percent
- System cost roll-up
- Cost of revisions (design change orders: scrap, rework, standard increase)
- Design change order (DCO) throughput and volume by distinction code
- Fixed costs
- Batch size costs
- Work order activity
- Corrective action status (internal and external)
- Simulation capability (what if)
- % on time, on quality of work orders
- Capacity levels (shop floor, facilities)
- Inventory accuracy
- Excess and slow moving inventory
- Facility and equipment utilization ratio
- Forecast versus actual units produced
- Pending changes—bill of materials, standard cost, routings
- Customer service level
- Standard receipts to inventory
- Summary of shipments (dollars, units by zone)
- First pass yield by assembly
- Supplier cost, quality and delivery performance
- Reporting on vendor activity
- Conformance and acceptance (incoming, in-process, final testing)
- Volume produced by commodity

Field Service and Support:

- Total service costs per product (labor, travel, other field, in-house, parts)
- Number of installations completed (net, cumulative, average)
- Number of preventive maintenance calls
- Product support costs
- Number of repair service calls
- Service contracts
- Warranty obligations
- Cost and time to repair
- Reliability measurements

Quality:

- First pass access yield
- Warranty cost
- Installation success
- Number of complaints
- Unscheduled service calls per product
- Calls per instrument for key accounts
- Mean time to repair
- Mean time between service calls
- Average number of calls per service rep
- Total scrap and obsolescence
- Volume produced
- Service level
- Corrective actions and recalls
- Total cost of recalls
- Customer survey results
- Number of returns
- Mean time between failure
- Number of design change orders

Regulatory:

- Shipment control
- ISO requirements and documentation
- Export commodity reporting
- EPA, NRC, hazardous waste info
- FDA information

Marketing:

- Customer placements
- Sales by zone, region, territory, representative, customer, product group and class, account, product.
- Market share data: gains, losses by product and location
- Gross profit by account and product
- Competitive activity
- Customer membership data, including sales and administrative fees
- Placements by location
- Won and lost data
- Pricing, discount
- Commissions
- Forecast (units)
- Revenue by business segment, product class, etc.
- Integration of buying group data

Engineering and R&D:

- R&D expenses
- New product sales
- Time to market
- Number of releases
- Patents, awards
- Infringements costs

IS:

- IS costs as % of sales
- Backlog and completed hours (project, support maintenance)
- Average time for request completion
- Process elapsed time for completion
- Sales per employee
- System availability
- System response time
- Cost of processing a transaction
- Value added ratio per process

▲

Business Processes

It is important to document the critical business processes within the organization. Determine which business processes require reengineering and prioritize these improvements. The efficiency of the company's key business processes will determine the company's success in the future. Business process improvements often result in IS projects or changes, and are therefore important to identify in the strategic planning process. The amount of change necessary to a process may also have an impact on the overall fit of the IS business application. If the business decides to complete major reengineering to a process that utilizes an aging business application system, it may be a good opportunity to look at replacing the system, or it will be one more factor in the replacement decision. Also identify how ready the organization is for business process changes and improvements.

It is often helpful to hire an external consultant to teach business process reengineering to the users and IS individuals participating on the project. Consulting can also be useful to facilitate business process reengineering because it is easy for individuals to get stuck in the mode of "We have always done it this way." People doing the work are not always good at reengineering; alternative motives such as empire building may interfere. Although the business process reengineering effort mainly involves the business, it is often initiated because of IS strategic planning. Once the business users are familiar with the methodologies, the users typically make considerable process improvements and changes, many of which have no impact on business application systems.

The first step in reviewing the business processes is to develop a business process map that graphically depicts the high-level, or macro, key business processes. This process map will also show the relationship between the processes. This map will facilitate understanding between all departments and provide the basis for the detailed business process identification. Note that the business process map shows the processes, not the organizational departments. Many processes will and should cross organizational boundaries. The business process map contains only the macro processes. Include the detailed processes such as order entry and shipping in the next level of detail. Identify an owner within the business (usually a high-level executive with organizational responsibility over the majority of the process) for each macro process on the map. This owner will be a key individual to champion change within the business process. Figure 4.7 shows an example of a business process map.

Next, identify the detailed, or micro, business processes within each of the macro business processes identified in the map. This may result in changes to the business process map as new processes are identified. The micro business processes that support the macro business process each

Business Process Map

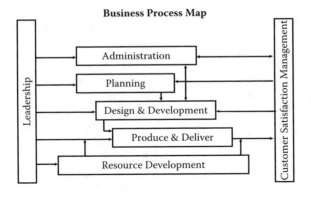

Figure 4.7   Business process map

have a distinct beginning and an end. The micro business processes can be identified through tasks performed by various departments in the company and by measures or output from the department. The output could be sent externally (for example, an invoice), internally (for example, a profit and loss statement), or required by external entities such as government agencies. Exhibit 4.12 shows an example of micro business processes.

Exhibit 4.12   Micro Business Processes Example

Administration
- Accounts payable
- Accounts receivable
- Credit and collections
- Internal audits
- External audits
- Shareholder
- Term negotiation
- Advertising
- Revenue accounting
- Payroll
- Billing
- Closing
- Pricing
- Tax
- Legal
- Regulatory
- Sales
- Invoicing

Leadership
- Long-term vision
- Organizational goals
- Involvement
- Mission statement
- Organizational design
- Development

Planning
- Competitive analysis
- Technological direction
- Market selection
- Business unit strategies
- Economic analysis
- Demographics
- Benchmarking

Customer Satisfaction Management
- Customer interviews
- Development of surveys
- Market research
- Complaint handling
- Warranty and claims
- Information requests
- Focus groups
- Survey execution
- Gap analysis
- Post-sales service
- Inquiries

Design and Development
- Feasibility studies
- Requirement definition
- Quality targets
- Approvals
- Full-scale development
- Supplier certification
- Life cycle development
- Preproduction build
- Reliability analysis
- Product release
- Deviation
- Tooling development
- Project planning
- Specifications
- Patent application
- Cost estimation
- Design review
- Testing
- Prototype
- Qualification
- Process design
- Engineering change
- Bills of materials
- Release

Produce and Deliver
- Request for quote
- Order entry
- Schedule
- Purchasing
- Parts ordering
- Receiving
- Manufacturing
- Provide a service
- Test/check
- Warehousing/storing
- Shipping
- Forecasting
- Production control
- Material planning
- Materials management
- Consignment process
- Expediting
- Create
- Maintenance
- Packaging
- Transportation
- Installation

Resource Development
- Hiring employees
- Employee involvement
- Performance reviews
- Well-being and satisfaction
- Employee records
- Medical programs
- Compensation
- Training and education
- Recognition and reward
- Health and safety
- Placement
- Suggestions
- Benefits

Identify business processes at a level of detail that makes sense for the company. One company identified the following macro and micro business processes:

- Customer interaction
  - Sales

- Order management
- Distribution
- Credit and collections
- Post-sales support
■ Product development and manufacturing
  - Design
  - Development
  - Procurement
  - Receiving
  - Payables
  - Manufacturing
  - Engineering change
■ Finance and administrative support
  - Finance
  - Human resources
  - Other support functions

Next, review the business processes to determine the level of efficiency in the current process. If a business process requires major restructuring or reengineering, often this results in an IS project. These projects may not have been requested, but these hidden projects may have more impact on the company than any of the projects on the original backlog list. The following process outlines one way to prioritize the work needed by business process area:

1. Identify basic opportunities to impact business performance. These could be the business objectives, or generic business opportunities. Identify the potential of additional business if the process improvement results in a competitive advantage. For example, one company identified the following potential business opportunities if processes improved:
   a. Determine the impact to external customers or entities (for example, customers, subsidiaries, buying groups, government agencies, ISO). This could be the result of an internal process that at some point has an impact on the final customer or a process that has obvious external impact. Measure the impact in terms of how much feeling (either positive or negative) the customer receives from the process.
   b. Determine the impact on quality of service or product. Measure the impact by the quality of product or the waste, defects, errors, and rework.
   c. Identify the business cost reduction opportunities. This would be any effect on costs and resources.

    d. Identify the impact on internal customers. Measure this in terms of how much positive or negative feeling the internal customers receive from the process.

    e. Identify the impact on the speed of the process. This would be the importance of speed in moving through the process, both internally as well as externally.

The company may have slightly different criteria for measuring the benefits of improvement in a process, but the ones identified above fit a large number of organizations. Confirm this performance impact by looking closely at the business goals and mission for the organization. Many of the words may be found in the mission or goals identified in the measures above, such as satisfied customers, profitability, speed, and high quality.

2. Next, rank each of the macro business processes identified in the business process map against the performance impacts identified above. A high number indicates that the process can have more impact on that performance area. For mathematical comparisons, use numbers 6 through 10; this keeps a factor from being too disproportionately large or small. For example, if a change is made in the design to deploy process, how much of an impact will it have on external customers, quality, business costs, etc.? Exhibit 4.13 is an example of the ranking for one company.

Exhibit 4.13   Rating Impact of Macro Business Processes

Performance Impact	Design to Deploy	Administration
Further impact external customers	8	6
Further reduce quality issues	9	8
Further impact business costs	6	9
Further impact internal customers	7	10
Further increase process speed	10	7

Next, take the micro business processes identified within each macro business process, and score the impact each micro business process can have on each performance impact on a scale of 0–10. Note a significant impact with a 10 while noting no impact with a 0. For example, "If we make a positive change to the purchasing micro process within procure to pay, how much would it impact external customers?" Multiply that number times the performance impact identified for that process. Note reasons for the rating. For example, Figure 4.8 shows an analysis for one company.

Business Process: **Procure to Pay** Owner: Date:

Organizational Processes	External Customers Further Impact (6)			Quality Issues Further Reduce (9)			Business Costs Further Impact (10)			Internal Customers Further Impact (8)			Process Speed Further Increase (7)			Total
	Desc	*Rate*	*Score*	*Desc*	*Rate*	*Score*	*Desc*	*Rate*	*Score*	*Desc*	*Rate*	*Score*	*Desc*	*Rate*	*Score*	
		0	0		0	0		0	0		0	0		0	0	0
Purchasing	Transparent	2	12	Correct specifications	5	45	Manual, high overhead	8	80	Many approvals, not user friendly	7	56	Takes too long	8	56	249
Receiving	Transparent	2	12	No barcode	2	18	Improve Efficiency	5	50	Traveler, lots of paper	7	56	< 24 hour cycle, no barcode	8	56	192
Receiving Inspection	Transparent, if no change to quality	2	12	For Instruments, high frequency, WIP Reject	8	72	High lot freq, all direct materials inspected	10	100	For Instruments, high freq WIP Reject	8	64		9	63	311
Raw Material Whsing/ Storing/Material Hand	Transparent	2	12	Good but not integrated	3	27	Excess Inventory, unnecessary handling	9	90	Increase efficiency high overhead	7	56	No automation, bin management	8	56	241
Accounts Payable	Transparent	0	0		0	0	Terms	9	90	Manual system	6	48	Slow, manual	8	56	194
Cycle Counting	> 99% Customer Service	0	0	Minimal	1	9	> 98% Accuracy	3	30	Lumpy Demand	7	56	Lumpy Demand, adequate	4	28	123
Supplier Quality/ Certification/2nd source	Transparent	0	0	Under developed Program	10	90	No Partners	9	90	High WIP Rej requires SF intervention	5	40	Cycle time, Inspection	6	42	262
Corporate Purchasing	Transparent	0	0	No impact	0	0	Cost Savings	10	100	No impact	0	0	No impact	0	0	100
OEM/Contract Purchasing	Distributor B. O.'s	5	30	Number of Complaints	7	63	Make/Buy Decisions	8	80	No impact	0	0	Number of days to process	6	42	215
Inbound Logistics	Transparent	0	0	Minimal	0	0	Reduce freight rates	10	100	Minimal	0	0	Reduce transit time	5	35	135
Performance Measurements	Transparent	1	6	Preventative and Corrective Action	8	72	Preventative and Corrective Action	8	80	Valid Measurements	8	64	Minimal Time	3	21	243

Figure 4.8 Business process rating

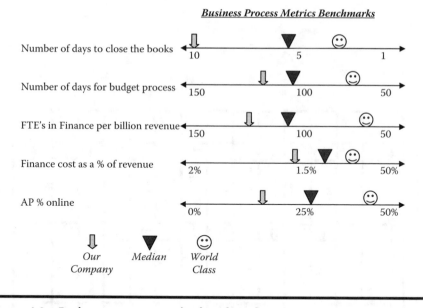

Figure 4.9   Business process metrics benchmarks

3. The rating totals can help indicate the priority of process improvements. Through this process, the company in the example above (Figure 4.8) found that in the procure to pay macro process area, the micro processes that would have the largest impact if they were to improve would be the receiving/inspection, supplier quality/ certification, and purchasing processes.

Use this mathematical model only as a general guideline. Review the chart and make sure it makes sense for your business. It can be useful in confirming known areas of inefficiencies and identifying inefficiencies not as obvious to the casual observer.

Companies also need to evaluate industry benchmark statistics to ensure their processes meet or exceed industry averages. Otherwise, what may seem like an efficient process may not be. As shown in Figure 4.9, the metric that has the most discrepancy from world-class levels or median levels can be the process to reengineer.

Business Requirements

Determining business requirements is another key component to the planning process, particularly if new applications may be necessary. Many companies take too long determining the detailed business requirements,

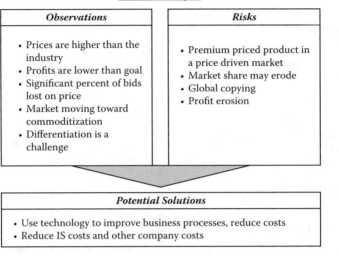

Business Analysis

Observations	Risks
• Prices are higher than the industry • Profits are lower than goal • Significant percent of bids lost on price • Market moving toward commoditization • Differentiation is a challenge	• Premium priced product in a price driven market • Market share may erode • Global copying • Profit erosion

Potential Solutions
• Use technology to improve business processes, reduce costs • Reduce IS costs and other company costs

Figure 4.10   Business analysis

and spend many months identifying their requirements. Several businesses can be utilized to complete this process in a few days, and are well worth the expense. Often these companies use a software tool and a database with thousands of common requirements requested by businesses. Assemble key users from all areas to go through the requirements in just a few days. It is critical during these sessions to involve individuals who are very familiar with the detailed business requirements. The individuals can simply answer yes or no if the requirement applies in the environment.

Another option rather than identifying all requirements is to identify only key or unique requirements. Someone familiar with vendor package functionality can be very helpful in this process as that individual can quickly recognize unique requirements.

Document Business Strengths, Weaknesses, Opportunities, and Threats

Document the strengths, weaknesses, opportunities, and threats (SWOT) of the business. This is important because these aspects may have an impact on IS, and there may be opportunities for IS to improve the weaknesses or capitalize on the strengths. Exhibit 4.14 shows an example of strengths, weaknesses, opportunities, and threats for a company.

One company identified observations, business risks, and potential solutions as shown in Figure 4.10.

▼

Exhibit 4.14   Business Strengths, Weaknesses, Opportunities, and Threats Example

Business Strengths:
- Technical innovation
- Reputation
- Product quality
- Market position
- Employees with long tenure
- High values
- Customer relationships
- Flexible

Business Opportunities:
- Use of Web technology
- Worldwide company growth
- Vendor-managed inventory
- Smaller lot sizes
- Business process improvement

Business Weaknesses:
- Profitability
- Cost competition
- Continuous improvement
- Silos by department
- Lack of competitive information
- Global presence
- Communication
- Reactive, firefighting
- Execution of projects
- Strategic planning, focus
- Internal controls and metrics
- Customer satisfaction metrics

Business Threats:
- Seasonality of product
- Larger competitors
- Reverse auctions on Web
- Legislature changes
- Federal funding changes
- Economic uncertainty
- Consumers desires changing
- Price pressures
- EPA and environmental regulations
- International competition

▲

Document Business Impact on IS

Documenting the impact the business situation and direction has on IS is one of the more important sections of an IS strategic plan. In this section, go back to the business situation, goals, strategy, strengths, weaknesses, opportunities, and threats and ask what impact each can have on IS. The following are some examples:

- If a company has a business strategy of globalization, IS should be able to handle global requirements.
- If a company has a strategy of acquisitions and divestitures, systems should be scalable to meet the changing business needs.

- If a business is continually in a firefighting and reactive mode, it increases the importance of the strategic plan and proactively identifying business needs.
- If a business is weak in project management and execution, IS can utilize project management methodologies and techniques to help the organization improve.
- If a company is very conservative, cost conscious, and risk averse, IS must be aligned with the business, have complete business justifications for expenditures, and minimize risks.
- In a highly competitive environment, ensure the planning process creatively analyzes customer desires to identify opportunities.
- If a company has high growth plans, ensure that the applications and systems are scalable and can handle the projected growth.
- If cost is an issue, ensure that applications are reusable.
- If the business users are technically immature, project schedules will need to account for additional training and documentation.
- If the business is not proficient in business process improvement, project schedules and resources will need to be allocated to assist with business process improvement.
- A company that is moving to smaller lots and just-in-time (JIT) principles needs to have business application systems that handle small lot sizes and lean manufacturing principles.
- If the business is moving toward 24x7, ensure that applications are designed for real-time processes and information.
- An entrepreneurial company with a high amount of potential change requires business applications that are broad and flexible, typically packages with table-driven customizable business workflows.
- A company in an industry with extreme price pressures needs to have business applications that have very detailed visibility to costs with flexible reporting and analysis tools to analyze and improve costs.
- A company with a business focus on six sigma, improving quality, and empowering employees requires business applications that monitor and measure quality.
- A company that has seasonality with significant overtime costs requires scheduling and modeling systems with the ability to plan labor hours and see the impact of future jobs so that work can be brought in to reduce the cost of overtime.
- A company that is in a market leader position must proactively utilize technology to maintain the leadership position and not become complacent.

■ A company that has low turnover of employees and employees with long tenure may have opportunities to improve and redesign business processes with a fresh look at industry best practices.

Review each business goal to determine how IS can help the business achieve the business objective. IS can assist the business in many different ways. Here are some examples:

■ Provide unique product and service features.
■ Reduce product development time.
■ Allow the delivery of customized services.
■ Open new channels and market niches.
■ Produce higher quality results.
■ Fill product positioning gaps.
■ Block channel access.
■ Increase buyer switching costs.

Typically, customers have a cycle of activities of acquiring and using resources. This cycle of activities may include establishing requirements, selecting and ordering, authorizing and paying for, testing and accepting, integrating and monitoring, upgrading, maintaining, transferring or disposing, and accounting for. Review the cycle to determine whether the company could do anything to make this process easier for the customer. Opportunities may exist anywhere within the cycle. For example, the Internet gives companies a new vehicle to provide products and services faster and makes them more accessible to customers.

Start by listing each business goal directly from the business plan. Briefly list and describe any way in which IS could help the company achieve the business goal. Most of these could be projects that business management might have mentioned in the past, but many might not have been formally requested. Often, these projects have the largest strategic impact on the business and typically use newer technology, but they have not been requested for a number of reasons. If the company was yours and you could use technology in any way possible, how would you achieve the business goal stated? Brainstorming sessions with the IS group as well as the IS steering committee can be very helpful to uncover some of these hidden opportunities. The purpose of the section is to get management throughout the organization thinking about how IS can help the company achieve its objectives. This information can be very enlightening for executive managers; they can begin to see the true potential value of IS. Because they are more familiar with viewing IS in only a back-office support role, this thinking may be new to them. Three examples are shown in Exhibits 4.15, 4.16, and 4.17.

▼

Exhibit 4.15   IS and the Business Goals — Example 1

IS and the Business Strategies

The following are some of the ways in which IS can play a role in each of the business strategies outlined previously:

1.   Provide superior product availability worldwide.
   -   IS must design systems that provide *real-time* data that will give the business immediate information, allowing it to respond in a timely fashion to the customer and industry needs.
   -   Design systems solutions to be *worldwide*, which will enable us to function as a worldwide supplier. This means that we must supply to our customers what is wanted, where it is wanted, and when it is wanted. Systems must be in place so that you can take an order anywhere in the world and fill it anywhere in the world depending on capacity and availability.
   -   Design systems to be *accessible* by the customer. Research what information we could provide to the customer to be easier to do business with as a supplier. This includes the ability for customers to enter orders after reviewing price and delivery information with the minimum amount of paperwork, providing order status and delivery information when needed.
   -   Utilize systems with business process reengineering to *eliminate non-value-added* steps throughout the business.
   -   A closer *link between the engineering and business systems* can reduce lead times of new products and product changes.
   -   We can improve the *make-to-order* system (for example, final assembly) so that we can efficiently tailor the product to the customer specifications with a minimum cost to us.
   -   Implement systems to provide a more comprehensive *feedback loop* from the customers. This includes customer expectations versus delivery performance as well as customer requests and feedback regarding the product.
   -   Implement systems that strengthen our *relationship* with our customers. This includes improved forecasting and inventory management systems so that we can effectively meet customer requests. Also provide tools for improved communications such as customer access to our system, via the Web, electronic data interchange (EDI), e-mail, and video teleconferencing.
   -   IS must provide vehicles that make us *easy to do business* with as a supplier. This includes tools for improved order capture process, such as the Web, EDI, phone response order placement, customer entry, remote order entry, and bulletin board order entry systems. This also includes vehicles for ease of payment such as credit card payment, monthly invoices, electronic payments, etc.

- We can improve the systems to handle "on sight" *inventory* management that includes replenishment and transfer.
- We can make *product selection* and configuration easier for the customer via improved Web functionality.
- We can provide the ability to make *delivery commitments* to our customers as well as vehicles that help us meet our delivery commitments.
- We can *benchmark* other global noncompetitor companies to determine how the companies are providing superior product availability worldwide.
- We can support the worldwide *super service center* concept by assisting with systems implementations at Germany, Singapore, and other sites as needed. We can ensure that IS planning addresses the global business needs rather than just our location.
- We can ensure that systems are in place to efficiently handle *export requirements* as well as facilitating worldwide transaction processing between subsidiaries.
- Design systems to support the quick-ship program and reduced *lead time* programs.

2. Deliver outstanding customer service and support.
   - An online *bulletin board system* can provide customers and employees (for example, subsidiaries, field sales, etc.) with immediate access to product information, ability to place orders, messages and notifications from the factory, answers to specific questions, engineering drawings, etc.
   - We could also use the voice-mail system to provide *interactive voice response* for customer information and requests. Enhance this with the video telephone to see the person with whom you are working.
   - Improved order management systems could make the ordering process efficient so that the company is *easy to do business with as a supplier.* Back-end systems such as Web ordering, electronic data interchange, credit card payment, monthly invoices, electronic payments, RFID, and bar coding would help the customer and reduce our order costs.
   - We can provide *pursuit and selling tools* and systems to improve the sales process. This includes product sizing and selection, discounting, quoting, project pursuit, customer profiles and tracking, project forecasting, competitive assessment, installed base analysis, account and territory management, agreements, and sales presentations.
   - We could provide *customer access* to order and agreement information via the Web.
   - Develop a Web-based system with the voice-mail or bulletin board system to provide *immediate delivery* of information, product literature, drawings, etc.
   - A total *integrated system* would provide the business with the ability to add functionality quickly and allow us to respond to customer requests. It would also provide worldwide consistency for ease of management.

3. Rapidly pursue targeted growth opportunities.
   - IS can assist by providing *worldwide reporting* through data warehouses. This will allow us to take advantage of global opportunities for new business as well as business improvements.
   - IS can assist by providing systems solutions that allow us to leverage the combined *family* of products and organizations.
   - We can implement *worldwide communication* and systems. The worldwide network must include access from customers and vendors as well as subsidiaries.
   - Systems must have *multilingual and multicurrency* capabilities.
   - We can provide tools for *marketing tracking*. This will allow us to track project pursuit, determine areas for increased pursuit, and be aware of worldwide activities for our multinational customers. An industry database or system can provide listings of potential customers to pursue.
   - We can implement a *quotation reporting* system that tracks quotations won and lost, competitors, reasons for loss, etc. This will allow us to improve our performance and win ratio for quotations. Worldwide project pursuit would identify growth opportunities.
   - We can support the worldwide *super service center* concept by assisting with systems implementations at Germany, Singapore, and other sites as needed. We can ensure that IS planning addresses the global business needs rather than just our location.
4. Create high-value, differentiated products for growth.
   - By integrating our environment and systems with the overall business direction, we can take advantage in the marketplace of our overall product family strength and ensure that future development is consistent to further support this strength.
   - We can provide tools for online imaging for engineering change orders and drawings that will assist in improving the process of getting *product to market* faster.
   - We can have a closer tie between the business computing environment and the *engineering computing environment* as there is some common information you can share rather than duplicating. This will reduce the cost of engineering new products.
   - An improved marketing and customer feedback system will help ensure that we are *developing the right products* for the industry and customer requests.
5. Be the best cost producer.
   - By investing in IS with business process reengineering, we can provide tools to improve the *efficiency and productivity* of the entire division that will improve our overall cost position. Teams throughout the division continuously improve their processes. Often, these improvements require changes within the system. By continuing to change and enhance our existing systems we can support these cost reductions as identified. Implement tools to support a paperless environment.

- The business is expanding manufacturing *globally* in various areas to reduce our cost of manufacturing. We can support this by assisting to implement systems in other places of the world (for example, England, Singapore, and Germany).
- *Global financial information* can provide improved visibility to the business. Quick, easy, and timely access to information can allow for improved business decisions.
- Use tools to develop systems *quickly* to handle the changing and growing business requirements.
- We can implement systems that are *flexible* to changing business needs (for example, requiring table changes rather than programming changes).

6. Manage the business globally.
   - IS can provide systems that have *real-time access* so that information is readily available to make improved business decisions. This includes having systems that are available 24 hours a day and data structures that are accessible.
   - Using tools, complete business processes in a *paperless environment* so that business can easily take place around the world. This will significantly reduce our costs and improve the overall business efficiency.
   - We can implement systems that are *portable* so that the company can move them to smaller or larger locations with a minimum of effort. Both software and data must be transportable to other hardware platforms and locations.
   - Utilize *data warehousing* concepts and software tools to pull information from all the differing systems and worldwide locations. The company can then easily analyze the information and provide management with the information it needs to manage a worldwide business.
   - Educate IS personnel about worldwide culture differences and increase their exposure to worldwide systems so that we can effectively address solutions for our new *worldwide view*.
   - IS can assist the business with utilizing new *technology*, such as PCs, laptop PCs, and software that will improve the business processing.
   - We need to ensure that systems are *worldwide* in nature and that the IS strategic planning includes the worldwide needs.
   - Implement improved tools for managing the worldwide *pricing* situation.
   - Modifying systems so that we function on a common *worldwide calendar* will allow us to easily interpret and analyze financial results and information.
   - Ensuring that systems are in place so that the critical worldwide *information needs* required to manage the business are readily available will assist the business in worldwide management. Key measures to manage the business must be consistent and readily available on a worldwide basis.

7. Maintain an environment where people want to work.
   - Support the *continuous process improvement environment* in the division by having systems that are easy to modify and flexible.
   - Ensure IS *job descriptions* accurately reflect the positions and responsibilities.
   - *Train* and tool IS personnel with up-to-date technology and skills.
   - *Communicate* tools and capabilities available to the division.

Exhibit 4.16   IS and the Business Goals — Example 2

IS and the Business Goals

The following are ways in which IS can play a role in each of the business goals outlined previously:

1. Achieve financial targets and credibility.
   a. *Financial information*: IS can provide improved financial systems that, in turn, will provide management with the necessary tools to monitor the financial health of the division and enable early detection and correction of problem areas. Apply consistent financial definitions and measurements. Improved analytical tools and ad hoc retrieval of the information will provide improved financial visibility and "drill-down" capability to isolate problem areas. Systems must also be available to improve the visibility of financial information for services, sales, and costs.
   b. *Financial and product forecasting information*: Consistent and reliable reporting of forecasts and expected financial results is critical. Improving visibility to outstanding quotations on a regular basis will provide financial and business planning for the future.
   c. *Project profit and loss information*: As the market emphasis and profitability shifts from hardware to services, we need to provide improved systems in the area of project management and engineering as this will continue to increase in importance. These tools include project scheduling, change order control, percentage complete, resource management, and financial information about projected and actual project profitability.
   d. *Worldwide information*: Worldwide information through a warehouse approach will provide business management with tools needed to manage the business and improve profitability on a worldwide basis.

e. *Increase productivity*: One of the main goals of IS is to eliminate waste and increase productivity throughout the division. This will reduce our overhead costs and allow us to meet or exceed our financial targets. IS can play a very important role in facilitating and coordinating the elimination of non-value-added tasks through business process redesign initiatives.

2. Merge to a common architecture.

a. *Common computing tools*: IS can provide a common set of tools that will assist technology in communication and migration of the platforms. This includes a seamless electronic mail system as well as common tools for business communication such as technical documentation, word processing, presentation graphics, and spreadsheets.

b. *Engineering*: For our customers, our product and services integrate the control system to their business application systems. Although we do this for our customers, we could do a better job of integration internally by coupling the engineering and manufacturing of our product closer to our business application systems. This results in a more timely solution to market. For example, engineering tools could provide worldwide access to designs and interface directly to the manufacturing system.

3. Transition selling and servicing organizations to achieve competitive advantage.

a. *Customer information*: It is imperative that we know exactly who our worldwide customer base is. Our customer base is an important asset for our future, and we need to treat it as such. We need an accurate, worldwide, easily accessible database with information about customers and what equipment they have. Understanding this information will allow us to improve customer service as well as increase potential sales. Examples of the kinds of information to include are:

1) Who the customer is
2) What hardware and software they have and how long they have had it
3) What industry and application it is used for
4) What devices it interfaces to
5) When and how it was serviced
6) All conversations and issues that have taken place
7) Customer contact individuals for various functions
8) Company contacts for various functions
9) Sales volume
10) Any agreements or special terms
11) Special notes about the customer

b. *Order entry and quoting*: It is critical that we structure our business and computer systems so that it is easy for customers to do business with us. Every point where a customer encounters us (configuration, quotation, contract negotiations, order, invoice, and order status) must be easy, quick, and accurate.

    c. *Enhancement and bug information*: We need to be responsive to customers who request an enhancement or discover a deficiency with the product. IS can provide a tool to track and report these enhancements and bugs. This will allow us to track bugs through the process and effectively manage completion of the effort, track and improve our quality, and communicate to the customers. The customers could have direct access to view status and enter problems.

    d. *Technical information*: Today we are wasting expensive engineering and technical resources by reinventing the wheel. A customer asks a question that has been asked and researched before within the organization. Utilize a tool to store all technical information with extensive "keyword" search capabilities to allow us to respond to our customers in a more timely, consistent, and cost-effective manner.

    e. *Service tools*: IS can become an integral part of servicing the customer. Use tools to monitor customer call tracking, but also aid in diagnostic expertise, questioning, and troubleshooting. A computerized system with artificial intelligence could have electronic documentation, automatic logging and reporting capability, problem detection information, and a direct interface to service management, as well as provide failure and servicing information for quality analysis.

    f. *Skills inventory and resource availability*: Provide a worldwide warehouse of resources and skills available so that the individuals can be used as needed.

    g. *Customer tools*: IS can assist in many areas to make it easy for the customer to communicate with us and improve customer service. One example of this would be an online bulletin board system with product announcements and alerts, ordering information, and new product releases. Link customers into an online communication system to send messages directly to employees. Other examples include direct web access to our systems, electronic data interchange (EDI), voice mail, video teleconferencing, graphical order entry and configuration, and one-stop shopping concepts. All of these methods can provide a partnership approach to ensure continued business.

    h. *Pricing information*: We need to have accurate and thorough information on profit margins.

4. Develop strong third-party relationships.

    a. IS can assist by using common third parties for additional services such as PC outsourcing support, application vendor packages, computer equipment purchases, etc.

5. Develop a strong corporate identity.

    a. IS can provide a clear direction for migration to common business application systems. Operating on common systems will improve the leveraging and communication, and allow us to function better as a single entity.

▼

Exhibit 4.17   IS and the Business Goals — Example 3

The following are the five business goals and possible ways in which IS could help our company achieve its business goals.

1. Customer delight
   - Design systems so that customers can access information easily and directly. Customers should be able to design and enter orders, and obtain cost, delivery date, and shipping information directly via technology (e.g., Internet, phone response, direct entry).
   - Systems should utilize electronic exchange, such as Web, EDI, electronic payment and invoicing, quotes, and acknowledgments.
   - Product selection and configuration of custom orders should be easy and feed directly into manufacturing.
   - Systems and processes should be designed to ensure maximum quality delivered to the customer. This includes catching design errors through the use of a configurator.
   - Provide services and information to ease customer responsibilities (e.g., bar coding on furniture for asset management, space management software).
   - All output of systems that touch the customer should support the corporate image.
   - Systems can provide business simulation capability to answer what-if questions.
   - Systems should provide complete error checking to catch errors immediately.
   - Systems should be flexible to adjust quickly to changing customer needs. These changes should be possible, for the most part, without IS involvement.
   - Systems should be easy to use to support the internal customer, or the next person in the process.
2. Superior sales growth
   - Provide pursuit and selling tools and systems to improve the sales process. This includes product configuration, time and territory management, sales pursuit systems, target market development, automated marketing lead information, and target market potential.
   - Systems should be flexible for changing sales territories, and actually proactively suggest optimum territory alignment.
   - Provide online bulletin board, fax-back, or Internet system to provide immediate access to product information, ability to place orders, answers to questions, and product literature.
   - Have tools and systems that are flexible to integrate new products.
   - Provide distribution planning systems.
   - Provide systems and tools that are easy and add value to the dealers and representatives.

- Provide tools that can analyze the impact of future price increases to maximize value and minimize customer costs.
- Provide systems and tools to support the design and introduction phase of the product development.
- Provide systems with simulation capability.
- Provide forecast information to drive manufacturing planning so that we can build the volume we sell.
- Provide configuration editing so that we can manufacture what we sell (ensure manufacturability).
- Interface to industry databases and information to proactively build pursuit information.

3. Financial excellence
   - Utilize business process reengineering to eliminate non-value-added steps throughout the business.
   - Implement tools and processes to support a paperless environment.
   - Standardize tools and equipment to reduce support costs. Utilize standard software packages whenever possible.
   - Provide tools that provide immediate financial feedback and information in a format that is understandable so that corrective actions can be taken.
   - Provide improved tools for inventory management and inventory turns accuracy.
   - Have flexible systems that can integrate future acquisitions.
   - Provide improved visibility to maintain and monitor standard and variance cost information.
   - Provide cost of quality measurement information, such as margin analysis, estimating tools, and quotes.

4. Employee excellence
   - Provide systems that are easy to use; make it easy to obtain information.
   - Train employees in the tools and processes to minimize frustration and improve their ability to do the job.
   - Provide up-to-date tools and technology.
   - Provide systems to track employee training and capabilities.
   - Provide employee performance tracking.

5. Business process improvement
   - Provide systems that are flexible to handle changes in the business processes.
   - Provide training and tools to facilitate business process reengineering.
   - Provide a structure and process for business process improvement.
   - Provide a tool to track and prioritize the business process improvements.
   - Provide quality measurements, such as value-added ratios.
   - Provide documentation and procedures for processes.

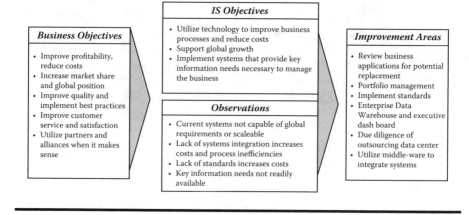

Figure 4.11   Business impact on IS objectives

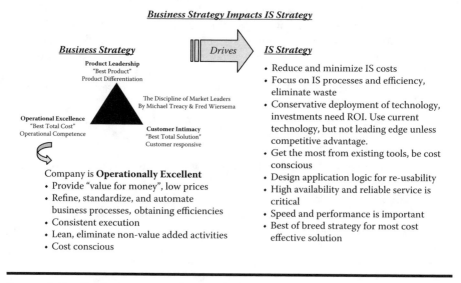

Figure 4.12   Business strategy impact

The process of looking at business goals can identify additional IS projects that were not previously on the backlog list. Add these projects to the list. Do not panic if the backlog seems to be growing; priorities will be identified that will ensure that the correct projects are in progress.

Figure 4.11 and Figure 4.12 shows examples of how two different companies summarized the ways in which the business strategy affects the IS direction. Figure 4.13 shows how a company reviewed each business goal and identified particular IS opportunities. Figure 4.14 shows an example of how business strengths, weaknesses, opportunities, and threats could have an impact on IS. Figure 4.15 is another example of how a company analyzed the business impact on IS.

IS Can Assist With Business Goals

Business Goal		IS Opportunities

Profitability, reduce costs

- Visibility to key metrics with executive dashboard
- Automate supply chain management with e-business capabilities
- Improved forecasting tools
- Pricing analysis and improved pricing functionality
- Reduce IS total cost of ownership with vendor packages, standardized desktop environment
- Redesign and improve the order process

Market and global growth

- E-business capabilities to expand market reach
- Replace custom applications with vendor packages that are scalable and have worldwide capabilities
- Global sourcing

Technical innovation

- Tools to facilitate the new product development process
- Document management
- Enterprise project management with visibility to development costs
- Flexible configurator

Customer service

- CRM to improve customer interface
- E-business capabilities with online access to order status, order entry, MSDS, COA
- Videoconferencing for increased customer face time
- Improve sales and customer service roles to utilize technology for efficiency so face time increases

Quality

- Document management
- Automate Certificate of Analysis process
- Improve visibility to quality metrics
- Software for business process mapping
- Embrace TQM methodology

Figure 4.13　Business goal impact

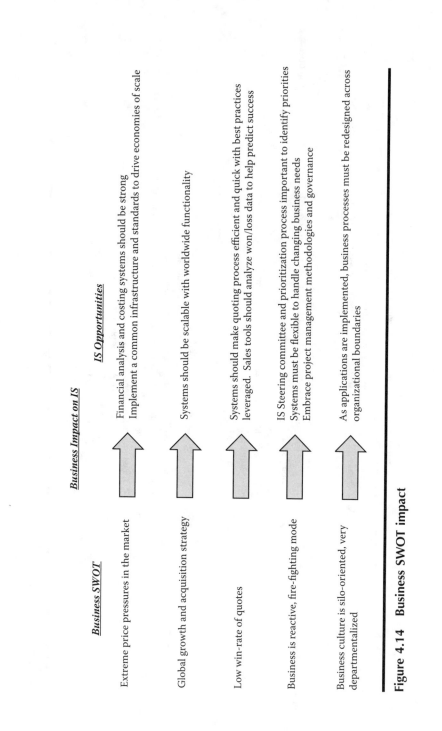

Figure 4.14 Business SWOT impact

Business Impact on IS

Business SWOT

IS Opportunities

Extreme price pressures in the market → Financial analysis and costing systems should be strong
Implement a common infrastructure and standards to drive economies of scale

Global growth and acquisition strategy → Systems should be scalable with worldwide functionality

Low win-rate of quotes → Systems should make quoting process efficient and quick with best practices leveraged. Sales tools should analyze won/loss data to help predict success

Business is reactive, fire-fighting mode → IS Steering committee and prioritization process important to identify priorities
Systems must be flexible to handle changing business needs
Embrace project management methodologies and governance

Business culture is silo-oriented, very departmentalized → As applications are implemented, business processes must be redesigned across organizational boundaries

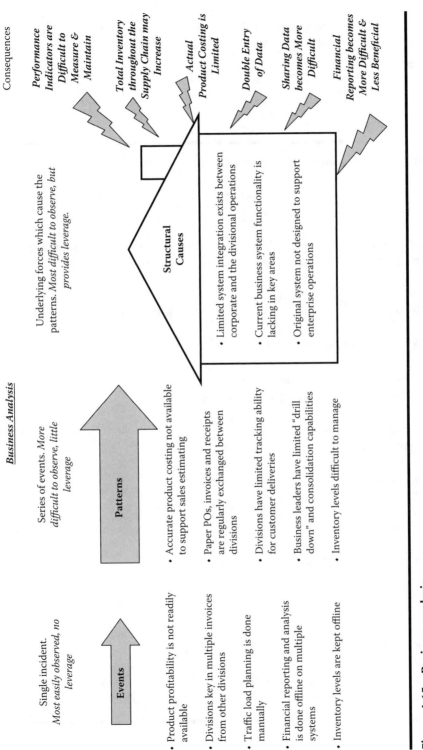

Figure 4.15 Business analysis

One company summarized the business strategic plan by identifying key success factors, key strategic issues, and boundary conditions that affect IS, as shown in Exhibit 4.18.

▼

Exhibit 4.18 Summary of Business Drivers Example

The business plan identifies better operating effectiveness through the following key success factors:

■ Creation of high performance customer oriented organization
■ Increased manufacturing efficiencies, consolidations, and outsourcing
■ Enhanced sales and customer support processes
■ Redefined financial and administrative processes that reduce cost

The key success factors that apply to IS are:

■ Improved operating efficiency
■ Improved operating effectiveness

The following key strategic issues may have a significant impact on business systems and support architectures:

■ Divestitures, acquisitions, partnerships
■ Investments in emerging markets
■ Third-party distribution
■ Automation of activities that connect the company with customers and suppliers
■ Company initiatives

The following are the boundary conditions for IS:

■ Implement the plan in segments; define each segment as a project.
■ Balance costs with benefits for each project.
■ Minimize external customer disruption.
■ Adhere to predominant Information technology industry standards.
■ Rely on proven information technology products and processes.

▲

Review and Confirm Business Situation Understanding

Meet with executive management and present a summary of the business direction to obtain confirmation on the information. If information is conflicting (which frequently happens), highlight the conflicting information, and come out of the meeting with consensus. Although a consensus on the direction is desired at this meeting, if executive management have not gone through a strategic planning process, it could take several meetings to obtain consensus.

In an example mentioned in an earlier chapter, executive management in one company thought it had a strategic business plan. After talking to the executives and obtaining conflicting information on the company's mission and direction, executive management came to the realization that its business plan consisted of financial targets and was missing key components. Executive managers from the various functions had slightly different approaches and opinions of how the company would achieve the agreed-upon financial targets. The business questions raised through the IS strategic planning process actually initiated the managers' process to develop a thorough business plan.

Upon obtaining agreement from executive management on the direction of the company, it is important to present the information to the IS steering committee. Although the steering committee will not be changing the vision, mission, and other information for the company, it is important to obtain their confirmation on the information, as well as to obtain additional detailed information. The next level of management may have a slightly different perspective.

It is also critical to present the same information to the IS group. This business information may be new information for the IS group, which is typically enthusiastic to hear information about the company direction as described by executive management.

Conclusion

Congratulations! You have now completed the first phase of the planning process, the visioning phase. You have completed the following:

■ Initiated the planning project by identifying the purpose, questions to answer, and scope. You identified the groups involved in the planning process and identified individuals across the business to interview. The project was announced and project communications vehicle established. Deliverables were initiated with a table of contents and structure.

- Business documentation was reviewed. Interviews, surveys, and workshops were held to obtain information about the business.
- The business was documented, including a description of the business, vision, goals, strategies, operating vision, information needs, business processes, business projects, and initiatives. Business and customer requirements were identified. Business strengths, weaknesses, opportunities, and threats were identified. The business situation was analyzed to determine the impact on IS.

You now know where you are going, and have a much better chance of getting to where you want to go! You are ready to proceed to the second phase of the planning process, the analysis phase, where you will turn your attention to the IS environment.

Notes for My IS Strategic Planning Project

_____

_____

_____

_____

_____

_____

_____

_____

_____

_____

_____

_____

_____

_____

_____

_____

_____

_____

_____

Chapter 5

The Analysis Phase

What's the use of running if you're not on the right road?

— German proverb

Now that you have a good understanding of your business and its direction, in the second phase of the planning process, you can turn your focus to IS. However, before developing the IS direction, it is critical to understand the current IS environment.

As shown in Figure 5.1, the second phase of the planning process is the analysis phase. In this phase, you will gain an understanding of the current IS situation, analyze how it meets the needs of the business, and develop recommendations. As Figure 5.2 shows, the analysis phase has the following components:

- Understanding the current IS situation
- Analyzing the current IS situation
- Developing recommendations and solution alternatives

Each of these components is discussed in more detail next.

Understanding the Current IS Situation
Review IS Documentation

Just as you reviewed business documentation in the first phase, begin by reviewing any IS documentation that exists. Following are examples of IS documentation that may be available:

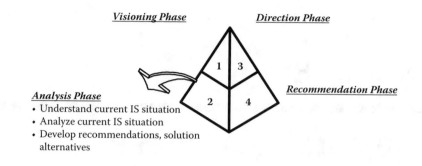

Figure 5.1   Analysis phase

- IS organization chart, names, titles
- Monthly and annual status reports
- Reports provided to management
- Strategic plans that may have been done in the past
- Assessments or audit results that may have been done in the past
- IS vision, mission, objectives, values
- Project lists, current priorities, project summaries
- List of backlog
- List of standards, policies, procedures, methodologies
- Process diagrams, IS forms
- Network diagram
- List of applications, high-level applications documentation
- List of desktop environment, standards, inventory information
- Steering committee presentations
- Executive management presentations
- Job descriptions
- IS survey results that have been done in the past
- Service-level agreements
- Metrics and key measures
- Help Desk call statistics
- Budgets and actual spending for the past three years (expense and capital)
- Governance documentation, members, and responsibilities of the IS steering committee

When reviewing the information, try to answer the questions in Exhibit 5.1.

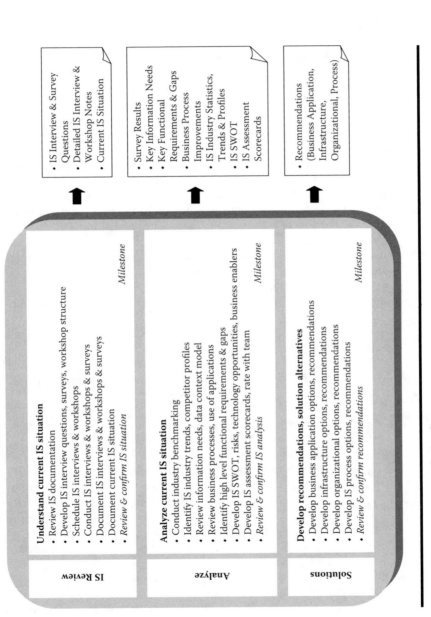

Analysis Phase

IS Review

Understand current IS situation
- Review IS documentation
- Develop IS interview questions, surveys, workshop structure
- Schedule IS interviews & workshops
- Conduct IS interviews & workshops & surveys
- Document IS interviews & workshops & surveys
- Document current IS situation
- *Review & confirm IS situation*   *Milestone*

Analyze

Analyze current IS situation
- Conduct industry benchmarking
- Identify IS industry trends, competitor profiles
- Review information needs, data context model
- Review business processes, use of applications
- Identify high level functional requirements & gaps
- Develop IS SWOT, risks, technology opportunities, business enablers
- Develop IS assessment scorecards, rate with team
- *Review & confirm IS analysis*   *Milestone*

Solutions

Develop recommendations, solution alternatives
- Develop business application options, recommendations
- Develop infrastructure options, recommendations
- Develop organizational options, recommendations
- Develop IS process options, recommendations
- *Review & confirm recommendations*   *Milestone*

Outputs:

- IS Interview & Survey Questions
- Detailed IS Interview & Workshop Notes
- Current IS Situation

- Survey Results
- Key Information Needs
- Key Functional Requirements & Gaps
- Business Process Improvements
- IS Industry Statistics, Trends & Profiles
- IS SWOT
- IS Assessment Scorecards

- Recommendations (Business Application, Infrastructure, Organizational, Process)

Figure 5.2.   Phase 2, analysis phase

▼

Exhibit 5.1 IS Questions to Answer

IS Management

1. Explain the IS organization, how it is organized, its roles, responsibilities, and skill set by area.
2. How many IS employees does your company employ?
3. Do other locations have IS? Where? How many IS employees?
4. What are the IS expenditures and budget?
5. What is the cost breakdown by category, such as labor, nonlabor, outside services, equipment repairs and maintenance, telecommunication, depreciation, and amortization? Be sure to include the amount of money the entire organization is spending on either leasing or owning (depreciation, amortization) of PCs, not just those charged to the IS organization.
6. How do the expenses by category compare to the past three years? What is the breakdown of expenses for business applications, PC, servers, or network?
7. How much capital money did the company spend each year on total IS purchases? How much money did the company spend for the past three years acquiring PCs throughout the organization?
8. What are the IS expenditures as a percentage of sales? How does it compare with the industry?
9. What are the planned projects? What is the backlog? For each project in progress, obtain:
   - Project name
   - Project description. This is an understandable description including why the project needs to be completed
   - Priority
   - Status: Is the project in progress, on hold, in test, etc.
   - What are the total estimated hours to complete the project?
   - How many hours have been completed to date?
   - What is the estimated completion date or elapsed time?
   - Who is assigned to the project from IS?
   - What business objective does the project support? An "infrastructure" project does not support a particular business objective, and can just be noted as infrastructure.
   - What is the total cost savings anticipated because of the project?
   - Who is the business individual or area requesting the project?
   - Who is the IS steering committee member sponsoring the project?
   - What capital outlay or additional expenses are required for the project?
10. What are the key performance indicators (KPI) that IS uses to measure success?
11. What are the key IS processes? Who is responsible for them? Are they documented and improved? Are ITIL (Information Technology Infrastructure Library) principles followed?

- Is there a formal change control process?
- What is the IS budgeting process?
- What is the process to acquire software and hardware?
- What is the process for communicating to the business?
- What is the process for managing computing assets and computing licenses?
- How are service levels and customer satisfaction monitored?
- What is the process for acquiring resources?
- What is the process for developing resources?
- What is the security process?

Business Application Environment

1. What business applications are utilized? By application:
   - Application name
   - Business purpose
   - Architecture
   - Date implemented
   - Programming language
   - Lines of code
   - Number of programs, reports, screens
   - Is it a vendor-supplied package? Include:
     - Vendor
     - Release installed. When was the last release implemented and how long does it typically take?
     - Latest release available
     - Maintenance agreement
     - Level of customization
     - Major areas of customization
2. Are the applications tightly integrated or interfaced? Include a diagram of applications and interfaces.
3. How many business users utilize the applications by functional department?
4. What business applications are used on the PC environment? For each application:
   - Application
   - Programming language
   - Vendor
   - Transaction processor
   - Database manager
   - Operating system
5. What critical business applications have user areas custom-developed utilizing PCs?
   - Language
6. Which percent of the applications are custom and which percent are vendor packages?
7. When were the application systems implemented?

8. How much is spent on vendor maintenance?
9. How many resources are required to maintain and support each application?
10. Processes:
    - What is the systems development process?
    - Is a change management process utilized?
    - Are project management processes used?

PC Environment

1. How many PCs does the company have?
   - By location and functional department?
   - By processor type?
   - By manufacturer?
   - By memory configuration? By disk configuration?
2. How many terminals are connected? Are any special devices necessary (for example, bar-code readers, optical imaging, point-of-sale devices)?
3. What is the standard PC configuration currently purchased?
4. Are PCs purchased or leased?
5. Is any plan or program in place to replace older equipment?
6. How much has the PC environment grown over the past five years? What has caused the growth?
7. How many different PC images are there? Include:
   - Image name
   - Operating system
   - Vendor name
   - Release level
   - Maintenance level
   - Utilities and productivity packages
     - Purpose
     - Vendor
     - Release
     - Maintenance level
8. How many printers, fax machines, and copiers are there?
9. How many Palms or handheld devices are there?
10. What standard PC software does the company utilize? (For example, word processing, spreadsheet, presentation, database, CAD/CAM, desktop publishing, etc.). What releases of software are used?
11. Help desk:
    - Are there multiple help desks or places for users to call?
    - Is the help desk automated (i.e., answering system, expert troubleshooting systems, reports, tracking)?
    - Is there a searchable problem management database to determine solutions?
    - What reports are regularly produced on the help desk activities?
    - Are documented help desk procedures in place?
12. Is there a user forum?
13. How is PC training handled?

14. Processes:
    - Are all calls to the help desk logged?
    - What is the process for PC support?
    - How are workstation standards determined?
    - What is the software distribution process?
    - What is the inventory/asset management process?
    - How is workstation deployment planned?
15. Metrics:
    - What is the average call volume per day/per week?
    - What are the calls per type of call (i.e., software, hardware, moves)?
    - What percent of the calls are resolved on the first call?
    - What is the average amount of time each problem is open?
    - What is the abandon rate of calls?
    - What are the five most common help desk calls?
    - Has a user satisfaction survey been conducted? Results?

Server Environment

1. On what hardware do the business applications operate? By hardware platform, include:
   - Machine, model?
   - Purchased or leased?
   - When was the hardware acquired?
   - How much disk, memory, MIPS, nodes?
   - How much tape capacity?
   - Are there any known performance or sizing concerns?
2. What operating systems? By operating system, include:
   - Name
   - Vendor
   - Release level
   - Maintenance level
   - Latest release level available
   - Latest maintenance level available
   - Number of exits coded by operating system (exit name, language, date last modified)
   - Number of system modifications by operating system (module name, language, date last modified)
3. What database, version (relational, hierarchical, object-oriented)?
   - Number of database instances
   - Number of tables/objects per instance
   - Size (number of rows) of tables
   - Number of indices per table
   - Number of stored procedures per database instance
   - Number of triggers per database instance
4. How many servers are there for business applications, network utility, server management, Web environment, development, or testing?
5. What systems software tools and versions are available?

6. Are systems management and monitoring tools used?
7. Is there a UPS or generator?
8. Outline the disaster recovery plan.
   - Is it tested?
   - Are backups stored off-site?
9. What is the number of support contracts in place? Include:
   - Vendor
   - Cost
   - Terms
   - Packages supported
10. Metrics:
    - Is availability measured and reported, service-level agreements established?
    - What percent utilization is each machine?
    - What is the average response time for online transactions?
    - How does system utilization compare to historic utilization?
    - Security violations?
11. Processes:
    - Is an automated problem management system and process in place?
    - What is the process for managing performance and capacity planning?
    - What is the process for disaster recovery?
    - What is the process for backup and recovery?
    - How is availability managed?
    - What is the security process?

Network Environment

1. Provide network topology diagrams for the WAN and LAN environments.
2. What locations are connected via the WAN?
   - Number of major nodes?
   - Number of end users?
   - Number of transactions/day?
3. What network technologies are used on the WAN? For each listed below, provide location, vendor, number, speed:
   - Fiber
   - Frame relay, Ethernet
   - MPLS
   - Internet
   - Point-to-point circuits
   - ATM
   - Hubs
   - Routers
   - Switches
4. What network technologies are used on the LAN? For each listed below, provide location, vendor, number, speed:
   - Ethernet
   - Token ring

- ATM
- Hubs
- Routers
- Switches
- Cabling
5. What network servers and operating systems are used?
   - File and print servers
   - Application servers
   - Database servers
   - Specialty servers for gateways
   - SMTP
   - Other
6. What external access is available?
   - Remote access
     - Modem pools
     - Private provider
   - Internet
   - Extranet
7. Network availability (WAN and LAN):
   - What hours is the network available?
   - Are there any known concern or growth areas relative to the network (WAN and LAN)?
   - What tools are used to manage network availability?
8. What electronic mail system does the company utilize?
   - How many people are connected?
   - Is it used for external entities such as customers and suppliers? How many are connected?
9. How is the company connected to the Internet?
   - How does the company use the Internet?
   - What are all the URLs for home pages?
   - How frequently do employees access the Internet?
   - What Web site application tools are used?
10. Is there an extranet? What is it used for?
11. Is there an intranet? What is it used for? What tools are used?
12. What are the data closets like? How many are there?
13. Does the disaster recovery plan include the network?
14. What security measures are in place?
    - Virus detection
    - Spam detection
    - Firewall
    - DMZ (demilitarized zone)
    - Passwords
15. Processes:
    - What is the security process?
    - What is the process to manage performance and capacity of the network?
    - What is the change management process for network changes?
    - What is the availability process?

- What is the backup and recovery process?
- What is the disaster recovery process?

16. Metrics:
    - What is the network availability objective or service-level agreement?
    - What is the reliability of the network? Is network availability data reported? How many unscheduled network outages have occurred in the past months? What were the causes?
    - What is the typical network load by application?
    - What is the percent utilization of the network lines and segments?

Data Center

1. Is physical security sufficient?
2. Review the data center:
   - Cooling
   - Electrical amps
   - UPS
   - Generator
   - Alarm
   - Sprinkler system
   - Location
   - Size

------------------------------------▲------------------------------------

Develop IS Interview Questions, Surveys, and Workshop Structure

If the IS department is small, hold individual discussions, or interviews, with each member to gather information. These individuals work with business departments on a daily basis and usually have a good understanding of issues and potential corrective actions. For very large IS organizations, use a workshop approach where teams break out to answer questions and report to the group. When talking to IS individuals, it is useful to:

■ Understand if they have any concerns or issues regarding IS. Internal problems can affect the end user or customer.
■ Identify suggestions on how to improve IS and the service the organization provides.
■ Understand what each individual likes and dislikes about his or her job and the IS group.
■ Understand any particular career interests or direction. In mapping the future organization, it is extremely helpful to know where individuals want to direct their careers. Again, satisfied IS employees are critical to providing good service to the business community.

Exhibit 5.2 provides an example of interview questions to use for IS individuals.

In addition to talking to the individuals in the formal IS organization, it may also be useful to talk to the informal IS support organization. There may be several individuals in the business that have IS-related responsibilities such as business analysis, report generation, or support of an engineering network or tools.

▼

Exhibit 5.2 IS Interview Questions

Your Job
1. What are your title, role, and areas of responsibility?
2. Explain the IS environment that you are responsible for (i.e., PC environment, network, or business application). Do you have any documentation that would help to better explain your area or your job?
3. How long have you been at the company?
4. What is your current skill set? How long have you been in IS?
5. What current projects are you working on? On what activities do you spend your time?
6. Are your work and projects clearly prioritized?
7. How much of your time is spent on support versus projects?
8. Do you have any concerns or issues relative to your job?
9. Do you have the tools and resources necessary to do your job? Do you have the training you need?
10. Are you getting the communication that you need? What other communication would be helpful? Are there any meetings or communication you would like to see eliminated?
11. What things do you like about your job and the IS group? Do you feel motivated to do a good job?
12. What things do you not like about your job and the IS group? What frustrates you about your job?
13. What are your career interests or direction?

The IS Organization as a Whole
1. What is the direction of IS as a department? What is the mission and vision of IS? What are the goals and objectives? Are any documents available that would be helpful for me to review?
2. What are the strengths of IS as an organization?
3. What are the weaknesses, or areas of improvement, for IS? What suggestions do you have on how to improve IS and the service the organization provides?

4. Opportunities?
5. Threats?
6. Describe the culture within IS.
7. How would you characterize the leadership team? Are you getting proper feedback and the direction you need?
8. What are some factors (strengths or weaknesses) in the company as a whole that impact the ability of IS to deliver? Is there anything that could be changed in the business to improve the IS environment and ability to execute?
9. What are ways that you think IS could assist the business? What are the specific business goals and how can technology support the business goal?
10. What are specific technologies that you think would be useful to implement? What industry trends do you think are particularly applicable in your industry?
11. Which technologies do you use today? What components, technologies, or projects do you think should be included in the technology roadmap? Do you have any opinions on the technical architecture and specific directions that should or should not be taken?
12. Do you feel that IS is aligned well with the business? Why or why not?
13. Do you feel that IS provides a strategic advantage to the company? Why or why not?
14. Is the company getting the proper value from IS that it should? Why or why not? What metrics do you think would help measure the value IS provides?
15. If you could stop the world and fix or change one thing in IS, what would that be?
16. What would you change if you ran IS?

▲

Surveys

Surveys can be useful tools for obtaining quantifiable information to compare from year to year. Follow the same survey guidelines provided in Chapter 4. The most important guideline is to conduct a survey only if you intend to do something with the information. Like interviews, conducting the survey sets an expectation for improvements. Exhibit 5.3 provides an example of a survey to use for IS.

▼

Exhibit 5.3   IS Survey

Survey for IS Employees
Response Key:

5—Strongly agree
4—Agree

3—Neither agree nor disagree
2—Disagree
1—Strongly disagree
N/A—Don't know or not applicable

Tools and Training

1. I have the tools and resources necessary to do my job.
2. I have the skills and training necessary to do my job.
3. I am encouraged by management to develop new skills.
4. I am able to get cross training to provide sufficient backup support.
5. Training is available for me to pursue.
6. Time is provided for me to take the training I need.
7. I am able to apply my training and skills to my job.

Job Feedback

1. The company appreciates the work I do.
2. The users I support appreciate the work I do.
3. IS management appreciates the work I do.
4. I receive feedback on my performance on a regular and ongoing basis.
5. The performance appraisal process is effective for me.
6. I have a clear understanding of my job expectations.
7. Opportunities for advancement are available to me.
8. I am able to pursue my desired career interests and direction.
9. I am fairly compensated for my work.

Communication

1. I am comfortable expressing my opinions, and my opinions are considered by IS management.
2. I receive the communication I need about the business.
3. I receive the communication I need about other areas of IS.
4. Communication between peers is effective.
5. I understand the direction and goals of IS.
6. I understand how IS activities support the business goals of the company.

Job

1. Although it may be variable, overall my workload is fair.
2. I like what I work on.
3. Priorities are clear and consistent; I know what I should work on.
4. I understand how my activities support the business goals of the company.
5. There is sufficient backup for my areas of responsibility.
6. I am able to get what I need from my manager.
7. I feel motivated to do a good job.

8. My physical work environment meets my needs.
9. I have input on estimates that are used for my work.

Overall IS

1. I respect IS management and feel the managers do a good job.
2. IS fosters a strong teamwork environment.
3. Individuals in IS have the right skills to support the organization.
4. IS is organized properly.
5. IS is able to get the funding necessary to support the organization.
6. Executive business management supports IS.
7. In general, IS is a productive organization.
8. The level of commitment and level of effort is consistent across IS.
9. IS is adaptable and flexible, and has a can-do attitude.
10. On a scale of 1–5, rate how reactive (1: very reactive) or proactive (5: very proactive) IS is.
11. Overall, I am satisfied with my job.

Open Questions

1. Other comments about my job.
2. List two or three things IS does best.
3. List two or three things IS most needs to improve.
4. Other comments about IS as a whole.
5. List two or three technologies available in the industry that would have a positive effect on the company if deployed here.
6. Identify one thing that IS should do or change next year.

Respondent Information

1. Which IS group do you work in? (Drop-down selection)
   - Desktop
   - Applications
   - Network/infrastructure
   - Telecommunications/other
2. My location is:
   - U.S.
   - International
3. My job classification is: (Drop-down selection)
   - Manager/supervisor
   - IS employee
   - IS consultant/contractor
4. I have worked at the company: (Drop-down selection)
   - Less than 1 year
   - 1 to 3 years

  – 3+ to 7 years
  – Over 7 years
5. Name: (Optional)

▲

Exhibit 5.4 shows an example of an e-mail that could be used to announce the IS survey.

The survey results will provide a wealth of information. Be sure the IS management team carefully reviews the results, determines appropriate action, and implements changes.

▼

Exhibit 5.4   IS Survey Announcement

IS Group,

As you are aware, we have started an effort to develop an IS strategic plan. The plan will identify the vision, strategies, priorities, projects, and action items for IS. As part of that process, we are interested in your satisfaction as an IS employee, because your satisfaction reflects on the service you provide your customers. We are interested in your honest feedback and comments on how we can improve the services we provide.

The survey should take less than five minutes of your time; it is a total of 30 questions, or five screens. Please complete the IS employee survey by clicking on the following link and answering the questions by April 7th: xxxxxxxxxxxxxxx.

The survey results will be summarized as part of the planning process, which is scheduled to be completed in the next 6 to 8 weeks. This will become an annual process so we can measure the progress from year to year. I thank you in advance for your participation and candid comments in this important process.

▲

Schedule IS Interviews and Workshops

Next, schedule the interviews, or one-on-one discussions. Similar to the business discussions, the IS interviews should be no longer than one and a half hours. Conduct the discussions in a private office or conference room.

Conduct IS Interviews, Workshops, and Surveys

The following are suggestions for the IS interview:

- Conduct the discussions in a flexible and casual manner. Listen carefully and ask probing clarification questions. Use the established questions as a guide, but ask more detailed probing questions as information is delivered.

■ Do not get defensive. Encourage open and honest communication. Weaknesses cannot be improved if they are not identified and discussed, even though that may be a painful process.

■ Cross-check information from interview to interview to ensure accuracy.

■ Ask for their involvement in the planning process. Their help is extremely important. It may be helpful to assign individuals within IS the responsibility to document certain aspects of the current environment or the direction.

■ Mention that they should feel free to send e-mails or have follow-up discussions if they think of additional items after the discussion.

Document IS Interviews, Workshops, and Surveys

Next, document the detailed notes of the interviews and workshops. Protect the privacy of individuals if they confide information that should not be shared. Document the results from the IS employee survey.

Document the Current IS Situation

If managers are not versed in the current situation, they will not be able to understand or approve the steps needed to get to the vision. It is important for everyone to have a clear understanding of the current environment before starting to develop the vision.

Many business managers are not able to answer basic questions about their current IS environment, yet they know the basics about other business functions such as marketing, engineering, or finance. Often, this lack of communication can be due to the failure of the IS area to communicate in a language and terminology that the business understands. It is definitely a challenge, but not impossible, to explain a technical environment to a nontechnical professional. For an IS professional who is extremely knowledgeable about the current environment, this step may seem too basic and not necessary. However, it is essential that all levels of business management understand the current environment, and the step is well worth the time. It is extremely important when presenting the information to attempt to summarize it with graphics and to be as brief as possible while still conveying the important information. When describing the current situation, avoid comments on strengths or weaknesses, which can be addressed with the analysis section. It can be helpful to keep track of the strengths and weaknesses, though, because such a list will prove helpful later in the analysis step.

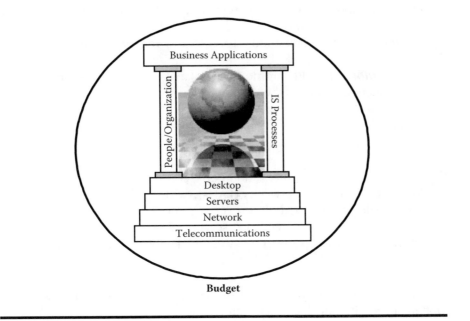

Figure 5.3   Components of IS

Begin by describing the major components of an IS environment, such as the following:

- Business application environment
- Desktop environment
- Server environment
- Network environment
- Telecommunications environment
- Data center environment

These environments are supported through the following:

- IS organization
- Processes
- Budget and metrics

Figure 5.3 shows an example of how one company introduced the components.

Another company looked at the following components in their environment:

Functional automation: Automation of business activities and business transactions

Decision support: Collection, retrieval, and presentation of business information

Documentation: Preparation, storage, and retrieval of electronic documents

Office automation: Electronic forms management, and personal/group productivity tools

When the same company looked at the technical architecture, it examined the following four components:

Client: Desktop computers, notebook computers

Network: Local area networks (LANs), wide area network (WAN)

Server: File, print, and utility servers; remote communications servers; application servers; database servers

Operating software: Operating systems, databases, system management tools, application development tools

Regardless of how you dissect the IS components, explain each component in additional detail, as outlined next.

Business Application Environment

Answer the following questions regarding each of the business applications in the detailed plan document:

1. What is each of the business application modules utilized by the company? Be sure to include all business applications, including those outside the responsibility of IS, such as critical user-built applications. What is the business purpose of each application?
2. When was each application originally implemented?
3. Is each application a vendor-supplied package, custom, or internally supported vendor package?
4. If the application is a vendor package, who is the vendor? Is the company on vendor-supplied maintenance and support? How much does the company pay for this support each year? Is the company on the current release? When was the last release implemented, and how long do upgrades typically take to implement?
5. If the application has been heavily modified, approximately how many modifications are there and what are the main areas of modifications?
6. What departments use the application? How many total business users use the application?

7. Are the applications tightly integrated or interfaced?
8. What programming languages is each system written in? What database language does each application use? Is the application Web-enabled?
9. What is the size of the systems in terms of lines of code? How many reports do the systems generate? How many programs comprise each system?
10. Are there any concerns or plans regarding the application?

A spreadsheet may be a good method to capture detailed business application information. Here are some of the basic headings of information to gather about business applications:

■ Business application name
■ Description
■ Business areas using application
■ Technical contact
■ Business owner
■ Number of users
■ Vendor package or custom or unsupported package
■ Vendor name
■ Annual vendor maintenance costs
■ Actual full-time equivalent (FTE) support resources
■ Language or architecture
■ Database
■ Hardware
■ Application interfaces
■ Year implemented
■ Total cost of ownership
■ Comments

Outline this application information in detail for each business application in the plan document, and summarize in presentation format with a few charts. Exhibit 5.5 shows examples of two application descriptions in the detail plan document. Write the application descriptions in business terminology, not technical jargon as much as possible.

▼

Exhibit 5.5   Business Application Example

Following are the specific business applications used by the company:

Oracle Enterprise Requirements Planning (ERP)

The following Oracle ERP modules are used:

- Customer
- Accounts receivable
- Accounts payable
- Purchase order
- Cost management
- General ledger
- Fixed assets
- Cash management
- Advanced pricing
- iExpense
- Order management
- Inventory
- Purchase order
- Material requirements planning
- Bill of material
- Engineering
- Work in process
- Quality module
- Financial analyzer

The Oracle ERP system was originally implemented in 1990 and is used in the United States, Canada, and England. The company has a total of xxx concurrent licenses, with an average of xxx users logged on during a typical day in the areas of customer service, production, scheduling, purchasing, and finance. The system is a vendor package with few custom modifications, although additional custom forms and reports have been developed. The system was recently upgraded in June to release 11.5.9 (Oracle 11i), which is Oracle's most current release. There is a production and test instance (including programs and databases). The company is on vendor support and pays $xxxK/year in support and maintenance costs. There are approximately x internal FTE resources to maintain and support the system on an ongoing basis. The system is written in Java, PL/SQL, and Oracle Forms 6.0 using an Oracle database, and operates on Hewlett-Packard hardware.

Goldmine Business Contact Manager

Goldmine is used by the sales group for tracking and managing sales activities. Goldmine Corporate Edition is a vendor package by FrontRange Solution Inc. that was implemented in 1993. The company is currently on release 6.5, which is the most current vendor release available. The system has been customized to be able to capture specific product and sales information. There are interfaces from Goldmine to the order management system for customer information. There are approximately xxx users of the system because it is used by all three divisions. Approximately xK e-mail mailings are done per month using Goldmine, approximately xK sales activities are scheduled per cycle, and approximately xK sales activities are completed per cycle. The company is on vendor maintenance and support, at a cost of $xxK/year. In addition, the company has spent $xK in consulting costs on Goldmine this year. The system is written in Delphi and uses a Microsoft SQL 2000 database.

▲

The following is an example of summary information that may be helpful to include in the overview presentation:

- Develop one summary diagram that represents all the business applications used by the company. Represent integrated modules with overlapping circles, and use arrows for interfaces. This diagram should be at a very high level. Include any external interfaces or connections, such as Web applications or interfaces to partners. Show interfaces to the other internal environments, such as, if the business applications have an interface to the engineering environment or to a computer-integrated manufacturing environment. Figure 5.4 and Figure 5.5 are examples of application portfolio summary diagrams.
- Identify the total percent of custom software versus vendor-supplied software. Custom and heavily modified applications require

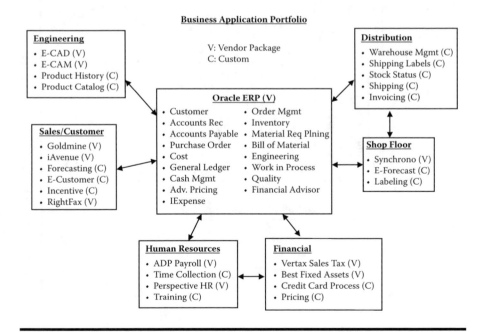

Figure 5.4   Business application portfolio

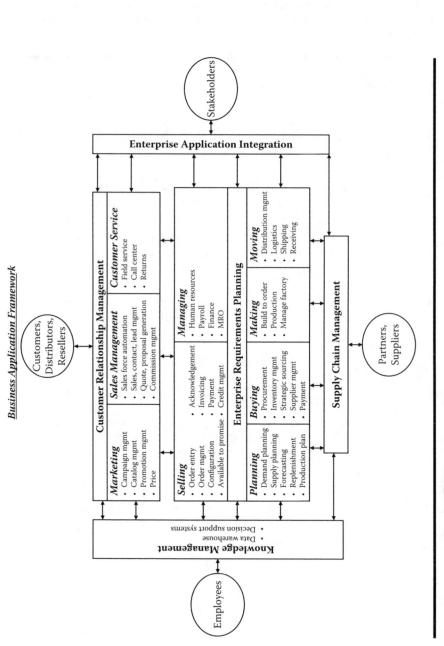

Figure 5.5   Business application framework

internal resources to maintain and support. The long-term cost of ownership of custom or heavily modified software is often greater than vendor-supported software. It is difficult and expensive for a company to keep custom software up to date with changing technology. Companies typically strive to keep custom software to a minimum (less than 20%) and use custom only for truly unique situations that can provide a competitive advantage.

- Identify the variety of databases. The more database languages (i.e., Oracle, SQL Server, DB2, Sybase, IMS) that a company is required to support, the greater the complexity, cost, support requirements, and additional skill set that must be supported. Companies typically try to standardize on a few database languages.
- Identify the variety of programming languages. Again, the more programming languages (i.e., Visual Basic, Oracle Forms, Access, Java, and COBOL) that a company is required to support, the greater the complexity, cost, support requirements, and additional skill set that must be supported. Companies typically attempt to standardize on a few programming languages.
- Identify the annual vendor maintenance and support costs. Understanding the cost of each application in the portfolio is the first step in making business value decisions. When asking for budget cuts, management may not be aware of the high amount of fixed cost.
- Identify the internal maintenance and support costs. To reflect the costs of applications, identify the amount of resources required to keep the application functioning and to carry on normal maintenance.
- Identify business users by country or department. Business management may be surprised to see who actually uses the applications throughout the company.
- Identify the year applications were implemented. This chart can depict the age of the applications and may be interesting to look at relative to the cost history.
- Identify the size of applications. It is helpful to relate the lines, function points, or complexity of code to things that are familiar to the average person to provide management with an understanding of the size of the systems that the organization owns and maintains. For example, at one company, the lines of code were compared to the number of lines of code in Microsoft Excel or in a Lincoln Continental (which was the car the company president owned). Compare the number of lines of code to the product that the company sells, if it involves software. The lines of code comparison can be especially helpful if you have custom systems

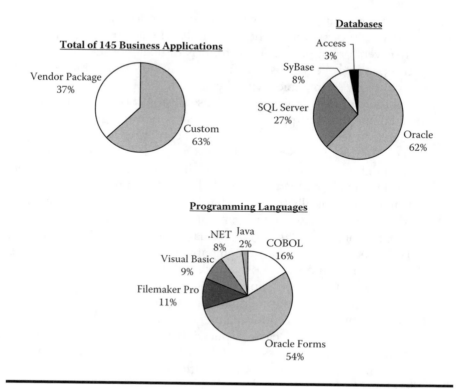

Figure 5.6   Business application summary

requiring resources to maintain. You may surprise management with the size of the system that the IS organization must maintain, especially if you correlate to the number of programmers maintaining Microsoft Excel or other products that have hundreds of programmers to maintain.

■ Identify how the usage of the system has increased over time. These charts would probably coincide with company growth and cost growth.

Examples of presenting this application summary information are provided in Figure 5.6 and Figure 5.7.

Desktop Environment

The desktop or client environment consists of the following components:

■ Desktop PCs and docking stations
■ Notebook PCs

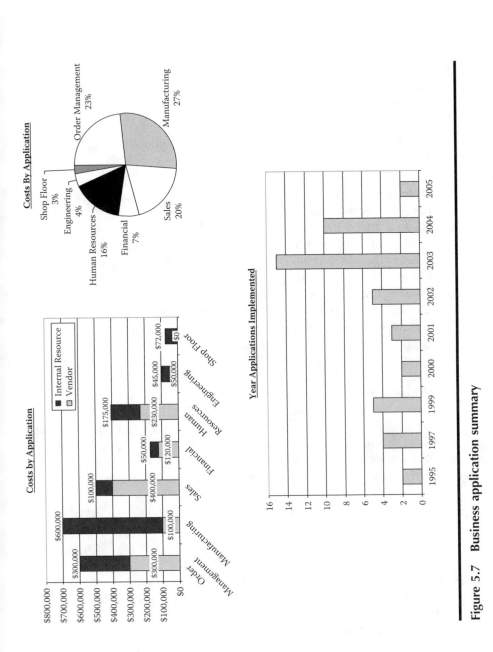

Figure 5.7   Business application summary

- Engineering workstations
- Terminals
- Personal digital assistants (PDAs), Palms, and other handheld devices
- Scanners
- Printers
- Fax machines
- Copiers

Answer the following questions regarding each component of the desktop environment:

1. How many PCs does the company have? How many PCs does it have by location and functional department?
2. What is the distribution by class of PCs (e.g., Pentium 4)? What percent are below industry standard (supported by vendors)?
3. What is the distribution by brand of PCs (e.g., Dell, Compaq, IBM)? Is the environment standardized?
4. What is the standard PC that is purchased?
5. Are PCs purchased or leased? If leased, how many years, who with, and what is the cost?
6. Is any plan or program in place to replace older equipment, or is it replaced as needed? What percent is replaced each year? Is a documented rotation guideline followed?
7. How much has the PC environment grown over the past five years?
8. What operating systems are used?
9. What standard PC software is used (e.g., word processing, spreadsheet, presentation, database, CAD/CAM, desktop publishing, etc.)?
10. What additional PC software is installed as necessary?
11. How many PC images are there? How long does it take to install a new PC?
12. Can users install software on their PCs?
13. How are software updates managed?
14. What security and virus protection measures are in place?

Answer similar questions for the notebook environment, engineering workstations, terminals, PDAs and Palms, scanners, printers, fax machines, and copiers. Format the answers by describing the environment in the detailed plan document, as shown in Exhibit 5.6. Quickly and thoroughly convey the information in just a few summary slides when describing this information to management, as shown in Figure 5.15 and Figure 5.16.

▼

Exhibit 5.6   Desktop Environment Example

Desktop and Client Environment

As shown by the diagram to the right, the worldwide desktop environment consists of:

- *xxxx* desktop PCs
- *xxxx* notebook PCs
- *xxxx* Macintoshes
- *xxxx* terminals
- *xxxx* bar-code printers
- *xxxx* printers
- *xxxx* fax machines
- *xxxx* copiers

The following table shows each of these by country:

	U.S.								
Desktop PCs									
Notebook PCs									
Macintoshess									
Terminals									
Bar-code printers									
Printers									
Fax machines									
Copiers									

Each of these environments is described below in more detail.

a. Desktop PCs

Hardware

The company has a total of *xxxx* desktop PCs. Figure 5.8 shows the percent by country.

All PCs are purchased rather than leased. PCs are purchased through several vendors, including <list of vendors>. Approximately *xxxx* new PCs are purchased each year on a worldwide basis.

Figure 5.9 shows the PCs that have been purchased over the past five years to demonstrate the rate of purchase.

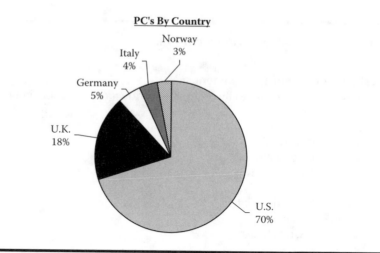

Figure 5.8   PCs by country

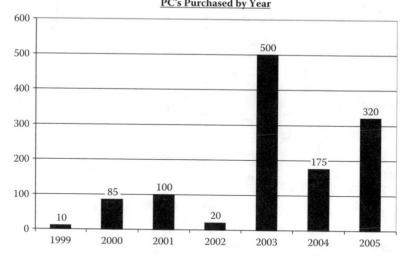

Figure 5.9   PCs purchased by year

Figure 5.10 shows how the PC environment has grown during the past few years.

Figure 5.11 shows the age of the PCs.

The standard PC that is purchased is a Dell Intel Pentium 4 processor, 3.0 GHz, 512 MB of RAM, 17-inch monitor and 60 GB hard drive. Figure 5.12 shows PCs by model and Figure 5.13 shows PCs by processor.

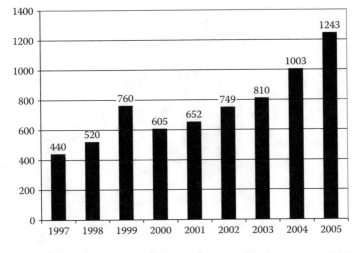

Figure 5.10 PC growth

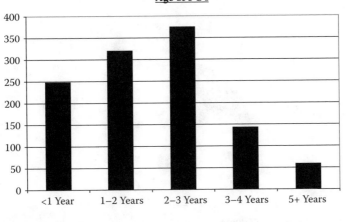

Figure 5.11 Age of PCs

The industry-standard PC is a minimum of a Pentium *xxx*, with *xx*% of the company's PCs falling below the minimum standard. With substandard hardware, some software packages may not operate properly and may require additional maintenance and support.

Accurate PC inventory information is maintained in the United States with a software package called <name of package>. PCs in the rest of the world are tracked and managed with <name of application>.

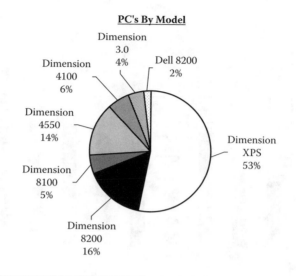

Figure 5.12   PCs by model

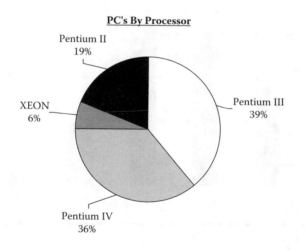

Figure 5.13   PCs by processor

When a business department needs a new PC, they <description of process>. PCs are budgeted by the user/IS. All PCs come with a three-year warranty that provides replacement parts and on-site repair by Dell. After the warranty expires, we purchase replacement parts and fix the PC. Old PCs that cannot be repaired are <description of policy>.

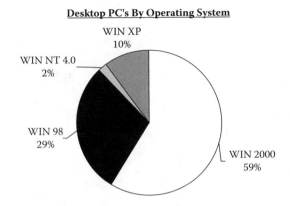

Figure 5.14   Desktop PCs by operating system

Software
The standard operating system used is Windows <name of OS>. However, the company has several other desktop operating systems to support, as shown by Figure 5.14.

The core set of software packages installed on PCs include:

- Productivity: _____ (e.g., Microsoft Office)
- E-mail: _____
- Internet: _____
- Virus protection: _____
- Documents: _____(e.g., Adobe Acrobat Reader)
- Others: _____

The company purchases *xxxxx* copies of Microsoft <name of program>, and *xxx* copies of <name of program>. The company pays approximately $*xxx*K/year in PC-based software licenses.

The standard set of software is loaded on PCs using Symantec Ghost software. The company has *xx* different images that can be loaded. It takes approximately *x* hours to install a new PC.

Additional software that is installed as needed includes:

- Project management: _____ (e.g., Microsoft Project)
- Flowcharting: _____ (e.g., Microsoft Visio)
- Palm synch: _____
- Others: _____

There are a total of *xxx* different PC-based software packages used at the company.

Users typically store files on the server, which is backed up nightly. Users are unable to install PC software on their PCs due to administrator rights.

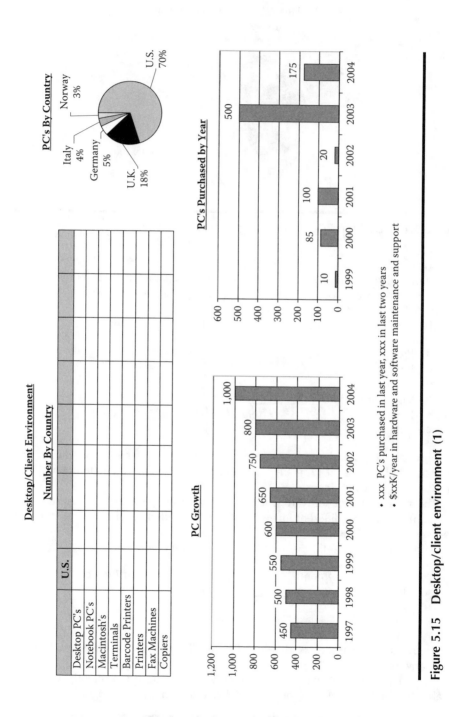

Figure 5.15 Desktop/client environment (1)

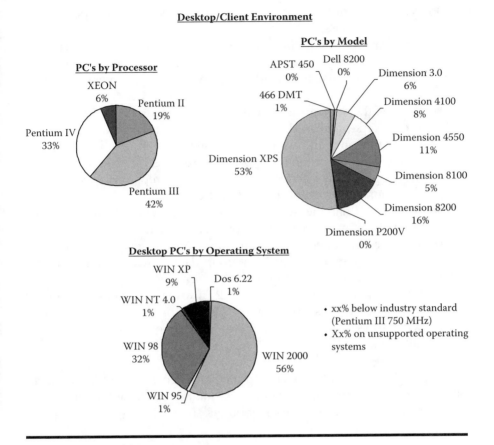

Figure 5.16 Desktop/client environment (2)

Server Environment

The server environment consists of the following:

- Server hardware
- Operating system software
- Other server software
- Disk
- Databases

Answer the following questions regarding the server environment:

- How many total servers are there? What is the business purpose of each server? How many servers are there by location or country? Are servers and data consolidated?

■ What is the distribution of hardware for servers? What percent by model and class?

■ What are the mission-critical servers? How are they protected? Is clustering, RAID 3, or RAID 5 used? Is there failover software? Are blade servers used? Is load balancing used? Is content switching used?

■ What is the standard server that is purchased?

■ Are servers purchased or leased? If leased, how many years, with what company, and what is the cost?

■ Is any plan or program in place to replace older servers or are they replaced as needed? What percent is replaced each year? Is a documented rotation guide followed?

■ How much has the server environment grown over the past five years? How many servers are purchased each year?

■ What are the operating systems used on the servers? What is the standard operating system? Is it up-to-date on releases and patches?

■ What other software is used on the servers?

■ What database languages are used? How many databases are there? How much data is stored in total? Is SAN or NAS technology used?

■ What tools are used to monitor and report CPU and memory utilization?

Format the answers by describing the server environment in the detail plan document, as shown in Exhibit 5.7. Summarize the information in a few summary slides in the presentation, as shown in Figure 5.25.

-------------------------------▼-------------------------------

Exhibit 5.7   Server Environment Example

The company has a total of xx servers. As shown by Figure 5.17, the servers are used for:

  Business application-specific servers: These servers are used for the major business applications for the company, such as ERP, payroll, human resources, shop floor, and engineering. These are a total of xxx business application servers.

  Utility services: These servers provide fundamental network services. These services include file and print sharing, e-mail, etc. There are a total of xxx utility services servers.

  Server management: These servers assist in the management and support of the network and server environment for things such as security, anti-spam, virus protection, and systems management. There are a total of xx server management servers.

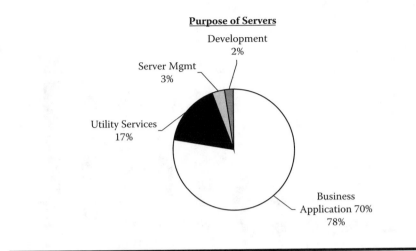

Figure 5.17   Purpose of servers

Development: IS use these servers for testing and development. There are a total of *xx* development servers.

The table below shows the servers by country:

	U.S.	*U.K*							
Business application servers									
Utility servers									
Server management									
Development servers									

Hardware

Approximately *xx* servers are purchased every year. Figure 5.18 shows the growth of the server environment over time.

Figure 5.19 shows the servers by model, with the majority being Dell Power Edge machines. Figure 5.20 shows the age of the servers.

Servers are purchased rather than leased. The standard server purchased is an HP/Compaq Proliant server (Intel Pentium IV Xeon 2200-MHz processor, 768 MB of memory, 3-36.4 Ultra SCSI drives, RAID 5 disk controller, CD-ROM drive, single power supply, and dual-processor-capable motherboard).

Maintenance and support contracts are carried on all servers. The company pays $xxxK/year in support agreements for hardware. This support provides 24/7, maximum of four-hour response, onsite service and hardware replacement.

Clustering technology is used to group servers for more efficient processing. SAN technology used for more efficient disk processing. The disk that is used is <type of disk>.

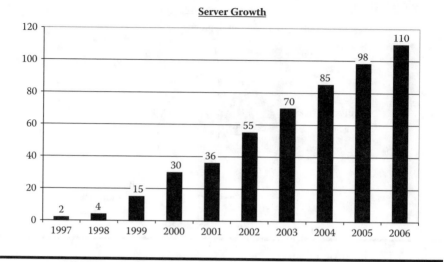

Figure 5.18   Server growth

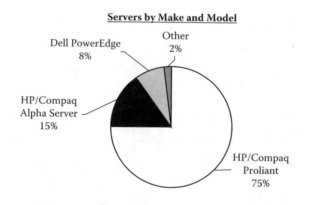

Figure 5.19   Servers by make and model

RAID3 or RAID5 technology is used to improve the reliability of the data.

Software

The servers operate on a variety of operating systems, as shown in Figure 5.21, with the majority using NT 4 Server.

Of the *xxx* business application servers, Figure 5.22 shows the breakdown of server by major business application area.

Databases

There are a total of *xx* database servers with *xx* total databases.

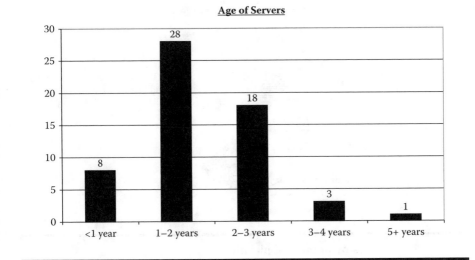

Figure 5.20   Age of servers

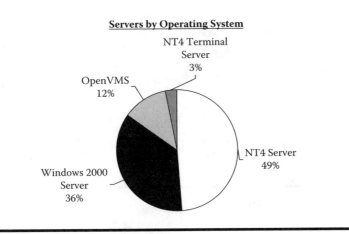

Figure 5.21   Servers by operating system

As shown by Figure 5.23, the majority (95%) of the databases are Microsoft SQL databases, with the remainder being one each of DB2, Sybase, Unidata, and Proprietary.

As shown by Figure 5.24, *xx* of the databases are production, and *xx* are used for staging, test, and development.

The production databases use *xxxx* of space. As a frame of reference, 1 terabyte of data equals 22,000 four-drawer file cabinets of information, so that is *xxxxxx* file cabinets of information.

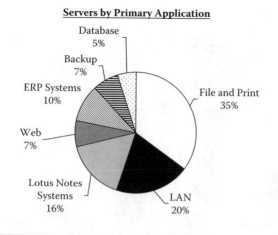

Figure 5.22   Servers by primary application

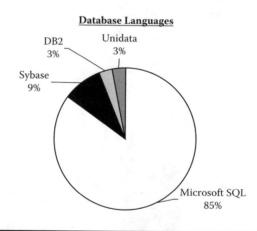

Figure 5.23   Database languages

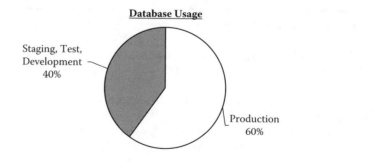

Figure 5.24   Database usage

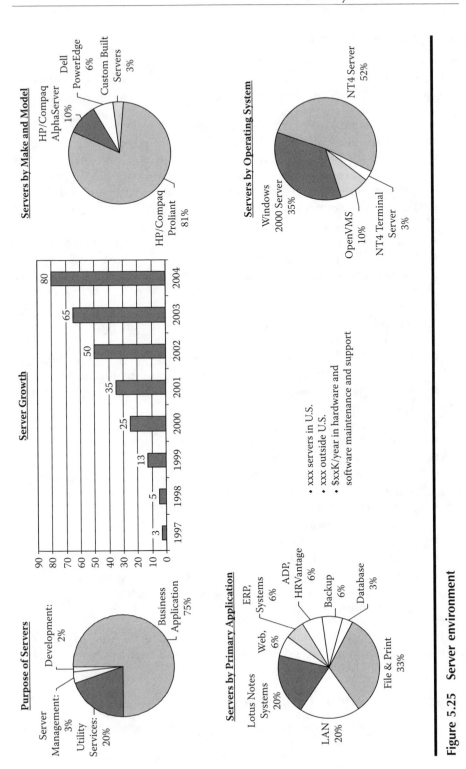

Figure 5.25 Server environment

Network Environment

Because of its technical nature, the network environment is probably the most difficult area to explain in understandable terms. Answer the following questions regarding the network environment in the detailed plan document:

- Obtain a high-level network diagram.
- What are the various locations that are connected via the network?
- How much does the company pay to support and maintain the network (annual costs)? What are the various maintenance and support agreements relative to the network software and hardware?
- Describe the data closets. How many are there and where are they located?
- What level wiring does the company use (i.e., category 6, category 5)?
- How many nodes are there on the network? (A node is any connection, such as a PC, printer, or server.) What are the nodes by country or location?
- How many defined network accounts, or users, are supported? Approximately how many are active in a given day? How many accounts by country or department?
- What is the network backbone and topology? What is the throughput of the backbone? What is the throughput to the desktop?
- How many hubs, switches, and routers are there? What brand and type are they?
- How is remote access provided?
- What is the network operating system?
- What software is used for e-mail?
- How is the security designed? How is the demilitarized zone (DMZ) designed?
- What firewall software is used for security and virus protection? How many firewalls are there?
- What is the reliability of the network?
- What are network key measures?
- How are outages monitored, and how are alerts handled?
- Are there any growth concerns or response bottlenecks relative to the network?

In the summary presentation, include a high-level summary with a network diagram and a few key points about the network.

Telecommunications Environment

Answer the following questions regarding the telecommunications environment in the detailed plan document:

- Describe the phone switch. When was it implemented? What brand is it? What company provides maintenance and support? What is the cost of maintenance and support? Is the software current?
- Describe the voicemail system. When was it implemented? What brand is it? What company provides maintenance and support? What is the cost of maintenance and support? Is the software current?
- Describe any call center software that is used. When was it implemented? What brand is it? What company provides maintenance and support? What is the cost of maintenance and support? Is the software current?
- Is voice-over-IP (VoIP) used? Where? What are the plans for further implementation?
- How many pagers does the company have? How much does the company pay for them?
- How many cell phones does the company have? What company provides service? How much does the company pay per user? Is there a backup plan? How many PDAs or Blackberry devices does the company have?
- Are there any teleconferencing and Web-conferencing capabilities? What hardware and software is used? What is the annual cost?
- Are there any videoconferencing capabilities? What hardware and software is used? What is the annual cost?
- How many calling cards does the company have? What is the annual cost?
- What provider is used for long distance? How much does the company pay per year?

In the summary presentation, include a high-level summary with a diagram and a few key points about the telecommunications environment.

Data Center Environment

Answer the following questions regarding the data center environment in the detailed plan document:

- What physical security is provided in the data center? Is access secure?
- Is cooling adequate?
- Are the electrical amps sufficient?
- Is an uninterruptible power supply (UPS) in the data center? How many amps of service is the UPS?
- Is there a generator? How many amps of service?

- What alarm, monitoring, and emergency notification exists?
- What type of sprinkler system is used?
- Is the data center located in an area to limit vulnerability to weather conditions?
- Does the data center have room for expansion?

In the summary presentation, include a few key points about the data center.

IS Organization

It is important to provide business management with a clear understanding of the responsibilities and activities of the IS organization. Any changes in the IS environment may affect the size and responsibilities of the organization, and it is important to understand the current situation.

The following are questions and information to obtain about IS resources and the organization:

- Include an organization chart with names and titles. If the organization is too large (i.e., hundreds of individuals), just include the top layers of the organization and summarize the lower levels.
- What is the total number of resources? How many are employees and how many are consultants?
- Where in the business organization does the top IS executive report?
- How many resources are there by each major job function (i.e., management, clerical, application programmers, help desk, network administrators, security, operations, systems programmers, database administration)?
- What are general areas of responsibilities and activities for each organizational group?
- What percent of time does each individual or group spend on support activities, maintenance, or project work?
- How many full-time equivalents (FTEs) are necessary for maintenance and support of each business application?
- What is the historical headcount for IS for the past five years? How much money has been spent each year on headcount and consultants?
- What is the average number of years of experience with the company for the IS employees?
- What is the average number of years of IS experience?

- What is the skill set of each individual?
- For each skill area or responsibility, who is the primary person responsible and who is the secondary? Are any areas not sufficiently covered?
- How many employees are supported by IS employees?
- What is the sales revenue per IS employee?

Exhibit 5.8 provides an example of how to present this information in the detail plan document.

▼

Exhibit 5.8   Organizational Example

Organization
The IS organization currently consists of:

- *xxx* employees
- *xxx* consultants and contractors

The vice president of IS reports to the CEO. Figure 5.26 shows the IS organization chart as of August.
Figure 5.27 outlines the major areas of responsibility for each group.

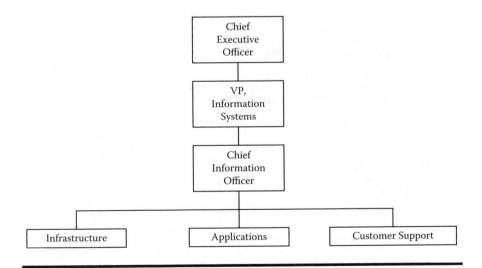

Figure 5.26   IS organization chart

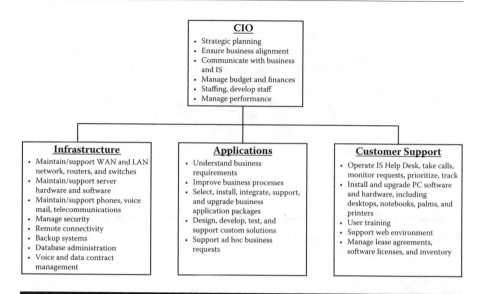

Figure 5.27   Major areas of responsibility

The following table identifies the staffing by area:

Position	Number of Individuals
Executive/senior management	
Middle/line management	
Project management	
Business analyst	
Application programming	
Network administration	
Database administration	
Operations	
Web	
Security	
Systems management	
Help desk	
PC support	
Finance/procurement	
Clerical	
Total	

The following table identifies the support personnel (FTE) by business application:

Business Application	Support FTEs
Manufacturing	
Shop floor	
Order management	
Financial	
Human resources	
Engineering	
Call center	
Sales	
Marketing	

The time spent on projects adds functionality and value to the business, and maintenance and support keeps the systems functioning at the current level. It is best to have an environment that minimizes support requirements, which allows IS to be able to add maximum value to the business. As can be seen by Figure 5.28, only a small portion of the resources is available for project work.

Figure 5.29 shows the historical headcount for IS. As can be seen by the chart, the staffing level has remained relatively stable in spite of the tremendous increase in PCs, business applications, and systems required to support.

Typically, consultants or contractors are used in IS if the skill set is not available in-house. Figure 5.30 shows the historical spending on IS contractors and consultants; Figure 5.31 shows the current composition of employees and contractors.

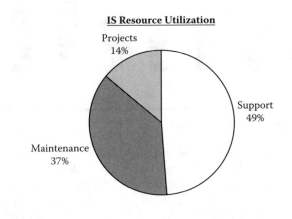

Figure 5.28   IS resource utilization

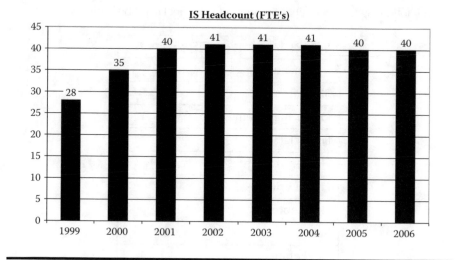

Figure 5.29   IS headcount (FTEs)

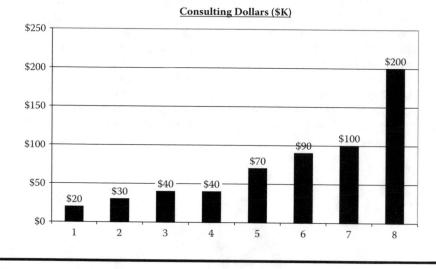

Figure 5.30   Consulting dollars ($K)

The IS group has a high tenure at the company, with the average number of years at the company being 8.2 years. The group is also very experienced in IS, with the average years of experience being 12.8 years. In addition, 64% of the employees have four-year college degrees. The current skill set also matches the environment well, although additional resources are necessary in the Web technology area.

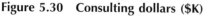

Figure 5.31   Employee/contractor mix

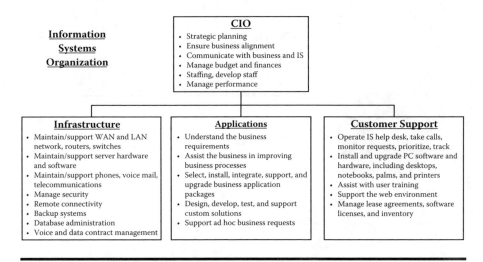

Figure 5.32   Responsibilities by area

For presentation purposes, summarize the organizational information and present it in terms that non-IS people can understand. Start with the organization of the group and then briefly explain the responsibilities of each group within the IS department. Provide a flavor of what the group does without going into excruciating detail. Figure 5.32 and Figure 5.33 are examples of a few slides that explain an IS organization.

Project Workload (Current and Backlog)

Assemble the project workload. This includes the projects requested by the various functional areas of the business as well as those in process.

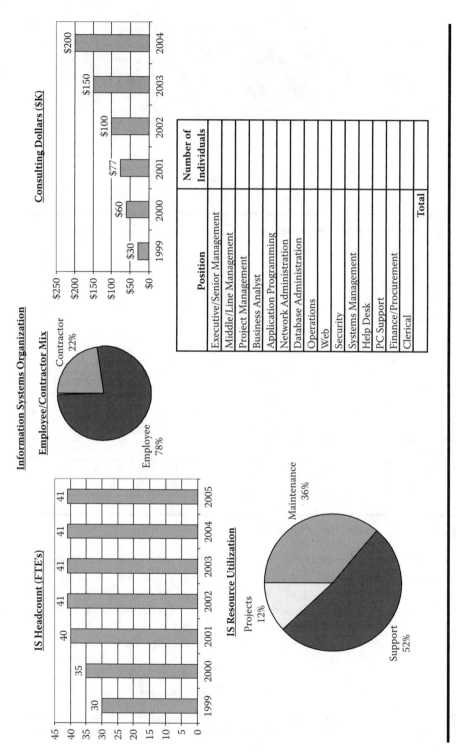

Figure 5.33   IS organization

Focus attention on the projects above a certain predetermined effort of work, projects that cross departmental boundaries, or projects that have capital or recurring costs above a certain level. IS management can prioritize small requests, normal support, or efforts below the established criteria. However, quantify the usual amount of smaller requests, support, and maintenance so that available project resources can be accurately represented. Exhibit 5.9 shows how one company categorized support and projects; Figure 5.34 shows how the company defined minor and major projects reviewed by the IS steering committee.

Exhibit 5.9   Project and Support Definition

Determine Type of Request

Definitions

Support

Problem identification
Problem resolution
Consulting (general Q&A)
Routine operations activities
    Examples:
        Purchasing
        Installation hardware/software
        Add users
        Facilities move
        Upgrades
        Report changes maintenance
        Backup
Ad hoc reporting

Projects (Major and Minor)

New service
Expanded service
Improved service

In addition to projects requested from the business, there are infrastructure projects, or projects that are necessary from an IS standpoint. Examples of these projects include network upgrades, desktop rotation, server rotation, disaster recovery, enterprise event management, problem management software implementation, security improvements, and wireless. For each project, capture the following information in a project spreadsheet, database, or project summary:

- Project name
- Project description: This is an understandable description including why the project needs to be completed.

Included in Existing Service Level & Cost Expectations	Change to Existing Service Level or Cost Expectations New Service Expanded Service Improved Service

COST
$25,000 $100,000

	$25,000		$100,000
Support	Support	Minor	Major
8	Minor	Minor	Major
1,000	Major	Major	Major

HOURS

Figure 5.34   Support, major and minor project classification

■ Business benefits: What business objectives does the project support? What benefits does the business plan to gain? What are the total cost savings anticipated as a result of the project? Projects could also be categorized as business continuance, medium business value, or high business value. An infrastructure project does not support a particular business objective, and can be noted as infrastructure or business continuance.

■ Business requestor: Who is the business person requesting the project? An infrastructure project would not be requested by a businessperson, and can be noted as "Information Systems."

■ Business sponsor: Who is the IS steering committee member sponsoring the project?

■ Priority: Priority can be a high, medium, and low priority based on an understanding of the project or the urgency of the requestor. Projects will actually be prioritized later in the planning process.

■ Status: Is the project in progress, on-hold, in test, etc.?

■ Estimated hours: What are the total estimated hours to complete the project? If exact hours are unknown, the project could be categorized as small, medium, large, or extra large with a span of hours identified for each category.

■ Completed hours: How many hours have been completed to date?

■ Estimated completion date: What is the estimated completion date or elapsed time?

■ Assigned to: Who is assigned to the project from IS?

■ Estimated costs: What capital outlay or additional expenses are required for the project?

- Recurring costs: Will any maintenance or support costs continue on an annual basis?
- Risk: Identify the risk as high, medium, or low.
- Dependent projects: Do any projects need to be completed before this project?

It can be tempting to assemble a project list for each area of the IS organization. However, one word of caution in doing this: if projects require assistance from other branches of the organization, it can be confusing to have multiple lists. With one combined list, the priorities are clear if assistance is necessary from various areas of IS. One list will reduce the chance for conflicting or unclear priorities.

Assemble all the project information and present a summary of the information to management. This can be done with two slides. The first slide can outline how many project resources are available. A significantly smaller amount of resources than the total resource pool is actually able to apply to project hours due to administration, sick, vacation, training, general support, and maintenance requests. The project resources can be determined by subtracting the resources to "keep the lights on" from the total number of resources. A simple table can show the following:

- Number of resources for each functional area of IS (for example, PC, network, operations, programming)
- The total hours available (number of people times 2080 for a 40-hour week)
- The number of nonworked hours (number of resources times total sick and vacation, etc.)
- The number of administration hours (number of resources times the number of hours typically spent in meetings and administrative duties)
- The number of support and maintenance hours (number of resources times the number of hours typically spent answering user questions, ad hoc queries, completing maintenance requests, etc.)
- The number of project hours available per year (total hours available minus nonworked minus administration minus support and maintenance)
- Project hours per week (project hours per year divided by 52)

An example is shown in Table 5.1.

Through this process, you will find that only a small portion of resources can actually be applied toward project time. In the example in Table 5.1, the company found that only 24% of its total resources were

Table 5.1 Project Resource Hours Available

	# of Resources	Total Hours/Year	Nonwork	Admin	Support	Project Hrs/Yr	Project Hrs/Wk
PC	4	8320	857	1248	4160	2055	40
Network	1	2080	200	312	1300	268	5
DEC Systems	3	6240	780	1080	2652	1728	33
iSeries Systems	5	10400	1000	1560	5200	2640	51
Technical Support	1	2080	200	240	1220	420	8
Total	14	29120	3037	4440	14532	7111	137

Time/tasks for management not included.

Open network positions not included.

24% of total resources for projects.

available for projects. This was one indicator of an aging, custom, or maintenance-intensive application portfolio. By ignoring this step in the process, many IS departments typically overcommit their resources. As mentioned in the example, this analysis can also identify potential problems with too much support and maintenance indicating custom or aging systems.

Now that you know how many resources you have, the second slide can show a summary of the backlog of projects. Again, a table showing the following can be useful:

- For each functional area of IS (e.g., network, PC, operations, programming), what is the total of outstanding project hours for each priority (high, medium, and low)?
- What is the total for all priority projects?
- What are the project resource hours available per year from the previous slide?
- What are the years of backlog for each functional group (project hours divided by project resource hours available)?

An example is shown in Table 5.2.

This analysis shows whether an area is overallocated with projects and where you need to shift resources. It also indicates whether an area of IS has aging systems or technology to address. In Table 5.2, it appears there are not enough resources in one area of applications. It also may indicate that those applications may be worth replacing due to the high backlog of requests.

Processes

Identify the various processes within the IS group. *A Practical Guide to Information Systems Process Improvement* (CRC Press, 2000), by Anita Cassidy and Keith Guggenberger, provides guidance in identifying processes. Figure 5.35 shows an example of the IS processes identified in one company.[1] Also, identify notes about each process area in the plan document. At this point, do not include editorial comments about what is good or bad; those things can be outlined in the strengths and weaknesses, and right now you should focus on what is good (or bad). Note the strengths and weaknesses to be used in a later analysis step. Exhibit 5.10 shows one example of notes about a process area.

Continue with key items in all the process areas. Summarize some of the key information from processes in the presentation, particularly any charts, or data.

Table 5.2 Current Backlog

	Priority "A" Hours	Priority "B" Hours	Priority "C" Hours	Total Project Hours	Project Resource Hrs/Yr	Years of Backlog
PC	1761	70	200	2031	2055	1.0
Network	368	250	173	791	268	3.0
Product related (DEC)	872	360	340	1572	1728	.9
Business application (iSeries)	3462	4764	11720	19946	2640	7.5
Technical support/op	1406	0	0	1406	420	3.3
Total	7869	5444	12433	25746	7111	3.6

New projects are added throughout the year.

Size of application backlog indicates total application replacement may be necessary.

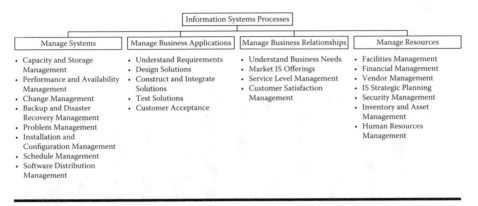

Figure 5.35   IS processes

▼

Exhibit 5.10   IS Processes

Processes are how the work is completed within the IS organization. In general, the majority of IS processes are informal and undocumented. The following are comments relative to each process area (shown here is just the first of four process areas).

Manage Systems Processes

■ Although a formal *disaster recovery plan* or business continuance plan does not exist, it is a project currently in progress. The company does have a contract with a disaster recovery company, <name of company>, to provide equipment in the event of a disaster. The cost of this contract is $xK/year; it is just a drop-ship contract for an equipment list.

■ *Backup tapes* are stored off-site on a daily basis. Daily tapes of the iSeries are stored for 5 days, 8 weekly tapes are kept, and 6 annual backup tapes are kept. Incremental backups are taken of network servers, with the last 5 versions of files kept indefinitely, and deleted files kept for 13 months. The company will be able to recover to the last 24 hours with a recovery time objective of 72 hours.

■ The *help desk* is the single point of contact for all PC hardware and software needs. Although some calls go directly to IS individuals, for the most part this process is followed. The IS help desk is available 24 hours a day, seven days a week at extension 1234. The help desk is staffed from 6 a.m. to 6 p.m. Support from 6 p.m. to 10:00 p.m. is handled through a rotation of individuals who receive a $xxx/week flat fee; they are required to be at home and call back within 10 minutes. Support on weekends and from 10 p.m. to 6 a.m. (M–F) is rotated among 10 IS individuals who get $xxx for a week rotation and respond within one hour. Attention paging software

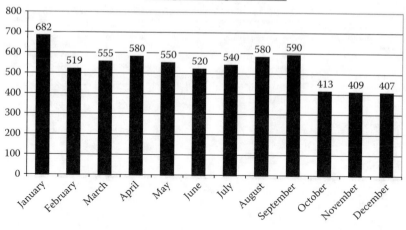

Figure 5.36   IS requests completed: 2005

is used to alert personnel of any issues, which costs $xxK/year in mainte-
nance. All calls or requests are logged into a custom Lotus Notes Dispatch
Tickets system. Users can also obtain assistance by submitting electronic
IS requests on the intranet. Users can also use the intranet system to track
the progress of their request. Calls are managed through the ACD system.

■ In 2005, IS completed 5,567 requests, or about 470 requests per month,
as shown by Figure 5.36. The departments utilizing IS the most in 2005
included sales op, customer service, and design services, as shown by
Figure 5.37. With approximately 300 PCs deployed throughout the company, we experience an average of 19 calls per PC per year (compared to
an industry average of 8 to 12 calls per PC per year).

■ The help desk uses DameWare *for remote control* of PCs for user support
and RemoteWorks by Xcellenet for software distribution. The cost for
DameWare is $xxx/year and for RemoteWorks is $xK/quarter for vendor
maintenance and support.

■ Some limited *capacity planning* is done based on monitoring file usage
CPU usage of all servers. Detailed charts are kept of capacity trends in the
TSM backup system due to the criticality of the system and the amount of
disk and tape storage that is used (7 terabytes of data).

■ A network monitoring system, Aprisma Spectrum, is used to monitor *network and server availability*. Additionally, an application monitoring system, BMC Patrol, is used to monitor some critical applications. Paging
notification software, Attention!, is used to alert IS personnel of problems
found by the monitoring systems. Network performance and availability is
not reported.

■ Tally Systems Census is used to track *PC inventory*, which is also used for
cross-charges. There is also a custom Lotus Notes database to track individual configuration information such as machine, software, and individual

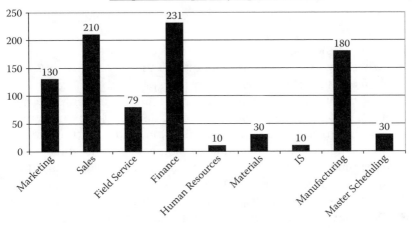

Figure 5.37 Completed IS requests by department, 2005

configuration. Software license compliance is tracked and managed manually. The company pays $xxx/year in maintenance and support for Tally Systems.

■ Detailed and up-to-date *network documentation* and diagrams are kept.

■ *Spare parts* and spare servers of critical network components are kept for backup.

■ *Ghost* software is used to install new PCs. It takes about 3 hours to configure a new machine. A new release of Ghost (Ghost Console) will reduce this time in the future to less than one hour and is planned for implementation. No software is currently available to automatically push updates to the desktop (i.e., SMS), but custom scripts are written.

■ The majority of *changes* are tested in a test system before implementing in production.

■ IS has an IS Support Center Online system on the intranet. This system provides:

    — *Services:* Ability to submit a trouble ticket, check the status of a trouble ticket, look up quick tips, search frequently asked questions, download software, submit questions, obtain PC information, and clean up.

    — *Information and news:* Information on system outages, latest news, help desk hours and availability.

    — *Custom applications:* Fixed-asset database, employee setup request, administrative tools, IS frequently asked questions.

    — *Administrative tools:* Provides the ability to unlock orders, order status, availability, security, ACD call detail, ACD call group, ACD call client, download maintenance, download reports, view PC inventory by division.

Budget and Metrics

Next, address the following questions relative to expenditures:

- What is the total IS budget for this year?
- What have been the IS expenditures the past five years?
- What is the breakdown of the IS expenses by category, such as labor, consulting, travel and entertainment, training, recruitment fees, shipping and postage, supplies, dues and subscriptions, hardware, software, telephone, depreciation, and amortization? Be sure to include the total amount of money the entire organization is spending on either leasing or owning (depreciation, amortization) of PCs, not just those charged to IS.
- What have been the capital expenses for the past five years?
- What are the major areas of capital expenses this year?
- What are the IS expenditures by country or department or application area?
- What are the IS expenditures as a percentage of sales for the past five years?
- What are the IS expenditures per employee for the past five years?

The best way to communicate the IS expenditures is visually with several bar and pie charts showing the composition and growth of the spending in both the detail document and the summary presentation.

Review and Confirm IS Situation

Meet with IS management to present a summary of the current IS environment and obtain confirmation of the information. This is an excellent time to correct any misunderstanding of the current situation before analyzing the environment, determining strengths or weaknesses, or making recommendations. Update the current information with any changes and proceed with the analysis phase.

Analyzing the Current IS Situation

Now you have documented the current IS situation, and in the previous phase, you documented the business situation and direction. Next, analyze the current IS situation against the industry situation and business direction to identify the gaps.

Conduct Industry Benchmarking

Industry benchmarking can be extremely useful when analyzing the current situation. You can purchase industry benchmark data from a number of companies (e.g., Computer Economics, Gartner Group, Giga, and Meta). For example, it is helpful to benchmark against a Computer Economics metrics for each industry and size company, including:

- IS budget as a percent of revenue
- IS spending per employee
- Overall IS budget
- IS budget comparison with last year
- IS departmental budget as a percent of the total IS spending
- IS spending by category
- Training costs
- Baseline costs
- IS capital spending by category
- IS staffing
- Workers supported per IS employee
- IS staffing mix
- Staffing changes from last year
- Contractor and temporary personnel percent
- IS reporting structure
- Technology implementation status
- Hardware trends
- Processes

Identify IS Industry Trends and Competitor Profiles

Technology and IS industry are continuously changing, which also affects the strategic direction. How do you provide management with an understandable overview of where technology has been in the past and where it is going in the future? Management needs to have an understanding of some of the basic trends and terminology because these factors may be involved in the new direction.

It is helpful to provide management with an index or appendix of technologies and the associated definitions. Categorize technology into tiers such:

Obsolete or trailing edge: This includes older "tried and true" technology, also known as legacy technology. However, unit cost may be too high to implement due to the age and support costs of the outdated technology. Projects may be planned to sunset (or replace) this obsolete technology with more up-to-date technology that is easier to support.

Ready to implement: This includes existing technologies that are available and proven, that have a defined cost saving, and for which the risk of implementation is low. These technologies may be implemented in some areas of the company, but not fully utilized or exploited.

Emerging or strategic technologies: This includes relatively newer technologies that are being implemented commercially but are more leading edge. These technologies have a higher risk of implementation and would not be cost effective at this stage.

Need further review: This includes technologies that are more experimental than commercial. These technologies are typically cost effective, and have a high risk of implementation. These technologies can be reviewed for possible future deployment.

Summarize the impact the industry trends have on the IS direction. Two examples are shown in Exhibit 5.11 and Exhibit 5.12.

▼

Exhibit 5.11   Technology Trend Impact — Example 1

Technology Trends	Potential Use
Data warehouse, business intelligence, knowledge management, data mining, business performance management	A data warehouse is a central repository for various data collected across the enterprise. The data is collected from various transactional systems and organized for improved analysis and access of information. We could use data warehouse technology to effectively analyze and correlate the information across the company. Data warehouse applications are typically separate from the primary business application (ERP). It is important to get the right information to the right individual so he or she can make better business decisions and retain knowledge gained within the organization. We can use this concept to provide more information rather than data, which will help individuals make better business decisions. The lack of information was cited as a weakness for the company.

Technology Trends	Potential Use
Enterprise application integration (EAI)	EAI consolidates and integrates the information and applications across the enterprise. EAI software lowers the total cost of interfacing applications when there are many different applications or points of integration. EAI provides a virtual system so that disparate systems appear as a unified application. For example, we may be able to use EAI to integrate as system like ERP and CRM.
Web services	Web services is a means of connecting and leveraging disparate data, systems, and software using "universal glue" (called XML interfaces via the Internet). It is used as an internal and external approach to enterprise application integration (EAI). This would be another option to integrate applications.
Web portals	A web portal is a window or gateway to specific services, applications, and information based on the needs of the department or customer. We could use this technology to personalize customer or supplier interactions. A portal gives a unified common interface to the enterprise business applications and decision tools, both externally and internally.
Web deployment technologies (.NET, J2EE, Java, XML)	This is a framework for Web services deployment. This technology can be used in additional development projects.
Executive information system (EIS)	EIS provides a graphical representation of company performance to support improved decision making (e.g., green light for adequate daily production throughput, red light for throughput lower than plan). A true EIS would provide real-time information, or dashboard, the ability to drill down into the detail, and all information without additional programming for each request.
E-procurement	E-procurement is the business-to-business purchase of supplies and services over the Internet. It reduces purchasing overhead, reduces the purchasing cycle, and facilitates more competitive pricing as suppliers submit competitive bids to win your business.

Technology Trends	Potential Use
E-business	This is using Web technology to totally reengineer business processes for efficiency.
Document management	Managing business documents and documentation, including the retention, storage, and retrieval. This technology can be very helpful for R&D notebooks and documents.
Customer relationship management (CRM)	This is an application that provides complete centralized information about customers.
Applications service providers (ASP)	ASPs provide complete applications and application outsourcing environment to companies. Effectively, this is a business application rental option.
Mobile commerce, wireless applications	With millions of Internet appliances ranging from phones to handhelds and pagers in the hands of consumers, the opportunity for e-business applications is great.

▲

▼

Exhibit 5.12 Technology Trend Impact — Example 2

The following are trends in the network industry that could impact our future:

■ *Network Protection:* Virus and worms are becoming more of a threat to companies operations than ever before. At one time it was taking several months for an exploit to be written once a vulnerability was identified. Today we are seeing exploits within weeks. Companies should be taking and planning for several actions:
  – *Anti-virus software:* Companies need to have anti-virus software installed on all PCs and servers with processes in place to enforce currency.
  – *Anti-virus e-mail checking:* Every e-mail received and sent needs to be scanned for viruses.
  – *802.1x:* The implementation of 802.1x will allow networks to interrogate any PC plugged into the network to ensure this is a corporate PC that is current on anti-virus software.
  – *Security client software:* Companies have been introducing client software to recognize improper behaviors and shut them down before damage can be done. These agents are not dependent on a list of known viruses, but monitor what programs are attempting to do and stops any behavior that is not acceptable. Cisco's Cisco Security Agent (CSA) is

an example of this. This type of software is relatively new in the industry and is maturing.

■ *Voice-over-IP:* Voice-over-IP (VoIP) will eventually replace traditional phone services. Companies investigating and converting to VoIP are typically companies that have outdated PBX systems that need replacing. VoIP offers many advantages, such as a local dial plan throughout all sites and phone portability. VoIP may or may not save long-distance charges. In-depth analysis needs to be conducted to determine data WAN costs versus long distance charges. According to a Meta Group survey of 276 North American companies, 62% of midsize enterprises and 63% of large enterprises (with 1,500 or more employees) have implemented some form of VoIP. It is widely accepted that everyone will convert to IP telephony. The only question is when.

■ *Wireless networks (802.11a, 802.11b, 802.11g standards):* Wireless networking has taken off in the industry to the point where access points and wireless cards are available in commercial stores. Depending on the culture of a company, the network staff probably needs to build a wireless network before someone else does. The key points to consider when deploying a wireless network are:

– What security to deploy. WEP, LEAP, and EAP are some of the options. Security is a must on wireless networks, and it is a wise move to implement the latest most secure option available.

– This is a public band available for anyone's use. Quite often, devices such as a cordless phone can interfere or interrupt 802.11 networks.

– This is shared bandwidth over the airwaves, where wired LANs provide dedicated bandwidth to the PC.

■ Increased reliance on the Internet.

■ Voice, data, video integration, streaming video.

■ 10-gigabit Ethernet: Increased network speed.

■ Load balancing: Using content switches to load-balance server pools.

■ IP version 6: The U.S. Department of Defense is expanding the current network address scheme.

■ Grid computing: Grid computing is applying the resources of many computers in a network to a single problem at the same time.

■ Nationwide high-speed cellular data networks.

■ Privacy issues.

■ Telecommuting support.

Server Trends

The following are trends with servers that may have an impact:

■ Decreased cost of a business transaction.

■ Increased interoperability and communication among diverse platforms.

■ Increased use of Java, HTML, XML, and other Web development and thin client technologies, XSL (Extensible Stylesheet Language for presenting XML documents).

- SAN storage devices; grouping storage together to share across servers. Reduces costs.
- Clustering.
- Fiber Channel storage.
- Hyperthreading CPUs' processor performance.
- Linux operating system for servers and desktops.
- Grid computing: Grid computing is applying the resources of many computers in a network to a single problem at the same time.
- Blade servers: Cluster-based systems that can be configured to include load-balancing and failover; hot-pluggable. Saves space and cuts costs.
- Server consolidation.
- Self-healing servers.
- 64-bit processing.
- Microsoft Windows Server R2 (2005 release): Will include support for Microsoft Visual Studio .NET development tools, features helping to deploy servers in branch offices, allow users to access intranet-based services without going through a virtual private network (VPN).
- Microsoft Windows Server Longhorn (2007 release).
- IBM FAST100: Entry-level disk array to compete with EMC, IBM's first write-once, read-many (WORM) tape cartridge.
- Storage virtualization technology: Capabilities for managing data on competing disk arrays. Provides high levels of scalability.

Desktop and Peripheral Trends

The following are trends with desktops and peripherals that may have an impact:

- Microsoft domination on the desktop.
- Embedded, smaller, and more powerful processors and chips.
- Replacement of desktop with laptop.
- Wireless, cellular, and mobile technology.
- Easy-to-use interfaces.
- Improved graphics, video, and sound.
- Increased video card power.
- Touch screens.
- Voice recognition.
- Multimodal access, handheld and PDA devices, palms, Blackberries.
- Computer telephone integration.
- Bar coding, RFID/EPC.
- Smart cards.
- Encryption, biometrics, and other security measures.
- IBM's Workplace Client Technology: A middle-ware approach to delivering server-based applications to a slimmed-down client that can run the Linux, Windows, and Mac operating systems. Supports a wide range of handheld and embedded operating systems as users move from device to device.

Competitor Profiles

For business management, this can be one of the most interesting sections of the plan. It is critical to find out what your competitors are doing with IS. It is amazing how knowing what the competitors are doing can establish an immediate sense of urgency to improve your IS environment!

So, how do you obtain information about your competitors? It actually sounds more difficult than it is. From the business review section of the planning process, you have a list of the competitors. Following are different methods of obtaining information:

- Ask them! You can find your competitors at IS organizations, training classes, and conventions. Even if you are honest and explain what company you are with, it will surprise you how many IS professionals are willing to tell you about their environment.
- Talk to employees within the company who used to work for a competitor. This can provide a wealth of information. Typically, in the marketing and sales or research and development sections of the organization, it is common to have individuals who have come from competing companies. Interview them and find out as much as possible.
- Review magazines, books, and journals. A literary search often reveals many different pieces about the IS environment of a company.
- Talk to vendors. Ask vendors to provide a list of clients utilizing their products.
- Look on the Internet. Review competitors' home pages and any other related information.
- Talk to customers of the competitor. Why did they choose the competition? Did the competition offer particular functionality that was attractive? Survey information may be available through the marketing and sales department from lost customers showing why the companies chose your competitor.
- Hire a consultant, provide a list of the companies, and pay to have a competitive analysis completed.

Following is some information that is helpful to find out about the competition:

- How many employees does the company have in IS? How many employees total are there in the company?

- What business application software is utilized? When did the company implement it? Is there a project in progress to replace it?
- Do their various divisions or locations operate on a central or common IS?
- What is the status of their PC environment and network?
- Can you obtain any information regarding IS expenditures?
- What functions does the company offer its customers (e.g., EDI, credit card, direct order entry, inventory tracking)?
- What particular technologies does the company utilize?

In addition to writing any information in the competitive profile section, it is useful to summarize the information in the strategic plan. Is the IS environment ahead or behind of competition? List the reasons why you are ahead or behind. What specific capabilities do you or do you not have in comparison to your competitors? Some things to look for include:

- Packaged software versus custom
- Strong or weak PC environment
- Strong or weak network, worldwide or local
- Outsourcing or staff within (for example, programming, PC help desk, PC acquisition)
- Integrated supply chain
- Utilization of technology (for example, bar coding, imaging, etc.)
- Use of the Internet
- Automated sales force
- Ability to take custom orders
- Speed of order delivery

Review Information Needs and Data Context Model

Review the list of business measures, key performance indicators, or key information needs identified in Chapter 4. For each business measure, identify the availability of the measure using the current systems. For example, create a spreadsheet with the business measure and the following columns:

- Whether it is available from the core business application systems
- Whether it is incomplete in the application systems
- Whether it is difficult to obtain, meaning that manual manipulation is required outside the system
- Whether it is not available

Total the information and summarize what percent is available and what percent is unavailable today. Do not be surprised if many of the key measures are derived by individuals manually keying information into a spreadsheet for analysis and manipulation rather than taken directly from the business application systems.

Review Business Processes and Use of Applications

Review the business processes identified in the previous phase and develop a list of key process improvement areas. For each process improvement area, identify whether it can be completed with the current application software or whether additional software is required. Also, identify business processes that do not have any automation today that could be improved using systems. Also, review the world-class benchmark business process statistics to identify key areas that can be improved. Review the business readiness for change.

Identify High-Level Functional Requirements and Gaps

Business Requirements Analysis

Review the list of business requirements developed in the previous phase. Identify whether the requirements are completed with manual processes rather than handled through the current business application systems. An example of the first few requirements is shown in Table 5.3.

Review the business interview notes, and identify any business requirements not sufficiently met with the current IS. The business requirements analysis can provide a very thorough and detailed picture of the gap of the current systems compared to what is required. Exhibit 5.13 shows an example of how to present this gap.

▼

Exhibit 5.13   Business Requirements Gap

The current systems lack the *breadth and depth* of functionality that is required. The appendix has a list of 250 detailed business application requirements specific for the manufacturing area, all of which are typically included in ERP software packages. Each requirement is rated by our personnel as to whether they need the requirement, whether they have it today and it is cumbersome or works well, whether it is desired, or whether it is a future need. The following is a summary of the requirements:

Table 5.3 Business Requirements Evaluation

No.	Question	Details	Division A					Division B				
			Manual Today	No, not needed	Maybe, don't know	Yes, needed	In the future	Manual Today	No, not needed	Maybe, don't know	Yes, needed	In the future
1	Do you do assemble-to-order manufacturing?					X					X	
2	Do you do batch processing?	Does the manufacture of your product involve mixing or blending chemicals, chemical compounds, basic raw materials, or food products?				X			X			
3	Do you do configure-to-order manufacturing?	Do you sell configured products assembled from features and options through a final assembly process?		X							X	
4	Do you do continuous flow manufacturing?	Wait and/or queue time between production operations is minimal or nonexistent. Most common in process industries where material is transported between operations via piping or other conveyance devices. Continuous flow versus work order process.				X			X			

#	Question	Description								
5	Do you do discrete manufacturing?	A discrete work order must be opened for the manufacture of a specific quantity, and then closed on completion.			X					X
6	Do you do engineer-to-order manufacturing?	Are your products/finished goods custom-engineered for specific customers? Do customers have unique product designs?	M		X	X				
7	Are you a job shop?	A job shop environment uses work orders to control production organized by functional work centers, such as drilling, press, etc.			X	X				
8	Do you do make-to-order manufacturing?	Do you produce finished goods once the order has been received, as opposed to picking standard products off the shelf?			X				X	
9	Do you do make-to-stock manufacturing?	Do you produce finished goods to a forecast and/or master schedule to be stocked until relieved by orders?	M		X					X
10	Do you do process manufacturing?	Process manufacturing adds value by mixing, separating, forming chemical reactions, dealing with formulas, batch sizes, and potency.			X	X				

Table 5.3 (continued) Business Requirements Evaluation

No.	Question	Details	Manual Today	Division A				Division B			
				No, not needed	Maybe, don't know	Yes, needed	In the future	No, not needed	Maybe, don't know	Yes, needed	In the future
11	Do you do repetitive manufacturing?	Repetitive manufacturers manufacture in high-volume, high-speed production by scheduling lines using work cells and JIT method.					X			X	
12	Does your business or organization consist of more than one company or division?	You require the software to maintain multiple companies; need to maintain separate balance sheets and be able to consolidate them.				X		X			

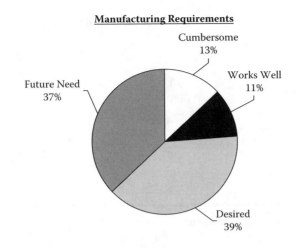

Figure 5.38   Manufacturing requirements

	Have Today				
Functionality	*Don't Need*	*Cumbersome*	*Works Well*	*Desired*	*Future Need*
Totals	71	24	20	68	67

As can be seen in Figure 5.38, only 20, or 11%, of the requirements are met with today's system. Some 13% of the requirements are met with cumbersome processes today; 39% are desired in the current system; and 37% are needed in the future. Although the company prides itself on its state-of-the-art manufacturing, much is accomplished due to manual work and personal heroics rather than using technology and repeatable processes.

A review of the total requirements shows that of the 138 requirements identified, 69% are manual or cumbersome today, 10% are needed in the future, and only 21% are automated today (see Figure 5.39).

Business Operating Vision Analysis

Review the business operating vision. Identify which requirements can be met and which cannot be met with the current IS. Analyze whether the current systems can address the business needs relative to global operations.

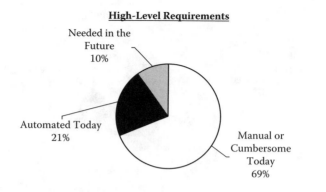

Figure 5.39 High-level requirements

One way to complete this analysis is to work with the IS steering committee and grade your current systems against how well the systems meet the requirements in the business operating vision with the following grades (or any other rating that the group agrees upon):

A: Excellent
B: Good
C: Average
D: Below Average
F: Fail, does not meet requirement at all

It may take a short discussion of each requirement to come to an agreement. Typically, this discussion can be very beneficial to identify strong and weak areas. Exhibit 5.14 shows an example of one company's grades on its business operating vision.

▼

Exhibit 5.14 Business Operating Vision Gap

Manufacturing

- Process manufacturing   D
- Discrete manufacturing   D
- Make-to-stock manufacturing   D
- Make-to-order manufacturing   F

Operate the business on a worldwide basis

- Partial design or manufacturing anywhere   F
- Consistent manufacturing processes/products   F

- Take an order anywhere, fill anywhere   F
- Coordinate worldwide project teams   F
- Worldwide procurement and sourcing   F
- Common customer support and service   F
- Multicurrency, multilingual   F

Utilize technology to operate efficiently and effectively

- Worldwide e-mail   D
- Paperless environment   D
- Minimize manual efforts   F
- Easy-to-use, flexible   F
- Electronic commerce   F
- Easy interfacing of systems   D

Easy to do business with from a customer standpoint

- Electronic commerce   F
- Capability to bundle sales   F
- Handle complex and multiple-site customers   D
- Utilize Internet for customer information   F
- Utilize external electronic services   F
- Interface to customer system   F

Have worldwide information needed to manage the business

- Provide timely visibility to key metrics   D
- Track and report contract compliance   C
- Timely roll-up of subsidiaries' financial numbers   D
- Timely financial close process   D
- Track the success of marketing techniques   F
- Sales force information   F
- Worldwide forecasting, budgeting, planning   D
- Worldwide inventory information   F
- Worldwide customer complaint/call information   F

▲

By reviewing the grades, the group may be able to come to some initial observations. Perhaps all the systems are inadequate, or perhaps several areas are in excellent shape while only a few areas are poor.

Environmental Business Requirements Analysis

Review the environmental business requirements. With the help of the IS steering committee, grade the current systems against how well the systems meet the environmental requirements. Additional observations can indicate weak areas, or perhaps the business has grown into new areas and the systems have not kept pace with the business changes.

External Business Requirements Analysis

Review the list of external business requirements, including customer and other stakeholder requirements. Identify requirements that are not sufficiently handled with the current systems.

Business Strengths, Weaknesses, Opportunities, and Threats Analysis

Review the business strengths identified in the previous phase. Is there any technology that can be utilized to capitalize on the strengths and provide a competitive advantage? For example, if a company strength is customer relationships, can customer relationship management (CRM) software be used to anticipate customer needs and send a personalized e-mail? If a strength is the flexibility of the company, are systems structured to handle flexibility? Also, it is important to review weaknesses. Can technology be utilized to strengthen any of the weaknesses? For example, if a weakness is prices, can improved cost analysis allow the company to reduce costs and prices? Review opportunities and threats for similar technology opportunities.

Develop IS Strengths, Weaknesses, Opportunities, Threats (SWOT), Risks, Technology Opportunities, Business Enablers

By comparing the current situation to the industry and business requirements, identify strengths and weaknesses of the IS environment in the following areas:

- Business application
- Technical infrastructure
- People, organization, culture
- Processes

Exhibit 5.15 shows an example of a detailed business application analysis.

▼

Exhibit 5.15   Business Application Detailed Assessment

Order Management and Marketing
Strengths:

- Order entry is accurate.
- Sales system provides a lot of good sales information (although difficult to use).

Weaknesses:

- System has no online verification of inventory, availability, restriction codes, storage temperatures, and order versus forecast.
- Inability to accept an order anywhere in the world, have visibility to it worldwide, and manufacture or fill the order anywhere in the world depending on capacity, availability, and inventory.
- Inability to handle order entry for shipments from all current distribution centers.
- Inability to handle international orders.
- Inability to support multicurrency and multilanguages.
- System does not currently support electronic commerce with customers, including invoicing, money transfer or payments, ordering. Systems are not able to do EDI, direct entry, or direct interface from a customer purchasing system.
- Inability to bundle sales and share information with other entities to support joint sales, common customer and membership information, and joint contracts. Inability to produce a combined sales report for customers with corporate information.
- Cumbersome program for handling credits and debits.
- Usage control program is inadequate for the international business needs of today.
- Inability to support a combined warehouse with other divisions.
- Cannot easily handle make-to-order.
- Inability to easily handle international shipping and receiving.
- Inability to handle complex and multiple-site customers and track membership of group purchasing organizations and hospital chains. Inability to interface with customer third-party intermediaries or distributors.
- No Internet home page currently for customers to have access of training availability, communications, product information, etc.
- No usage of external services and sources of customer information.
- Contract compliance information not meeting all the needs.
- Inability to track the success of various marketing techniques.
- Sales force has very limited information available, and it is not timely. Marketing has limited visibility to the consolidated sales information; it

takes much manual effort to obtain it, it is not timely, and it is of questionable accuracy. This includes won/loss information, placement information, customer information, and general visibility to what is happening in the field.

▪ Inability to interface information from the customer system for automatic reordering or test result information.
▪ No visibility to worldwide customer complaint and call information.

Manufacturing
Strengths:

▪ Provides the basic inventory management and MRP tools
▪ Systems built around capabilities of IS
▪ Personnel who are trained and experienced
▪ Above-average lot control and tracking system
▪ Above-average expiration and ship date logic

Weaknesses:

▪ Does not handle worldwide sourcing and procurement
▪ Limited cost information
▪ Not user friendly
▪ Limited visibility to hours required to build a system
▪ No tie of shop floor hours to payroll
▪ Poor CRP capabilities
▪ Poor inventory, supplier, and distribution management tools
▪ Inaccurate allocation screens
▪ No "what-if" capabilities
▪ Limited visibility to change
▪ No visibility of run rate versus standard
▪ Must do quality check on all reports before using for inaccurate and incomplete information
▪ Many manual workarounds to bridge the needs with system capabilities
▪ Overall limited reporting capabilities on manufacturing activities
▪ Below-average distribution capabilities (e.g., backorders manually have to be tracked)
▪ No system expert (however, we do have module experts)
▪ Does not support consistent manufacturing processes and products; no common bill-of-material or part numbering
▪ Limited cost information

Finance
Strengths:

▪ Data is accurate in cost to six decimal places to the right.
▪ Ability to transfer information from sales system and general ledger to Excel.

Weaknesses:

- Financial close process very cumbersome, time-consuming, and not timely. It takes three weeks to close the books for a month and disseminate financial information. By the time management has the information, it is too late to be useful or make timely business decisions.
- Different worldwide calendar makes financial comparisons difficult.
- Roll-up of subsidiaries' financial information not timely.
- Limited capabilities for forecasting and budgeting.
- Financial reports are time-consuming and cumbersome to generate.
- Limited worldwide information available.
- No visibility to worldwide inventory.
- Chart of accounts maintenance is complicated and labor intensive.
- It is very difficult to budget spending at a project level. You cannot easily accumulate expenses for projects that continue over a year-end.
- Inability to track customer profitability.
- Foreign currency is not handled properly.
- Limited reporting capabilities in accounts receivable. Reports not available other than month-end.
- No online visibility to spending or budget. Find out after it is too late.
- Unable to point sales from one division to different general ledger account numbers.
- Requires many manual journal entries in general ledger.
- Unable to keep financial data on the system for more than three years.

After submitting the detailed strengths and weaknesses, in a meeting with the IS steering committee, brainstorm and list the strengths and weaknesses for the business applications as a whole. The interaction during this process can help everyone understand the situation in other areas of the business. Exhibit 5.16 shows an example of the overall strengths and weaknesses assembled by one company for the detailed plan document; Table 5.4 shows another company's application strengths and weaknesses in the summary presentation format.

Exhibit 5.16   Business Application Summary Assessment

Strengths

- It works! The system is getting the job done and allowing the business to function today.
- It is reliable and is generally available during the stated daytime hours.

■ Overall, the systems are tailored to our business rather than fitting the business to the system. This allows us to continually make process improvements in the business and change the system to meet those requirements. Therefore, we have flexibility in how we do our business, rather than being constrained by the system (provided we have the resources to accommodate the changes in a timely fashion).

Weaknesses

■ Although our systems collect a lot of data, all areas lack in ease of ability to analyze the data and turn it into valuable information. Simple analysis questions or "what if" questions require significant manual manipulation and independent searching. As a result, there is considerable demand on the programming group and a large backlog of projects.

■ Due to the high number of custom systems, the systems require a high level of maintenance and support to keep them functioning.

■ Many of the key measures to manage the business are not available from the systems, or are derived through extensive work on PCs and manual processes.

■ The systems are not user friendly. A lot of training is required to become proficient with the systems and therefore a limited number of individuals have access to information.

■ Reporting is cumbersome. Users need to submit programming requests to see a different view of the data.

■ The systems do not currently support a paperless environment. All processes utilize considerable manual effort.

■ The systems require much manual maintenance, duplicate entry, and external manipulation of data. Many workarounds and external "islands of information" have developed over the years to accommodate deficiencies in the systems.

■ Quality of data is questionable.

■ Information is stored in several different places, and labor is required to keep information updated in several places. Information is inconsistent.

■ The systems are slow, and have capacity and space issues.

■ Nightly processing requires too large a time window, reducing system availability.

■ Capabilities are currently limited for worldwide communication, interaction, and sharing of files.

■ Current systems (other than the new software) do not meet the desired computing architecture requirements that are outlined in subsequent sections. The systems are not open, which means the systems are difficult to integrate for worldwide information and ease of obtaining information. The systems are not client/server or graphic user interface (GUI) based, which means utilizing the power of the PC so that the systems are easy to use. The systems are not a packaged supplier solution because they have been significantly modified and are not maintained by the supplier. The systems are not real-time, which means that the systems are not available 24 hours.

Table 5.4 Application Strengths and Weaknesses

Business Applications	
Strengths	*Weaknesses*
■ They work ■ Customized ■ Handles volume, throughput ■ Relatively stable ■ Interface broker ■ Warehouse functionality ■ Web-based functionality ■ Electronic EDI ■ Scalable costs	■ Not designed for current business ■ Manufacturing functionality weak ■ Information access ■ Data integrity ■ Size/volume limitations ■ Visibility to costs, profit ■ Architecture out of date ■ Risk ■ Not flexible, requires programming ■ Customized, not best practice ■ Warehouse, shipping systems ■ Interfacing data ■ Ease of use, "green screen" ■ Standard ERP functionality lacking ■ CRM lacking ■ International ■ Fragile ■ Not real-time ■ Tools ■ Costs relative to functionality

One large multidivisional company summarized the gap in the business application systems by placing them on a grid identifying efficiency, effectiveness, and number of systems as shown in Figure 5.40.

Next, review the technical infrastructure. Grade the current systems against technical requirements as shown by Exhibit 5.17.

---------------------------------▼---------------------------------

Exhibit 5.17 Technical Infrastructure Assessment

	Current Systems Grade
Configurability	
Table-driven logic	C
Configurable logic	C
Workflow	F
User-defined fields	C
User-defined tables	C
Forms tools	D
Metadata	F

Flexibility

Relational database structure	F
Extensible database	F
Interoperability and reusability	F
Program calls	F
Service-oriented architecture	F

Information

Real time	C
Business intelligence	F
Graphical user interface	A
Query by example	C
Electronic reporting	C
Drill-down	C
Ad hoc reporting	D
Screen and reporting functionality	C
Built-in data warehouse	F
Extract transform and load	F
Microsoft Excel add-ins	F

Integration

Web services	F
Integration management	F
Enterprise applications interface	F
Application programming interfaces	F
Support Simple Object Access Protocol	F
EDI	B

Security

Transaction history	B
Single Sign-On	F
Secure Socket Layer	F
Role-based security	C
Record-based data access	F
Built-in disaster recovery tools	C

Scalability

Web enabled	F
Efficient application design	C
Multi-tier distributed computing	F
Real application clusters	F
Monitoring	C
Open systems	F
Enabling Technology	
Effective-date controlled data	C
Integrated device electronics	F
E-mail integration	F

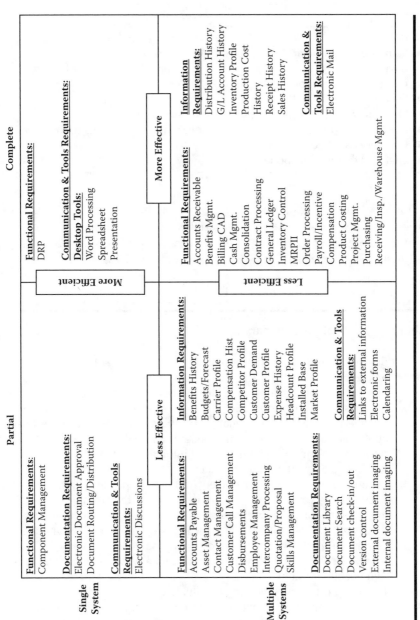

Figure 5.40 Application summary

Table 5.5 Technical Infrastructure Analysis

Technical Infrastructure	
Strengths	*Weaknesses*
■ Reliable ■ Standard PC hardware/software environment ■ Up-to-date technology ■ Security, firewalls, UPS, anti-virus ■ Standard network components ■ Management tools ■ Internet cost-effective WAN ■ Gigabit Ethernet backbone	■ Large, complex server infrastructure ■ Microsoft Office 97 ■ Potential limitations of Internet for WAN ■ Gauntlet firewall ■ Server failover ■ Some single points of failure ■ SAN

Identify the strengths and weaknesses of the technical infrastructure. Table 5.5 shows a summary of the analysis at one company.

It can be helpful to summarize the overall gap of business applications and technical infrastructure, as shown in Exhibit 5.18.

▼

Exhibit 5.18 Analysis Summary

- Business Applications: The business applications have the largest gap from where we need to be. The majority of the items listed in the business operating vision are a result of lacking deficiencies in our business application systems. The strengths and weaknesses that were identified also provide more specific information on the gaps. The area of the business application is the area of most concern, and will take the most time and resources to improve. Rather than building on what we have, this area requires total overhaul and replacement.
- PC and LAN: This area of our environment is positioned for the future. There are, however, improvements necessary in the areas of support, communication, consistency, and tools to better utilize this environment. Standards and controls, although not perfect, are moving in the right direction. During the past few years, the company has invested fairly well in this area. Although our PC environment continually needs upgrading, it is not significantly lacking.

  To meet our future computing architecture and the business requirements of easy access to information in a meaningful format, the PC is a very critical piece of our environment. We must aggressively continue investments and upgrades in this area.
- Product-Related Computing: There are improvements we can do in this area, but in general, the systems here seem to be meeting the requirements.

The systems are old, patched, have been added onto over the years, are written in a variety of languages, and have redundant and inefficient data structures. Redesigning and changing the technical architecture of these systems would help significantly but is not as urgent as the improved business application systems. These systems are very company specific, and we would probably not find packages that would address these requirements. Once we obtain a new technical environment for the business application systems, we must evaluate these systems to be rewritten for the new environment and possibly eliminate a separate environment.

■ Network: The basic infrastructure of the local network is such that we can build on it for the future. There are weak areas and links that we must strengthen, and we must increase the capacity to be able to handle our new computing architecture. The network will become our most critical piece of our environment in the future. We must place focus on strengthening our external network to other locations, customers, suppliers, and other external entities. Our networking capabilities will become our advantage or disadvantage in the marketplace in the future.

In summary, our business application systems are the area of largest concern and need of improvement at this time. We need to continue to build on and strengthen the PC and network areas. We can migrate the product-related computing to the new architecture over time.

▲

Review the strengths and weaknesses with the organization, people, and culture, as shown in Table 5.6. Identify the strengths and weaknesses relative to processes, as shown in Table 5.7.

Develop IS Assessment Scorecards; Rate with Team

In addition to qualitative information in the strengths and weaknesses section, it is helpful to have quantitative data that can be compared from year to year. The surveys provide some quantitative data, but scorecards can also be helpful. Develop scorecards with industry best practices and rate your performance with the IS management team. Rating the scorecard as a group is a valuable exercise, establishes a common base, and communicates issues across functions. Include sections and ratings for:

■ Strategy
■ People/organization
■ Processes
■ Business applications
■ Technical infrastructure

Table 5.6   Organizational Assessment

IT Organization, Culture	
Strengths	*Weaknesses*

■ Knowledgeable people
■ Have made improvements
■ Fun environment
■ Strong IS values
■ Institutional knowledge
■ Good backup skills
■ Upper management commitment
■ Customer service focus
■ Resources allocated per division
■ Flexibility
	■ Leadership
	■ Decision making
	■ Trust, respect
	■ Too many meetings
	■ Organization structure
	  – Managers, span of control
	  – No project management
	  – Manufacturing application
	    knowledge
	  – Clarity in roles
	  – Business analyst role
	  – Worldwide coordination
	  – Skill set capacity
	■ Accountability
	■ Teamwork

Table 5.7   IS Process Analysis

IS Processes	
Strengths	*Weaknesses*

■ Some documented policies,
  procedures
■ Job descriptions
■ System change log, SCR process
■ Project management framework
■ Partial disaster recovery process
	■ Informal processes, inconsistent,
	  undocumented
	■ Project management not implemented
	■ Complete test system, process
	■ Documentation
	■ User training
	■ Prioritizing
	■ Governance, overall steering
	  committee
	■ Business continuance plan
	■ Communication

Ratings on a scale of 1–5 can be used as follows:

1. No systematic approach is evident to the criteria. Results do not exist or are poor.
2. The beginning of a systematic approach is evident but major gaps exist.
3. A systematic approach to the criteria with good performance.

4. A sound and systematic approach to the criteria with good to excellent performance.
5. Criteria are fully implemented without any significant weaknesses or gaps in any area.

Exhibit 5.19 is one example of a scorecard.

▼

Exhibit 5.19   Scorecard

Criteria   Ranking

Strategy

1. IS is a true business partner with business departments. 1 2 3 4 5
2. A formal, consistent process is used for joint development (business and IS) of an IS strategic plan. 1 2 3 4 5
3. A comprehensive IS strategy exists with all opportunities identified and prioritized jointly by the business and IS. 1 2 3 4 5
4. The IS strategy is aligned and integrated with the business strategy. 1 2 3 4 5
5. A clear business vision as well as business objectives and priorities is communicated. 1 2 3 4 5
6. IS delivers strategic business value to the business. 1 2 3 4 5
7. The entire IS organization has a strong customer focus. 1 2 3 4 5
8. IS competitive comparisons have been completed. 1 2 3 4 5
9. There is a clear and consistent IS vision and objectives communicated. 1 2 3 4 5
10. The vision for technology is known and marketed throughout the business. 1 2 3 4 5
11. Goals and plans have clear, measurable objectives. 1 2 3 4 5
12. There is a mind-set throughout the business open to and aggressively pursuing technology opportunities. 1 2 3 4 5
13. Action plans are tracked and monitored against the goals. There is a monthly review of actions to plan. 1 2 3 4 5
14. The technology strategy is seamless and consistent across all parts of the business. 1 2 3 4 5
15. Customers and key business partners are tied into the IS environment and strategy. 1 2 3 4 5
16. Back-office systems have a clear direction on how to support e-business and are moving in that direction. 1 2 3 4 5
17. Business areas drive project efforts, not IS. 1 2 3 4 5
18. There is a process for continually planning and adjusting the IS strategy. 1 2 3 4 5

19. All employees understand the IS strategy.	1 2 3 4 5
20. Priorities are clear and consistent across IS.	1 2 3 4 5
21. There is proper funding to meet IS initiatives.	1 2 3 4 5
22. A balanced IS scorecard is used based on the IS goals and objectives.	1 2 3 4 5
23. Long term directions and expectations are not compromised to meet short-term demands.	1 2 3 4 5
24. IS is viewed by the business as a business enabler rather than an overhead expense.	1 2 3 4 5
25. The business is perceived as an IS leader and functionality is provided to demonstrate leadership.	1 2 3 4 5
26. Regular strategic planning meetings are conducted to achieve alignment.	1 2 3 4 5

People/Organization

1. A business leader sponsors each project.	1 2 3 4 5
2. Users are active participants on projects.	1 2 3 4 5
3. IS resources understand the business.	1 2 3 4 5
4. IS management provides a strong customer focus.	1 2 3 4 5
5. There is a strong commitment to learning.	1 2 3 4 5
6. IS management actively manages performance improvement.	1 2 3 4 5
7. Accountability with proper authority is given to individuals for each objective.	1 2 3 4 5
8. There is strong executive management support for IS in the business.	1 2 3 4 5
9. IS executives participate in senior management meetings and decision-making activities.	1 2 3 4 5
10. Responsibilities are identified and documented.	1 2 3 4 5
11. Individuals are held accountable for performance.	1 2 3 4 5
12. There is appropriate backup of responsibilities and knowledge.	1 2 3 4 5
13. The organization is flat with the appropriate levels of management and span of control.	1 2 3 4 5
14. IS management is easy to reach and has regular contact with employees, users, and suppliers on values and performance improvement issues.	1 2 3 4 5
15. Continuous improvement, innovation, and learning is practiced throughout the IS organization.	1 2 3 4 5
16. There is a strong business sponsor with a passion for e-business.	1 2 3 4 5
17. The appropriate business units are responsible for Web content.	1 2 3 4 5
18. Cross-functional teams exist to improve processes throughout the business.	1 2 3 4 5
19. Proper orientation and training is provided.	1 2 3 4 5

20.	Resources have up-to-date technology skills.	1	2	3	4	5
21.	Resources are trained in a variety of areas rather than specialized in a narrow function.	1	2	3	4	5
22.	Reward systems (compensation and recognition) support the belief and performance related to goals.	1	2	3	4	5
23.	The skill set of the team is adequate to do the job.	1	2	3	4	5
24.	Resources include technical specialists as well as business generalists.	1	2	3	4	5
25.	Employees freely provide input into the decision-making process.	1	2	3	4	5
26.	Employees feel empowered so they can respond quickly.	1	2	3	4	5
27.	Employees take ownership of projects.	1	2	3	4	5
28.	Project management is recognized as a key skill and critical factor for successful projects.	1	2	3	4	5
29.	Resources are devoted to developing project management skills.	1	2	3	4	5
30.	Employees are encouraged to be innovative.	1	2	3	4	5
31.	IS is a team-oriented organization.	1	2	3	4	5
32.	Communication flows throughout the IS organization.	1	2	3	4	5
33.	IS relies on external resources to complement the staff.	1	2	3	4	5
34.	External resources transfer knowledge to the existing employees.	1	2	3	4	5
35.	Career progression is based on a demonstrated growth in capability and skill.	1	2	3	4	5
36.	Employee satisfaction is taken on a regular basis and actions taken as necessary.	1	2	3	4	5
37.	Performance expectations are effectively communicated and reinforced on a regular basis.	1	2	3	4	5
38.	Performance reviews include 360-degree feedback including input from users, peers, and management.	1	2	3	4	5
39.	A formal skills development and training program exists with preestablished skill requirements.	1	2	3	4	5
40.	Resource allocations are flexible as teams are created to support specific business initiatives.	1	2	3	4	5
41.	Employees are developed to utilize their full potential.	1	2	3	4	5
42.	Employees are utilized in areas of their strengths.	1	2	3	4	5
43.	Sufficient resources are assigned to reach the e-business goals.	1	2	3	4	5
44.	IS has a dedicated financial resource.	1	2	3	4	5
45.	The CIO is positioned as a member of the corporate board or executive committee.	1	2	3	4	5
46.	Internal relationship managers/account executives are employed to work with the business.	1	2	3	4	5
47.	Leadership development programs are used.	1	2	3	4	5
48.	A project management office exists.	1	2	3	4	5

Processes

1.	IS processes are defined and documented.	1	2	3	4	5
2.	IS processes are continually improved.	1	2	3	4	5
3.	There is a systems development process that manages application life cycle, including version releases, code freezes, testing plans and cycles, change management, source code control, and documentation.	1	2	3	4	5
4.	Projects are only begun with a formal business case in place.	1	2	3	4	5
5.	Changes are grouped in a release mode and the change management process is managed.	1	2	3	4	5
6.	There is a test plan that is used for testing.	1	2	3	4	5
7.	Stress tests are completed when necessary.	1	2	3	4	5
8.	Changes are documented.	1	2	3	4	5
9.	There is a process and escalation procedure for unhappy customers.	1	2	3	4	5
10.	Business processes have been engineered to support the use of each application.	1	2	3	4	5
11.	A formal process is in place to listen to all customers, to understand requirements, and improve processes.	1	2	3	4	5
12.	Emphasis is placed on problem prevention.	1	2	3	4	5
13.	Service-level agreements are defined and agreed upon with users.	1	2	3	4	5
14.	Service-level agreements are met.	1	2	3	4	5
15.	Metrics are used to measure the efficiency and effectiveness of processes.	1	2	3	4	5
16.	Metrics exist for assessing specific impacts of technology on the business.	1	2	3	4	5
17.	Individuals review metrics and report on a regular basis and take appropriate action.	1	2	3	4	5
18.	It is a regular practice to track, rate, and improve customer service.	1	2	3	4	5
19.	User problems are handled quickly.	1	2	3	4	5
20.	Expectations are properly managed.	1	2	3	4	5
21.	Time frames provided are realistic.	1	2	3	4	5
22.	Projects are implemented on time and on budget with the expected business functionality.	1	2	3	4	5
23.	Projects are properly planned with small project milestones.	1	2	3	4	5
24.	IS proactively provides support.	1	2	3	4	5
25.	Regular communication flows between IS and the business. Communication is regular, deliberate, and organized.	1	2	3	4	5
26.	IS participates in business unit meetings and may be stationed in business units.	1	2	3	4	5

27. A safe and healthy work environment is provided.   1 2 3 4 5
28. Vendor agreements are managed.   1 2 3 4 5
29. Policies and practices reflect commitment to regulatory, legal, and ethical compliance.   1 2 3 4 5
30. Benchmarking is done against world-class organizations. 1 2 3 4 5
31. Portfolio management or other project prioritization methodology is used regularly.   1 2 3 4 5
32. IS awards are won and showcased.   1 2 3 4 5
33. Project management methodologies are used regularly and consistently.   1 2 3 4 5
34. IS audits are performed on a regular basis.   1 2 3 4 5
35. A charge-back model is used.   1 2 3 4 5
36. IS issues regular P&L statements.   1 2 3 4 5
37. Forecast demand for IS services and systems is based on metrics.   1 2 3 4 5
38. Vendors are consolidated.   1 2 3 4 5
39. Risk is formally managed.   1 2 3 4 5
40. Customer surveys are done on a regular basis.   1 2 3 4 5

Business Applications

1. Functionality is designed from the customer viewpoint. 1 2 3 4 5
2. Complete business requirements are understood before a technical solution is developed.   1 2 3 4 5
3. Redundancy is minimized in data and applications.   1 2 3 4 5
4. Business applications are designed for maximum flexibility to ensure responsiveness to users.   1 2 3 4 5
5. Business applications are designed for maximum maintainability to improve customer service.   1 2 3 4 5
6. Business applications are designed for reusability to lower development costs.   1 2 3 4 5
7. Business applications are designed for integration for ease of use and accessibility of data.   1 2 3 4 5
8. Business applications are designed for consistency to reduce training costs.   1 2 3 4 5
9. Business applications are designed for usability to exploit technology power and reduce user training needs.   1 2 3 4 5
10. Each project is audited to ensure the business benefits were achieved.   1 2 3 4 5
11. IS delivers vendor-supported standard packages rather than custom solutions.   1 2 3 4 5
12. Business solutions are designed to meet or exceed the business requirements   1 2 3 4 5
13. IS proactively offers and suggests new technology solutions to assist with the business.   1 2 3 4 5
14. All key information is available online. There is quick and easy access to information.   1 2 3 4 5

15. Business processes are redesigned to take advantage of
    new technology.   1   2   3   4   5
16. The data collected is complete, reliable, timely,
    accurate, and useful.   1   2   3   4   5
17. Transactional data is consolidated to reduce user
    redundancy and input while improving accuracy.   1   2   3   4   5
18. The information architecture is built to support
    business knowledge necessary to make the business
    decisions.   1   2   3   4   5
19. Updated documentation exists for the functionality
    and systems.   1   2   3   4   5
20. Navigation is consistent and easy to follow.   1   2   3   4   5
21. Solutions are scalable to accommodate changing
    business requirements.   1   2   3   4   5
22. There is an attractive and consistent look and feel on
    the Web that fits the environment.   1   2   3   4   5
23. Customers can quickly find answers to their
    most-frequently asked questions.   1   2   3   4   5
24. There is a process defined for updating Web content.   1   2   3   4   5
25. Automated e-mails are utilized to develop a customer
    relationship.   1   2   3   4   5

Technical Infrastructure

1. The infrastructure is simplified and standardized to
   reduce costs and improve support.   1   2   3   4   5
2. The infrastructure is automated to reduce costs and
   enable proactive service and support.   1   2   3   4   5
3. The infrastructure uses redundancy of technology to
   maximize availability.   1   2   3   4   5
4. The infrastructure is integrated.   1   2   3   4   5
5. Single points of failure and redundancy are addressed.   1   2   3   4   5
6. Disaster recovery plans are in place.   1   2   3   4   5
7. Backup processes are in place.   1   2   3   4   5
8. Documentation exists for the technical architecture.   1   2   3   4   5
9. Proper security policies and procedures are in place.   1   2   3   4   5
10. There is a planned, consistent, and up-to-date
    architecture.   1   2   3   4   5
11. Key metrics are captured and reported on a
    regular basis.   1   2   3   4   5
12. Proper security and firewalls are in place.   1   2   3   4   5
13. The infrastructure is scalable.   1   2   3   4   5
14. Software licenses are managed.   1   2   3   4   5
15. Information is restricted to those who need access.   1   2   3   4   5
16. There is sufficient capacity.   1   2   3   4   5
17. Network management tools are utilized.   1   2   3   4   5

18. IS develops proactive solutions based on a clear understanding of the root cause of problems and the associated implications of the solution rather than reactive solutions.   1 2 3 4 5
19. IS implements proven technology to enable business and process change.   1 2 3 4 5
20. IS is innovative to proactively address business requirements.   1 2 3 4 5
21. Proper standards exist, including Web browser, Web development application software, hardware, and software.   1 2 3 4 5
22. Systems and data are centralized or distributed to optimize performance while minimizing systems administration responsibilities.   1 2 3 4 5
23. Legacy systems and infrastructure are replaced as necessary to meet the business requirements and minimize support costs.   1 2 3 4 5
24. Anti-virus measures are in place.   1 2 3 4 5

Summarize the scorecard ratings in the plan document and the plan presentation. Include the detailed scorecard ratings in the appendix of the plan for future reference. An example of a summary is shown in Exhibit 5.20.

Exhibit 5.20   Scorecard Summary

IS Best Practices Scorecard
It is helpful to develop quantitative metrics, or scores, in addition to the qualitative strengths and weaknesses as progress can be quantified and improved on an ongoing basis. Anything that is not measured cannot be fully valued or improved. A quantitative scorecard was developed that identifies industry best practices. The scorecard and ratings are included in the appendix. Sections are included for:

- Strategy
- People/organization
- Processes
- Business applications
- Technical infrastructure

Ratings were developed on a scale of 1-5 as follows:

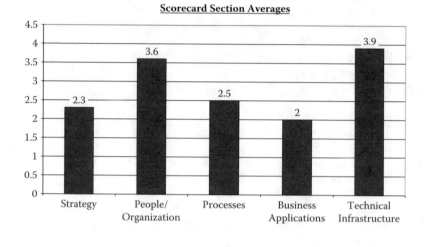

Figure 5.41   Scorecard section averages

1. No systematic approach to the criteria is evident. Results do not exist or are poor.
2. Beginning of a systematic approach is evident but major gaps exist.
3. A systematic approach to the criteria is evident with good performance.
4. A sound and systematic approach to the criteria is evident with good to excellent performance.
5. Criteria are fully implemented without any significant weaknesses or gaps in any area.

The average by section is shown in Figure 5.41.
The following are conclusions relative to the IS scorecard:

▪ The scorecard aligned very closely with the qualitative strengths and weaknesses identified earlier.
▪ The technical infrastructure and the people are strengths.
▪ The areas of improvement are strategy and business applications.
▪ Overall the average was 3.0, which is higher than other companies that have been assessed.

Other scorecards can also be helpful to communicate where the company is relative to the industry. Exhibit 5.21 shows an example of other potential quantification methods that could be used to communicate the current situation.

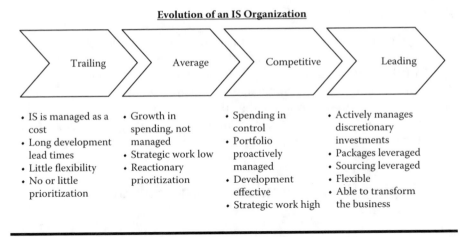

Figure 5.42   Evolution of an IS organization

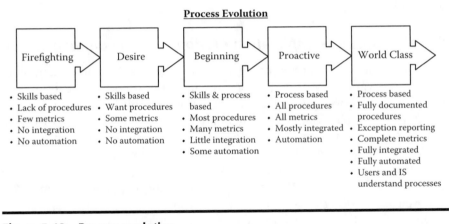

Figure 5.43   Process evolution

Exhibit 5.21   Other Ratings

Figure 5.42 shows the phases often identified for an IS organization.

Based on the descriptions and definitions for this evolution, we are currently between the "trailing" phase and the "average" phase.

World-class IS organizations have solid IS processes in place. Figure 5.43 shows an evolution of companies relative to IS processes.

Based on this model, we are currently between the "Firefighting" and "Desire" modes of operation.

Review and Confirm IS Analysis

This is a critical milestone to obtain confirmation before proceeding to ensure that the state of the current environment — which will be the basis for the recommendations — is understood by everyone. Present the IS situation analysis to the IS management team. Obtain their confirmation on the situation. It is important that the IS organization objectively view the situation and the issues before improvements can be made. Update the information with any input received.

Developing Recommendations and Solution Alternatives

Before developing the complete plan, it is helpful to identify the various recommendations that will be incorporated into the plan in the next phase of the planning process.

Develop Business Application Options and Recommendations

Using weaknesses identified earlier, identify specific recommendations to address the various weaknesses or gaps in the business application area. The options will not be reviewed in detail until the third phase of planning, but it is helpful to outline the general options that will be reviewed. Sometimes, management may eliminate some alternatives and save analysis.

For example, if the business application environment has so many gaps that it needs total replacement, the recommendation may be to evaluate replacing the ERP system. Options may include upgrading to a new release, writing a custom system, selecting a new vendor package, or outsourcing applications. Initial discussions may rule out some options, such as writing a custom system or outsourcing.

Some environments may require specific enhancements that can be listed, such as:

■ Improve the supply chain systems and business processes.
■ Implement radio frequency identification (RFID) for product tracking.
■ Improve visibility to costing information.
■ Improve customer information.

Keep in mind this list of recommendations is only an initial list. Specific costs, business benefits, and priorities will be determined later. The purpose is to give the business an idea of the recommendations and possible solutions for the current situation. An example of a few business application recommendations is provided in Exhibit 5.22.

▼

Exhibit 5.22   Business Application Recommendations

- *Human resources and payroll:* Consider replacing payroll and human resources systems with an integrated vendor-supplied package. As part of the selection effort, do a cost/benefit analysis of outsourcing payroll to a company such as ADP. Leading vendor packages such as PeopleSoft/Oracle should be considered as an integrated solution.
- *E-business:* Develop and document a strategy on how the company can utilize e-business and the valuable Internet technology to assist with the business objectives. Identify the strategy for new technologies such as e-enabling the business processes, implementing e-procurement, Web services, Web portals, etc. IS should be more involved with the communication department in establishing the direction for the Internet and Web hosting. Back-office applications should have a plan to become Internet enabled. Educate the business on the benefits and use of e-business. E-business should be mentioned as an aspect in the business plan because e-business is a method to handle the growing business and ensure the effectiveness and efficiency of the company.
- *Engineering interfaces:* Improve the systems and integration from CAD, product data management, and document control. New product development should be able to occur quickly. Engineering systems and front-end systems should be integrated.

▲

Develop Infrastructure Options and Recommendations

Identify the specific recommendations necessary for the desktop, network, and server environments. Often, this is a list of projects or improvement areas, but it may also include options. An example of a few technical infrastructure recommendations is provided in Exhibit 5.23.

▼

Exhibit 5.23   Technical Infrastructure Recommendations

- *Establish a complete test environment:* A complete testing environment must be implemented and maintained. This environment should be used for testing of all business application and technical infrastructure changes. Changes need to be implemented in a test environment prior to production to help minimize the problems associated with changes.
- *Review and improve network and server infrastructure:* Review and document all single points of failure in the environment and evaluate the cost and benefits of additional redundancy. Increase the use of clusters and SANs. As mentioned in the process section, implement improved systems

management tools to improve the proactive management of the network. Consider replacing Intellops with HPOpenview, Tivoli, or new features of XP. Consider and evaluate the cost of outsourcing the network monitoring and management as an option. As stated in the process section, review the design and use of the two data centers to ensure efficient use, backup, and maximum redundancy. Review and improve network performance in problem areas such as MJR and garages. Ensure proper tools exist for detecting and solving network issues.

■ *Standardize hardware and software environments:* Additional variety in the environment costs money in support and long-term cost of ownership. Strive to reduce the variety. Establish and enforce standards, which would also require management support. Consider staying more current in desktop software and hardware to minimize support costs. Although new hardware may cost more in the short term, the long-term cost of ownership is less. Replace low-end PCs (anything below a Pentium III). Consider leasing desktop equipment as an option. Implement an ongoing obsolescence plan. Standardize desktop operating system. Eliminate the old IBM Mainframe and VAX as is planned. Be sure to sunset and actively move old equipment out. Projects should address historical data or machines will stay around forever. Make sure these machines are removed and a plan is developed in the future for timely removal of old equipment.

■ *Wireless technology:* Define the company's strategy relative to wireless technology. Identify a direction and policy for use of PDAs, Palms, and synchronization. Provide a leadership role in the wireless area.

---▲---

Develop Organizational Options and Recommendations

Identify the specific recommendations for the organization, culture, and skills. An example of organizational recommendations is provided in Exhibit 5.24.

---▼---

Exhibit 5.24   Organizational Recommendations

■ *Recruit and refill key CIO position:* The CIO position is a critical position and should be filled as a CIO rather than director or lower position. CIO responsibilities, and recommended characteristics and skills, are outlined in the appendix. Use a structured process for selection of CIO and involve the business. Today, the IS organization is very tactical focused and does what is requested of them. The group is lacking a strategic visionary person that can provide a close link to the business executives. The assessment process and the surveys indicated that IS had a disconnect at the executive level, and this was a significant area for improvement. The CIO should participate in the strategic discussions and identify ways in which technology could benefit the business. The CIO would lead the development of the IS strategic plan, which is also a significant area of improvement.

■ *Actively manage individual performance improvement:* Managers and supervisors must actively manage and improve individual performance. Ensure expectations are documented, communicated, specific, measurable, and consistent. Deal with performance issues rather than hoping they go away. Work with unions as necessary. Do not allow substandard performance; it impacts the entire group.

■ *Define outsourcing/contractor strategy:* The ratio of consultants to full-time employees should increase over time to provide organizational flexibility as priorities change. Although contractors or outsourcing may cost more money initially, it provides more organizational flexibility in the future. IS needs to have flexibility with resources as a different skill-set may be required for a new direction. Document a strategy to define how and when IS should effectively use consultants and outsourcing. Consider/evaluate outsourcing pieces of IS support.

―――――――――――――――▲―――――――――――――――

Develop IS Process Options and Recommendations

Identify the major process areas that require improvement. An example of business application recommendations is provided in Exhibit 5.25.

―――――――――――――――▼―――――――――――――――

Exhibit 5.25 IS Process Recommendations

■ *Implement a formal systems development methodology and project management process:* The single, most significant improvement that can be made in IS is to implement a formal systems development methodology and project management process. Today, there is little formal structure or project management to projects. As identified in the weaknesses, many projects move from identification to programming to implementation. Many projects have no schedule, no resources identified for each step, and no milestones, purpose, objectives, or measures for success. Project meetings often do not have agendas, minutes, action items, etc. Project delivery can be improved significantly by going through a formal structure of initiation, feasibility, requirements development, design, programming, testing, documenting, training, and implementation. All projects, whether business application or infrastructure, should go through the systems development process. The systems development process should include:

–   An initiation process that provides all users with a consistent method to request IS projects or changes, which is publicized across the business.

–   A complete list of IS backlog should be kept, reviewed, and managed.

- All projects should formally identify the business justification, which includes the total cost of ownership estimate.
- All project costs should be estimated up-front, tracked, managed, and reported. This includes user and IS labor.
- The systems development process should include a formal testing process for all projects to ensure every project gets proper testing.
- All projects should have a post-project review process to identify areas that went well and areas to improve for subsequent projects.

Consider possible project management packages and tools with an off-the-shelf systems development methodology to avoid writing a custom process. Even though projects have user project managers, IS should have a partner project manager assigned for each project that provides the project management expertise and process.

■ *Implement a complete testing process:* Develop and document a formal testing process. Test plans should be developed and include stress tests, parallel tests, performance tests, and integration tests when necessary. Ensure that all projects, including both business application projects and technical infrastructure projects, go through the testing process. Integrate the change management process and the testing processes. Ensure that nothing goes into production without first going through the testing process and test system.

■ *Implement a formal change management process:* A formal change management process and quality control function should be implemented. This process should be scaled so that it can be used for smaller requests as well as major projects. For smaller requests, changes should be grouped and implemented in a release mode to increase the overall stability and reduce the risk to the environment. The change management process for larger projects should be integrated into the systems development methodology.

▲

Review and Confirm Recommendations

Now you are ready to present the current IS situation, situation analysis, and recommendations to executive management. Review the current situation for each area of the environment, such as business application, desktop, server, network, organization, and processes. Summarize the industry information. After each section, summarize the strengths and weaknesses of the environment. Finally, present the recommendations. The presentation should be about one and a half hours.

Conclusion

You have completed phase two, the analysis phase, and have completed the following:

- Reached a complete understanding of the current IS environment through interviews with the IS group. The current environment was documented, including the business application area, technical infrastructure, organization, processes and budget.
- Reviewed and documented the industry trends, benchmark statistics and competitive profiles.
- Assessed the current IS environment, including strengths, weaknesses, opportunities, and threats (SWOT). Scorecards and surveys were utilized to provide quantitative information to be compared from year to year.
- Identified initial recommendations and alternatives.

Congratulations! Everyone is now grounded in the current situation and is ready to discuss the future!

Notes for My IS Strategic Planning Project

References

1. Cassidy, A. and Guggenberger, K. *A Practical Guide to Information Systems Process Improvement*. CRC Press, Boca Raton, FL, 2001, p. 78.

Chapter 6

The Direction Phase

The great thing in this world is not so much where we stand,
as in what direction we are moving.

— Oliver Wendell Holmes Sr. (1809–1894)
American physician, professor

Now it is time to develop the IS direction, identifying where IS must be in the future for your company to meet its business requirements. As a basis, you have a good understanding of both the business direction and the current IS situation gained through the first two phases.

As shown in Figure 6.1, the third phase of the planning process is the direction phase. In this phase, you will determine the high-level direction and plan for IS in the future. This is an important phase — it will set the compass for the future. As shown in Figure 6.2, the direction phase has the following components:

- Developing the IS vision and direction
- Developing the IS plan
- Identifying IS projects

Each of these components is discussed in more detail in this chapter.

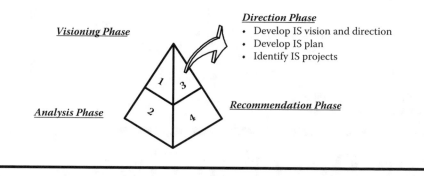

Figure 6.1   The direction phase

Developing the IS Vision and Direction

Often, a company begins IS strategic planning by identifying the technical requirements the IS department desires in a new system. This list may include technical terms and acronyms. These terms mean nothing to business management and it is not clear what requirements in the business direction are driving those technical requirements. Before determining the technical architecture and requirements, take a step back and build the high-level IS direction based on the business direction. The high-level IS direction establishes the framework for the detailed plans.

Developing the IS Vision and Mission

I have seen several groups argue for hours about what is a mission, what is a vision, and how objectives are different from strategies. Entire books are written on the topic of developing a good mission. Rather than these statements being the end-all, it is more important to get involvement in developing these direction statements. After presenting the business direction and current IS environment to the IS group as well as the IS steering committee, these groups can assist in developing the statements for the direction of IS. The steering committee can update and refine a draft started by the IS organization. The groups can decide what is necessary and develop the words that best fit the environment and company. Perhaps one company desires a charter, mission, vision, objectives, and strategies, while another company would like to make it simpler and have only a vision and objectives. The key is to involve the group and develop statements that make sense for the company. Examples are provided here to give you ideas and initiate the thought process, but your statements must address the concerns and needs at your company.

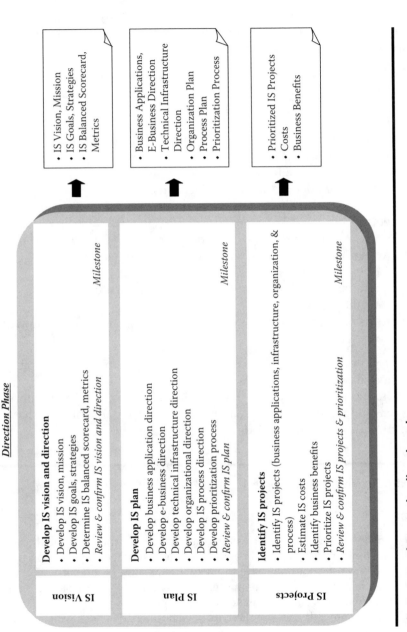

Figure 6.2 Phase 3, the direction phase

Vision

A vision is a concise statement on where you want to go and what you aspire to be. Develop this by looking at the company's vision statement and objectives and identifying how IS can assist the company. Following are tips in developing a vision:

- A vision identifies where the group is going and what it is going to become.
- A vision communicates hopes and dreams, and provides a picture of the desired future.
- A vision is an inspiration to get there; it touches hearts and spirits; it moves people.
- A vision helps all employees see how they can contribute and provides guidelines for daily decisions.
- Focus on what the group wants to create, not what you want to get rid of.
- Focus on the end result, not the process for getting there.
- An impossible vision discourages people; an ambitious vision motivates people.
- There is a thin line between a vision and a hallucination, so make sure the vision is ground in reality.
- A vision should stand the test of time and not require updating every year.

The following (Exhibits 6.1, 6.2, 6.3, 6.4, 6.5, 6.6, and 6.7) are examples developed at several companies.

Vision statements vary and that there is no right or wrong, although some may disagree with that statement. The important thing is that the vision provides a meaningful direction for the group.

▼

Exhibit 6.1   Vision — Example 1

Vision:

- Anyone can get any information (site, geographic area, or global level) at any time, anywhere, and in any way, given the proper security constraints.
- The end user does not have to know the location of the data.
- Maintain data in only one master place within the organization.
- Implement systems to enhance end-user productivity.
- Systems are able to support competitive business demands with immediate response to quickly changing business needs.
- The IS group adds a competitive edge to the company's product line.

▲

Exhibit 6.2   Vision — Example 2

Vision:
We seek to be an integral partner in the achievement of the company's vision and mission through the appropriate application of information technology to business needs.

Exhibit 6.3   Vision — Example 3

We will have business systems that:

- Take advantage of global "sameness"
- Are purchased whenever practical
- Have integrated data that is entered only once
- Provide consistent definitions of information
- Support functional and cross-functional business processes
- Deliver the *right* information, at the *right* place, at the *right* time, in the *right* format
- Are flexible to support changing environments
- Can be accessed by office, home, and mobile workers
- Provide capabilities to external customers and suppliers

Exhibit 6.4   Vision — Example 4

The strategic role of the IS group is to be:

- A provider of information technology (which means assessment and acquisition of new technology), which will assure that company use of IS and applications provide strategic advantage in our business markets
- A provider of information services, the infrastructure and environment that assures companywide information sharing that meets customer requirements
- A strategic business partner of the business units to provide timely and cost-effective IS solutions to business needs
- A proactive agent of change, providing management and staff with decision-making, quality information through automated and integrated IS and processes

Exhibit 6.5   Vision — Example 5

Vision:

- Have delighted customers
- Proactively address business needs
- Provide competitive advantage to the company
- Be recognized in the industry as a world-class IS organization
- Have IS employees with a passion and commitment, people who carry the fire and love their job
- Provide enterprisewide business solutions
- Have a superior functioning team

Exhibit 6.6   Vision — Example 6

Vision:

- The IS group is an essential and valued component of the business.
- Business partners actively see IS as a business partner.
- IS proactively addresses business needs with a sense of urgency.
- Agile business processes are enabled by technology.
- IS employees have a passion and commitment.
- IS processes are agile, efficient, and effective.
- The IS environment is simple, standard, and easily maintained.
- IS solutions provide the business with a competitive advantage.
- IS decisions are made in the company's long-term best interest.

Exhibit 6.7   Vision — Example 7

Vision:
The IS group will transform the City to be more integrated, citizen-centric, efficient, accountable, and accessible.

Mission

A mission statement for IS is a concise statement of what the group does. It includes a statement of why the IS group exists, what business it is in, and what purpose and function it provides for the company. Look at the company mission for ideas or themes for the IS mission. Here are some tips in developing a mission for IS:

- A mission is a statement of the group's purpose, i.e., the reason for the group's existence.
- A mission answers the question "why" rather than just explaining what the group does.
- A mission clarifies what business the group is in from the customers' viewpoint.
- A mission should be clear, concise, informative, compelling, interesting, and inspiring.
- Address what the group does, what customers are served, what service is provided, and what sets you apart from other groups.
- A mission should stand the test of time and not require updating every year.

The following (Exhibits 6.8, 6.9, 6.10, 6.11, 6.12, 6.13, 6.14, 6.15, and 6.16) are examples developed at different companies.

Again, you can see a wide variety of mission statements. Although some planning experts may disagree, the most important part of a mission is that it makes sense to the group rather than following strict planning guidelines. It is not worth spending hours forming a perfect statement. Although vision and mission statements are important, do not get consumed in this step of the process.

Exhibit 6.8   Mission — Example 1

Mission:
The mission of the IS group, in partnership with the business units, is to facilitate the availability of timely and accurate information needed to manage the day-to-day and strategic direction of the company by the deployment of systems and tools. This information will assist the company in achieving its objectives and becoming one of the top ten in the marketplace.

Exhibit 6.9   Mission — Example 2

Mission:
The mission of the IS group, in partnership with the business community, is to develop, implement, and maintain worldwide business system solutions that provide secure collection, storage, and access to information. We will accomplish this by matching the business requirements with the appropriate technology.

Exhibit 6.10   Mission — Example 3

Mission:
The mission of the IS group is to develop, implement, and maintain high-quality, efficient, and effective business systems that provide the information needed to support the daily operation and strategic business direction of the business at a level superior to the competition with customer satisfaction as the end goal.

Exhibit 6.11   Mission — Example 4

Mission:
Our mission is to facilitate improvements in operating efficiency and effectiveness by delivering worldwide integrated business systems and services. The business strategies will drive our efforts to ensure that our contributions provide the highest value to the corporation.

Exhibit 6.12   Mission — Example 5

Mission:
The mission of the IS organization is to provide timely, cost-effective, high-quality IS and services that meet or exceed our customers' requirements for achieving business goals and objectives.

▼

Exhibit 6.13   Mission — Example 6

Mission:
The mission of the IS group is to partner with our customers to build value-added business solutions and provide reliable, high-quality technology solutions and services on a timely and cost-effective basis.

▲

▼

Exhibit 6.14   Mission — Example 7

Mission:
The mission of the group is to provide technology solutions that help the business be successful.

▲

▼

Exhibit 6.15   Mission — Example 8

Mission:
In partnership with business departments, IS provides business solutions that provide secure collection, storage, management, and access to information.

▲

▼

Exhibit 6.16   Mission — Example 9

Mission:
The IS group drives efficient management of City government by:

- Leading change and business process improvement
- Implementing business needs-driven technology
- Providing information, tools, and methodologies to continually improve results-based management
- Providing easy access to City products and services through efficient and reliable IS

▲

Values

It can also be helpful to identify the values that will guide the actions and decisions of IS. Exhibit 6.17 shows an example of values.

▼

Exhibit 6.17   Values Example

Values:

- *Citizen and stakeholder centered:* We will work to provide citizens and stakeholders with access to information to achieve greater transparency in government.
- *Technology-enabled:* Services, information, and business processes will be electronic and enabled by technology.
- *Proactive:* Service delivery will be proactive, pushing services out to the citizens.
- *Integrated:* Cross-department service integration will be the norm through the use of a common foundation of technology, standards, and policies.
- *Results-oriented:* IS is about delivering results, not technology. IS will assist City departments to be more results-oriented in the way they design and deliver services.
- *Cost-effective:* Solutions and services will be selected and implemented in a way that provides the highest value and return from the public's investment.
- *Secure:* Information and access will be provided responsibly with the necessary security.
- *Professional:* IS will deal with customers with honesty, integrity, courtesy, and respect.
- *Passionate:* We will take pride in and show enthusiasm and commitment for our work.

▲

Develop the IS Goals and Strategies

Goals

Goals state how you are going to achieve the vision and mission. The following (Exhibits 6.18, 6.19, 6.20, 6.21, 6.22, 6.23, 6.24, 6.25, and 6.26) are examples of goals from different companies.

▼

Exhibit 6.18   Goals — Example 1

IS Goals:

- Implement solutions in partnership with the business units. Champion each project (business-requested projects, not infrastructure projects) by business management to ensure that business issues drive technical solutions.
- Align IS projects and priorities with business priorities and direction. Likewise, the strategic direction of the company will determine the strategic direction of IS.
- Provide responsiveness and flexibility to address changing business requirements rather than simply utilizing technology.
- Meet external customer requirements and assist in solving our customers' business issues.
- Maximize productivity and reduce costs throughout the business.
- Provide real information for business decisions (as opposed to endless amounts of data). Information must be available anytime (24-hour access), anywhere in the world, in any way (flexible formats), for anyone (with security). Support worldwide information requirements and business objectives.
- Minimize IS investments through the use of standardized hardware and packaged software, whenever possible. This will minimize support requirements and provide for maximum growth and flexibility to take advantage of future industry developments.
- Minimize risk to the company by utilization of proven technology, yet not out-of-date technology.
- Educate the users and maximize their ability, through tools and training, to get information without dependence on the IS group and utilize new capabilities and leading technology in providing a competitive advantage for the business.
- Balance IS resources and expenditures with the business demands and the return on investment (ROI) to the business.

▲

▼

Exhibit 6.19   Goals — Example 2

IS Goals:

- The IS group will provide support, guidance, and advice to all areas of the business. This assistance will include the application and use of technology, in addition to suggestions on business process improvements. We will provide continued support after project implementation to ensure that we meet the business needs.
- We will design systems for ease of use to maximize the business productivity.

- We will provide superior communication to ensure information sharing throughout the organization regarding technology and computing. We will understand the business and communicate in a language that is understandable. All areas of the business will know who to call for assistance.
- We will treat our technology users as we would a customer and serve them with a positive attitude.
- We will implement solutions in partnership with the business. User involvement is key to the success. Business management will own, initiate, and sell each project to ensure that business issues drive technical solutions rather than having technology looking for a problem. We will not initiate projects without the appropriate business commitment and support.
- We will choose directions and tools to provide responsiveness, timeliness, and speed to address the key business needs.
- We will balance the IS group resources and expenditures with the business demand and the return to the business.
- We will have a broad knowledge to be able to apply various technologies and assist in all areas of the business.

Exhibit 6.20   Goals — Example 3

IS Goals:

- Implement high-quality business solutions with a focus on customer satisfaction.
- Develop systems that support the growth and profitability goals of the company.
- Assist the company in improving its strategic position in the marketplace.
- Support the business by improving efficiency, productivity, information flow, and information access.
- Provide tools that will allow employees to make better and more timely business decisions.
- Reduce overhead costs.

Exhibit 6.21   Goals — Example 4

IS Goals:

- Support corporate objectives and goals by providing information management technologies, systems, and services that meet business requirements.
- Communicate and execute the IS organization vision and strategic plan.

- Effectively and efficiently provide and manage the companywide IS infrastructure.
- Team and collaborate with the business units to fulfill their information sharing needs.

Exhibit 6.22   Goals — Example 5

We will strive for the following goals in all systems:

- Flexibility
- Performance
- Availability
- Cost management
- Risk management
- Viability
- Manageability
- Supportability
- Scalability
- Interoperability
- Reduced complexity
- Single system image
- Extensibility

Exhibit 6.23   Goals — Example 6

Goals:

- We will improve customer confidence in our capabilities.
- We will research new technologies that can assist the business.
- We will design systems to support the global business objectives.
- We will continuously improve IS processes.
- We will use vendor-supplied software and standard tools whenever possible.
- We will implement highly available integrated systems.
- We will provide business systems that provide accurate business information.
- We will use technology to enable and improve business processes.
- We will develop and retain skills and self-managed employees.

▼

Exhibit 6.24   Goals — Example 7

Strategic Goals:

- All worldwide customers receive equal priority.
- All new systems must provide local flexibility while preserving strategic consistency.
- Cost, balanced against risk and benefit, should be an important factor in all architectural decisions.
- We will maintain a worldwide focus and functionality for all systems.
- Systems must accommodate a range of users, from power users to casual users.
- Systems must strive to empower users, extending the concept of end-user computing.
- Systems must be built in a consistent, user-friendly fashion minimizing complexity, user training, and costs.
- Systems will utilize Internet support and technologies for electronic commerce.
- The implementation of new functionality will not interrupt current business flow.
- Supporting the existing business must be the top priority.
- Systems must be available to each geographic location to support their hours of operation.
- New systems must provide acceptable levels of performance to support the business functions.
- New systems must interact with the appropriate network and systems management components.
- New systems should present a business view rather than a technical view.
- Systems should be capable of being enhanced in an efficient manner.

▲

▼

Exhibit 6.25   Goals — Example 8

Goals:
The computing architecture will:

- Provide system performance, availability, and reliability consistent with business needs
- Support client/server architecture
- Enable office, home, and mobile computing
- Use scalable components
- Minimize variety within each architecture component

- Include tools for managing utilization of components
- Rely on a minimum number of vendors that:
  - Have a global support infrastructure
  - Support multiple prior versions of their products
  - Provide products that are compatible with multiple brands of other components

Exhibit 6.26   Goals — Example 9

Goals:

- The computing architecture will be adhered to for all future systems.
- Systems will be developed with a client/server model. A three-tiered application architecture (presentation, logic, data) will be employed on a three-tiered technical architecture (workstation, application server, enterprise server).
- Data and function should be distributed as necessary to meet business and performance needs.
- Systems will employ graphical user interface design when appropriate.
- Object technology will be used where appropriate to develop flexible, timely systems.
- A global network will be in place to service users worldwide.
- Data integrity, concurrency, and throughput should be managed by a transaction monitor.
- Elimination of a single point of failure should be balanced against cost.
- Systems should provide national language support where reasonable.
- Products selected should adhere to industry-accepted standards (open).
- There should be a high degree of interoperability between the application development tools and the systems management tools.
- Systems will be deployed using relational database technology.
- Systems will be displayed graphically.
- Multimedia will be deployed as necessary and will be balanced against cost.

Strategies

As you describe how you will achieve your goals and mission, strategies are detailed directional statements. Clearly state the strategies in the strategic plan; it can save the IS group from many emotional arguments and political battles throughout the year. Strategies are an area of the strategic plan worth devoting more time to, because the strategies should be statements that guide future selections and directions. In fact, some companies use the strategies as a scorecard to rate alternatives when evaluating packages or options.

Exhibits 6.27, 6.28, 6.29, and 6.30 are examples of IS strategies.

▼

Exhibit 6.27   Strategies — Example 1

IS Strategies:

- The IS steering committee will guide the IS direction and priorities.
- We will treat users of our services as our customers and participate in business process improvements in the business areas. We will facilitate sharing of information throughout the organization regarding technology and computing by providing superior communication. We will understand the business and communicate in a language that is understandable by the business.
- We will design systems for maximum availability (e.g., 24-hour availability, 7 days a week), worldwide connectivity, and optimum dependability.
- We will not constrain solutions by hardware or software platforms. We will utilize the power of various hardware platforms as needed. Likewise, one software solution will not meet all the business needs. We will integrate solutions as business requirements dictate. IS individuals will be cross platform knowledgeable.
- We will maintain information only once and have it available to everyone given proper security clearance. Information will be easily accessed and timely, and users will have the proper tools and training to be able to present the information in the desired format to support business decisions.
- We will implement new technology so that we are compatible with the industry. However, we will ensure the technology is proven to minimize the risk to the business.
- We will design systems and solutions to maximize external customer satisfaction. We will also utilize technology to minimize the costs of our entire supply chain.
- We will handle worldwide information exchange electronically and transport it through the communications facilities with little user effort.
- We will leverage resources and solutions with other corporate entities whenever it makes sense.
- We will have a base of experts on staff and also manage the use of consultants where it makes sense.
- We will utilize the power (for example, processing and ease of use) of the PC in our systems and projects to graphically summarize and present information so that it is meaningful to the business.
- Systems will support ISO 9001 and Sarbanes–Oxley standards.
- We will provide a process for continued evaluation of hardware and software solutions.

▲

▼

Exhibit 6.28   Strategies — Example 2

IS Strategies:

- We will implement and design systems for ease of use. We will design systems to enhance end-user productivity. This will result in less user training and will support cross-functional users.
- We will provide tools that allow for easy access to information. We will design systems with the vision that anyone can get any information at any time, anywhere, and in any way, given the proper security. This means that there must be a worldwide communications network with proper security access that then allows users to simply connect to the application and information required.
- We will provide guidance and expertise without controlling the user.
- We will provide solutions that cross platforms (mainframe, PC) and utilize various hardware and software tools.
- Systems and information will be available 24 hours a day, 7 days a week.
- We will provide timely and ongoing training and support in applications, technical tools, and additional support as needed. This includes a value added help desk for PC, printing, and local area network support.
- We will implement new technology to keep our tools provided to the business current with the industry. However, we will ensure the technology is proven to minimize the risk to the business.
- We will handle information exchange within the worldwide business electronically and utilize e-business whenever possible.
- We will provide worldwide information to support the business. The IS strategic direction will address the global system and information needs.
- Rather than producing endless amounts of data, we will utilize the power of the PC in our systems and projects to graphically summarize and present information so that it is meaningful and useful to the business. We will provide the information with minimal manual manipulation and intervention.
- We will provide tools and capabilities to automatically load data into the systems to reduce unnecessary and redundant efforts.
- We will utilize vendor package solutions whenever possible to reduce the maintenance requirements, but also tailor solutions as necessary to meet the business requirements.
- We will provide updated equipment, including PC hardware and tools that propel the division to meeting the business requirements.
- We will provide continuous improvement in the systems and applications for the business. We will implement large projects in small pieces to reduce the overall risk to the business, and so make the projects easier to manage, staff, and implement.

Internal Strategies:

- Personnel: We need to provide career and personal growth for the IS employees so that they continue to expand themselves to provide improved solutions for the business. This can be done through active career path counseling and programs, updated job descriptions that reflect the positions accurately, job rotation both inside and outside the group to obtain exposure to the business and other areas of IS, increased recognition, and increased training in both technical and business areas.
- Technical: The IS group must stay current with new and emerging technologies so that we can deploy them to benefit the business at the right time. We will reserve time for technical research and development to stay current with technology. Training must be a priority in this fast-changing field so that skills and methods do not become obsolete.
- Prioritization: It is critical with limited resources and many areas to apply technology that the IS group carefully prioritize projects and work in partnership with the business. We will follow the IS steering committee process and priority setting process to obtain maximum productivity.
- Communication: Communication is critical to eliminate redundant efforts and leverage whenever possible.
- Global: As a global focus and design are critical to our business, the IS organization must become educated in what this means and how to design systems globally.
- Standardization: Whenever possible, we must encourage common hardware and software to reduce the amount of support requirements necessary.
- Staffing: IS planning is critical to be proactive with the proper staff mix and knowledge base. We will plan staffing in accordance with the business needs of the future.
- Documentation: Documentation is critical as it allows us to continue support of the business applications. We will continue and improve documentation to reduce the support requirements and learning time required for business applications.

Exhibit 6.29   Strategies — Example 3

Information System Strategies:

1. Leverage: Whenever possible and practical, we will attempt to leverage IS solutions that exist within other divisions, as long as the solution meets the business needs of our division. This results in the lowest overall cost solution. We will modularize and structure solutions to take advantage of

reusable program code and allow for leveraged solutions that will result in lower cost.

2. User partnership: User management must own, initiate, and sell each project to ensure that business issues drive technical solutions rather than vise versa. As application systems are enablers that allow employees to do their jobs more efficiently and effectively, we will require end-user sponsors and team participants to successfully develop or implement any business application system. We will not initiate projects without the appropriate end-user commitment and support.

3. Vendor-supplied packages: Whenever possible, we will choose vendor package solutions. We will review and select vendor packages for each project unless significant business objectives are not met through any available package solutions. Whenever possible, we will implement vendor packages with no or as few modifications as possible. This minimizes the overall cost of ownership of the business application.

4. Open systems: We will develop systems with the open systems concept for maximum cross-system portability and interoperability access. Although open systems are a vision for our future direction, true open systems are not in abundance in today's vendor marketplace. As open systems become more available in the marketplace, we will replace systems with open systems. In the meantime, we must embrace vendors that are committing to open systems and use vendor products with proven portability.

5. Accessibility: We will design systems with the vision that anyone can get any information at any time, anywhere, in any way, given the proper security. This means that there must be a worldwide communications network with proper security access that then allows users to simply connect to the application and data required. Databases must be SQL compatible to increase the compatibility of data across the locations.

6. Systems development tools: We will design business systems so that the systems are able to meet the needs of rapidly changing business requirements. We will utilize tools and techniques to minimize the time and cost required to implement new or modify existing systems. We will routinely utilize prototyping and well-defined specification and implementation procedures.

7. Warehousing: If the company requires worldwide information, we will utilize a common data warehouse rather than dictating a single worldwide solution.

8. User interface: We will design systems whenever possible and practical, to enhance end-user productivity. This will result in less user training and will support cross-functional users.

9. Data: Although we store data in several places, we will design systems so that we enter and maintain data in only one data storage location. Although we can duplicate the data for reporting purposes, one source must be the owner, maintainer, or master of the information. This will result in more accurate data and less overhead in maintaining the data in multiple locations and formats.

10. Information: We will summarize, sort, and present information so that it adds clarity, visibility, and meaning to the business rather than just data. Our systems and projects will strive to produce information critical to business decisions rather than endless amounts of data.

11. Information exchange: We will exchange worldwide information electronically and transport through the communications facilities with little user effort. Conversion of document formats must be available for text, spreadsheet, graphics, voice, and image. Information exchanged outside the organization must also be electronic whenever possible through industry-standard electronic data interchange or the Web.

12. Infrastructure: The IS group will initiate projects requiring maintenance or enhancement to the infrastructure.

─────────────────────────── ▲ ───────────────────────────

─────────────────────────── ▼ ───────────────────────────

Exhibit 6.30   Strategies — Example 4

IS Strategies:

■ Open (or Open Database Compliant — ODBC): Implementation of systems based on open technology will be the most effective method to meet the business requirements of worldwide information and providing solutions independent of hardware platforms. ODBC will allow technically different systems to be interfaced to share any information the business requires. Purchased or internally developed software must conform to this standard because the benefits obtained by implementing an open systems architecture can be eroded if one piece of the architecture does not meet the standards. ODBC will also provide the company with a leveraged position for negotiating with vendors.

■ Relational database structure: A relational (SQL)-based data access will provide the maximum flexibility to meet changing business requirements, ease of obtaining information, and maximum data integrity.

■ Client/server, graphical user interfaces (GUIs): In efforts to provide systems that are easy to use and present information in meaningful ways to users, we will utilize the power of the PC and integration of various hardware platforms. Standard GUI designs will ensure that systems are easy to use with minimal training. It also reduces application development time. Both the PC and network environments are critical components of a client/server GUI environment.

■ Vendor-supported software: We are not in the business of providing business application software. Other companies are, and can do it better and less expensively than custom writing our software to fit our business. We will utilize packaged, unmodified, vendor-supplied software whenever possible and utilize our resources in areas that are truly unique and provide a competitive advantage in the marketplace. We will change the business process to fit a standard package rather than changing the system to fit our process. Although we will not utilize beta software, our strategy will be to stay relatively current on vendor-supplied releases and rewrites.

- Real time: We will design and implement systems so that updating of information occurs immediately rather than through batch processing. This will support the objective of 24-hour availability as well as the timely information requirements. We will build backup measures into the design of the network and systems to ensure continuous availability. Systems must be reliable with minimum downtime. We will design systems so that information is available online with distributed printing capability to minimize handling costs and provide timely information.

- Connectivity: We will design the computing environment for optimum connectivity rather than stand-alone islands. The objective is to be able to electronically share and pass information *from* anywhere in the world *to* anywhere in the world. We can obtain significant value to the business by sharing information, eliminating redundancy of efforts, and increasing the speed of communication through a solid networked environment. We will leverage this network with the entire organization for efficiency and cost reasons. This connectivity requires complying with certain technical standards and guidelines.

- Integration: We will design systems so that the user enters information only once. This will reduce effort, eliminate redundancy of data, and improve data integrity.

- Data integrity: The accuracy and dependability of our information are foremost. Therefore, we will implement application solutions that ensure the data is correct at all times. This implies sufficient edits to ensure that the user enters the data properly as well as taking sufficient data collision precautions through application design standards.

- Software design: The core of tightly integrated set of applications (financial, manufacturing, distribution) will be provided by one software supplier to minimize the amount of bridges and interfaces necessary.

- Electronic exchange: Information exchanged within or outside the organization must be electronic whenever possible and through industry-standard electronic data interchange (EDI).

- Disaster recovery: We will design recovery in the event of disasters or problems with each application. We will design recovery up to the last business day, with disaster recovery within one business day.

- Security: We will implement applications and software with the utmost security to ensure that we protect our critical business information. We will protect and secure the worldwide network as much as possible, and take sufficient measures for overall security, including virus checking, password protection, and other software security measures.

- Documentation: Appropriate online and printed system help will be available for users of the systems. This will provide immediate aids to system navigation as well as minimize training time for new and existing users.

- Maintainability: For areas of the business for which we cannot meet their requirements with standard vendor-supplied software applications packages, we will design systems so that the systems are easy to modify and quickly tailor to changing business needs or business process improvements.

■ Table driven: Systems developed with tables rather than hard-coded values are more flexible to changing business needs. Maintenance costs of systems are considerably less because users are able to make changes to meet the business needs.

■ Bar coding: We will utilize bar coding whenever possible to reduce the amount of manual labor required to maintain information.

■ Imaging: Whenever possible, we will store and retrieve documents online for efficiency.

■ X.500 e-mail standard: We will use this standard electronic mail protocol to allow for compatible communications.

■ ISO certified suppliers: If possible, we will select suppliers that are ISO certified for our software providers.

■ Other technologies: We will deploy other technologies, such as videoconferencing, pen-based computing, CD-ROM, and executive IS, as the business requirements dictate.

▲

As shown in Figure 6.3, strategies may be somewhat conflicting at times. Keep this in mind while documenting strategies to try to be as specific as possible. The clearer the strategy, the easier decisions will be on a day-to-day basis.

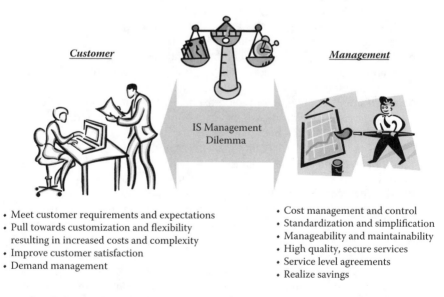

* Meet customer requirements and expectations
* Pull towards customization and flexibility resulting in increased costs and complexity
* Improve customer satisfaction
* Demand management

* Cost management and control
* Standardization and simplification
* Manageability and maintainability
* High quality, secure services
* Service level agreements
* Realize savings

Figure 6.3   Conflicting strategies

IS goals and strategies typically apply across IS, to the business applications, technical infrastructure, organization, and processes. Both the business and IS groups must understand these statements and realize what aspects in the business make them important. Figures 6.4, 6.5, 6.6, and 6.7 show examples of how various companies tied the business goals to the IS strategies. You may also want to tie the IS goals to the IS strategies, and to the resulting metrics, as a company illustrated in Figure 6.8.

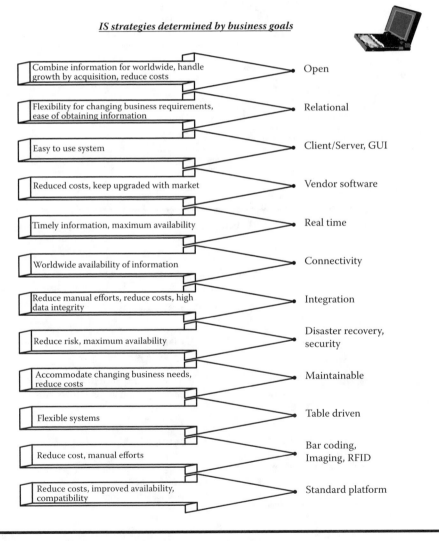

IS strategies determined by business goals

Business goal	IS strategy
Combine information for worldwide, handle growth by acquisition, reduce costs	Open
Flexibility for changing business requirements, ease of obtaining information	Relational
Easy to use system	Client/Server, GUI
Reduced costs, keep upgraded with market	Vendor software
Timely information, maximum availability	Real time
Worldwide availability of information	Connectivity
Reduce manual efforts, reduce costs, high data integrity	Integration
Reduce risk, maximum availability	Disaster recovery, security
Accommodate changing business needs, reduce costs	Maintainable
Flexible systems	Table driven
Reduce cost, manual efforts	Bar coding, Imaging, RFID
Reduce costs, improved availability, compatibility	Standard platform

Figure 6.4   Business goals and IS strategies

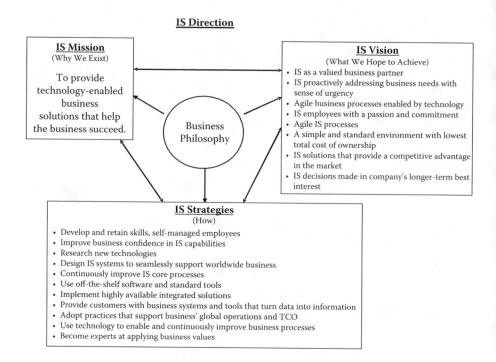

Figure 6.5   IS mission, vision, and strategies

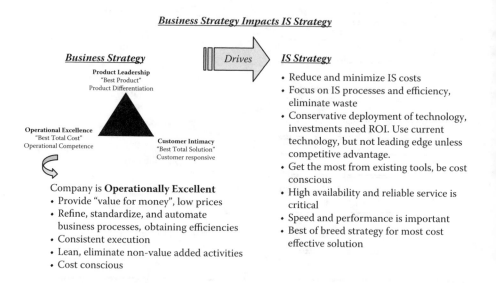

Figure 6.6   Business strategy impacts IS strategy

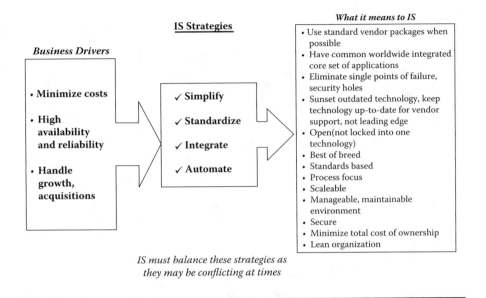

Business Drivers

- Minimize costs
- High availability and reliability
- Handle growth, acquisitions

IS Strategies

✓ Simplify
✓ Standardize
✓ Integrate
✓ Automate

What it means to IS

- Use standard vendor packages when possible
- Have common worldwide integrated core set of applications
- Eliminate single points of failure, security holes
- Sunset outdated technology, keep technology up-to-date for vendor support, not leading edge
- Open(not locked into one technology)
- Best of breed
- Standards based
- Process focus
- Scaleable
- Manageable, maintainable environment
- Secure
- Minimize total cost of ownership
- Lean organization

IS must balance these strategies as they may be conflicting at times

Figure 6.7   IS strategies

Determine the IS Balanced Scorecard and Metrics

Measuring IS performance has been an area that has received much attention and press. Determining the appropriate metrics to measure IS performance has always been a challenge for management. Many companies spend countless hours gathering and reporting data to executives who do not really care about the metrics IS continues to report. For example, many IS organizations report how many calls they completed or how many maintenance requests were completed. What do the numbers actually mean? Although the metric may provide a relative performance from month to month, that is arguable because one request may be simple or very complex and there is no way to judge if the number reported should be more or less. With too many metrics, people become confused about what is important. The administrative burden in collecting and reporting the data can be nonproductive. The key to success is selecting a small number of metrics that are relevant to the business and that represent the true leverage points.

One way to identify metrics is to ask members of executive management what is important to them and how they would measure the success of IS. Another method is to benchmark against industry metrics, as discussed in the industry benchmarking section in the previous chapter, "Conduct Industry Benchmarking." However, the best metrics are those that tie back directly to the direction, because it is important to measure

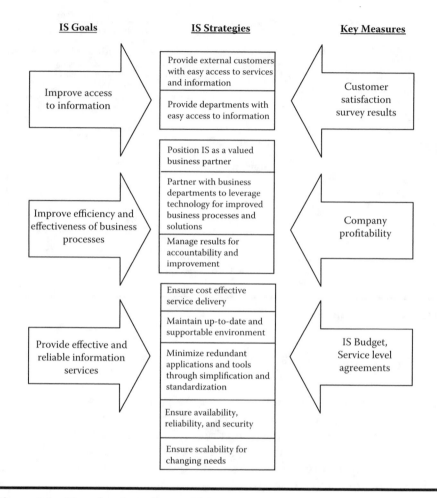

Figure 6.8 IS goals, strategies, and key measures

progress to the direction, not just metrics for the sake of metrics. An excellent method to determine metrics is to use the balanced-scorecard approach. This provides a balanced measurement around four areas: financial, customer, internal processes, and individual innovation or learning. The balanced scorecard emphasizes that no single measure provides a clear picture of how an organization functions but that a set of key indicators is required. This allows an organization to focus on what is important to define the success of the organization over time. The following are questions within each balanced-scorecard area as it relates to IS:

> *Financial*: How much money is the organization spending on IS? Where is the money being spent? What was the budget and how did actual

spending compare? How much money is spent keeping the business functioning (e.g., legacy systems support and maintenance) versus moving the business forward (e.g., new development projects that meet the business priorities)? How much revenue is generated from IS initiatives, such as e-commerce? How does IS perform in the eyes of senior management? Examples of financial metrics include IS costs as a percent of revenue, percent of IS costs on development, IS budget actual versus plan, and revenue related to e-commerce.

Customer: How does IS perform in the eyes of external and internal customers? How satisfied are customers? How well is IS meeting service-level agreements? How does IS address the customers' concern about time, quality, performance, service, and cost? How many business interviews and focus groups have been held? Examples of customer metrics include annual customer satisfaction survey results, customer satisfaction on random surveys of help desk requests, post-project customer satisfaction, and service-level agreement performance.

Internal process: How well are the IS processes formalized, documented, followed, and measured? How is time being spent within the IS organization? How does IS impact the business processes? How does your execution compare to industry standards? How many joint IS and business planning meetings have been held? How many IS steering committee meetings have been held? How many IS projects are directly linked to a documented business goal? What is the system availability? What is the system response time? How many security breaches or outages have been experienced? Examples of process metrics include number of function points or XP velocity points delivered, availability, and percent of the organization required to support and maintain systems.

Organizational learning and people: What is the ability of the IS organization to learn and improve? How well does the group keep pace with changing technology? Are career plans formalized? What skills and training are required? What recruiting and retention programs are implemented? How satisfied are the employees? Is the organization positioned to meet challenges of the future? Examples of people metrics include IS employee satisfaction, IS turnover or retention, and training hours per IS employee.

The following is one method of determining key metrics integrating the IS direction with the balanced scorecard that has been very successful:

■ With a group of individuals such as IS management team or the IS steering committee, review each statement within the IS vision, mission, goals, and strategies. Ask the group how to measure that, or how you will know that you have achieved the objective. If multiple measures are given, write down both. Move quickly and do not dwell on each item; take the first response and move on.

■ You will end up with a long list of metrics. Review the list and categorize each metric as high, medium, and low in terms of the value the metric provides.

■ Take the metrics rated as high priority, review them to ensure the metrics are measurable, and review them in relation to the vision, mission, goals, and strategies. Discuss whether they make sense or whether there is any need to add metrics or change them. Review each metric to identify the appropriate category within the balanced scorecard.

■ Narrow down the list of metrics to the key metrics. There should be one or two metrics within each area of the balanced scorecard.

■ Identify the frequency with which each metric will be measured, such as monthly, quarterly, or annually.

■ Identify the target for each metric.

You should have no more than about six or eight key measures to measure the overall success of the IS organization. There may be many more metrics that are measured within each work group. For example, the help desk may have many detailed metrics, such as number of calls, mean time to close requests, mean time to respond, percent answered on the first call, and so forth. Operations may be another area with many detailed metrics. However, it is critical to focus on the few key metrics that measure the overall progress to the goals and direction. Following are six critical metrics that should be considered for inclusion:

Percent of the IS budget spent on maintenance versus new development: Typical organizations may spend 80% of IS costs on keeping systems functioning and only 20% on new initiatives. World-class organizations strive for a 50%/50% balance between maintenance and new development.

Customer satisfaction: Both annual surveys and random surveys after service has been completed are excellent metrics of IS performance.

Percent of IS projects directly linked to a documented business goal: This metric represents the alignment of the IS priorities and work with the business plan.

Comparison of IS budget to plan: Meeting budget targets demonstrates an environment that is predictable, planned, and under control.

Availability: In most environments, providing a reliable, secure, and stable environment for business operations is critical.

Percent of IS staff exceeding average performance criteria on performance reviews: Some companies that are artificially driven to a standard distribution of performance ratings may not be able to use this metric effectively. However, it can be a good measurement of the competence and accomplishments of the organization if done properly.

Review and Confirm the IS Vision and Direction

This is an important milestone to review the high-level IS direction with both the IS group and the IS steering committee. Update any areas that may require changes or additions.

Developing the IS Plan

Develop the Business Application Direction

Next, identify the specific direction for the business application area. Begin by identifying principles that will guide the business application area. Principles are a reflection of the general culture and values. They provide guidance for IS decisions and investments in the future. There should be similar themes reflected through the IS mission, vision, strategies, and principles.

One example of a business application principle that if not stated can cause emotional arguments is the use of packaged versus custom software. In the past, companies have tended to migrate to custom solutions as both business users and the IS individuals claim they have unique requirements. Due to the high cost of custom solutions, and the increased availability of packaged solutions, many companies are migrating away from custom solutions. Yet, without a clear guiding principle, on a project-by-project basis it can be easy to fall into custom software claiming "We are unique" or to spend hours arguing about custom versus packaged solutions. Exhibit 6.31 and Exhibit 6.32 show how two companies addressed the custom versus packaged issue with a guiding principle.

▬▬▬▬▬▬▬▬▬▬▬▬▬▬▬▬▬▼▬▬▬▬▬▬▬▬▬▬▬▬▬▬▬▬▬

Exhibit 6.31 Custom versus Package Direction — Example 1

Custom versus Packaged Business Applications Direction
We will invest the majority of resources (people and money) in areas and systems that are strategic and unique to the business. We will choose the lowest-cost

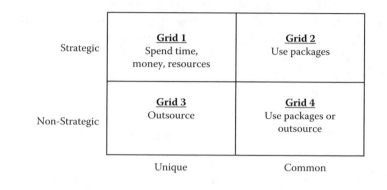

Figure 6.9   How to implement a system

solution in terms of overall cost of ownership (e.g., vendor package, outsourcing, etc.) on the nonstrategic support systems. This will allow us to concentrate resources on areas that are most strategic to the business. We will use the matrix in Figure 6.9 as a guideline to determine how to implement a system:

- Grid 1: Systems that are strategic and unique to the business must be the area where we invest time, money, and resources. We will custom build systems in this area, because we will need to tailor these systems to the business. An example of a system in this area is a customer information system that would include specific information about how the customer is using our product.
- Grid 2: We will purchase vendor-supplied packages for applications that are strategic but have common requirements unless we will gain a strategic advantage by significantly enhancing the system in some way. An example of a system in this area is a customer bulletin board system.
- Grid 3: Systems that are nonstrategic but unique to the business will be outsourced. This could either be a vendor package solution with modifications or a custom-built solution. However, if the needs are not strategic, we should not invest considerable resources. We will determine the least costly alternative in terms of implementation and total cost of ownership. An example of a system in this area is a configurator to order and build our model number.
- Grid 4: For systems that are nonstrategic and common, we will utilize vendor packages, or outsource the function. We will install and maintain systems in this area with minimum time, worry, and resources. We will accept it, even if it does not fit the business exactly. Even though these systems are still very important to the daily functioning of the business, the idea is to spend as little time and money on systems in this area in either implementation or maintenance. Examples of systems in this area are accounts payable, accounts receivable, and the general ledger.

With this basic framework and strategy, the challenge of the steering committee and the IS group is to define what projects are strategic and nonstrategic to the business. With the IS steering committee, we will map the application areas on the grid above to determine possible solutions. We will do this by examining what impact the application would have on the business goals and mission. This will focus attention on facts rather than emotions. Rather than arguments on custom versus package, the business can identify whether the application is strategic or nonstrategic by linking it to the business goals.

Exhibit 6.32   Custom versus Package Direction — Example 2

Application Direction

We will use the grid in Figure 6.10 to map our business applications and determine the proper solution accordingly.

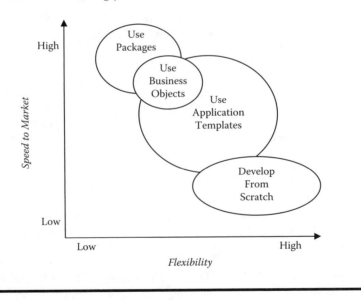

Figure 6.10   Mapping business applications

Exhibit 6.33 provides an example of additional business application principles developed by a company.

▼

Exhibit 6.33   Business Application Direction

Business Application Direction:

- **Common core application architecture**

  After deciding to buy or make business applications, companies have two options as to their overall application strategy. On one end of the spectrum, companies are choosing the best-of-breed approach. Here, they select the best vendor package for the specific business application. They may have vendor packages from many different vendors and integrate the packages through various tools and methods available today. On the other end of the spectrum, companies go with a single supplier and obtain all vendor packages from one vendor regardless of the fit so that it will easily integrate in the environment. Our application strategy should be in the middle of these two strategies. We should obtain the core set of ERP applications from a single vendor, but when necessary obtain other vendor packages to meet specific needs and integrate those packages. Noncritical applications will be from the single vendor to minimize cost of ownership and reduce integration costs. This strategy will provide us with the best functionality at the lowest overall cost of ownership.

- **Business process reengineering**

  We will implement new applications and technology after analyzing, simplifying, and redesigning business processes. We will not automate a flawed process. Improved processes are more streamlined, efficient, and cost effective, and automation of those processes will be easier to implement and maintain. We will reengineer business processes to fit the software and industry best practices unless a strong business reason prohibits it.

- **Business information**

  We will design and implement applications to provide critical business information, rather than endless amounts of meaningless data. Information should be summarized, sorted, and presented in ways that it adds clarity, visibility, and meaning to the business. Data warehouse and reporting tools should be provided so that users can service themselves and obtain information directly rather than relying on IS for reports and information. Tools and data warehouses will lower the overall costs rather than developing custom reports. Training should be provided to the users so that they are able to easily obtain necessary information. Applications should be designed with the vision that anyone can easily get any information at any time, anywhere, and in any way, without assistance from IS if that individual has the proper security.

- **Integrate**

  Applications must be integrated and share information rather than interfacing data back and forth. We will design applications for optimum connectivity rather than stand-alone islands of information. We will design business applications so that data is entered and maintained in one place. Although data may be duplicated for reporting purposes, one source should be the owner, maintainer, or master of the information. Data duplication should be kept to a minimum. This will result in more accurate data and less overhead in maintaining the data in multiple locations and formats. We will implement a common method of application integration through an enterprise applications interface (EAI). EAI implements a basic technology framework to connect disparate systems into a single entity that delivers information sharing between applications, partners, and customers. All new applications must provide an EAI connection to access and share data across the organization.

■ **Interoperability and reusability**
We will construct applications with methods that substantially improve interoperability and the reusability of components. This enables the development of new applications as needed by the business. Sharable components must be built as sharable from the beginning; it is difficult and expensive to do so after the fact.

■ **Scalability**
We will design applications to grow as the business grows. The applications must be scalable in size, capacity, and functionality to meet changing business and technical requirements. This reduces the total cost of ownership by reducing the amount of application and platform changes needed to respond to increasing or decreasing demand on the system. Scalability must be reviewed for both upward and downward capability.

■ **Relational database structure**
For transactional applications, a relational-based data access for business applications will provide the maximum flexibility to meet changing business requirements. It will also ensure ease of obtaining information and maximum data integrity.

■ **Open systems**
Implementation of business applications based on open technology will be the most effective method to meet the business requirements and provide solutions independent of hardware platforms. This allows us to select the most economical solution without impacting applications and increases flexibility because technology components can be purchased from many vendors. Open systems will allow technically different systems to be interfaced to share any information the business requires.

■ **Web enabled**
Business applications must be designed for a thin-client Web-based architecture. This will result in the lowest overall cost of ownership due to the client requirements and will allow us to take advantage of a new class of applications: Web services, or server applications that exchange XML-formatted data with other applications over the Web. The use of Web services is a cost-effective way for us to integrate existing, stand-alone applications into larger business (and business-to-business) systems.

■ **Business usability**

In efforts to provide business applications that are easy to use and present information in meaningful ways to the business, standard graphical user interfaces should be used. This will ensure that systems are easy to use with minimal training.

■ **Real time**

We will implement business applications so that updating of information occurs immediately rather than through batch processing or copying of information. Information will be entered at the process rather than after the fact in a manual entry process. This will allow us to see what is in operation on the manufacturing floor at any given time.

■ **Table driven**

We will implement applications with tables rather than hard-coded values, because they are more flexible to changing business needs. Maintenance costs of systems are considerably less, as business users are able to make changes to meet the business needs. This will also allow users to be self-sufficient in making changes to business applications and processes.

■ **Secure**

The importance of designing security into applications cannot be understated in today's world when dealing with customer information and the intellectual property value of an organization. Sensitive information and intellectual property must be protected at all costs by the following means:

a. Access to all applications should be tied to Active Directory.
b. Sensitive data should be encrypted within the database.
c. Sensitive data should not move unprotected over the Internet.
d. Any application that lives outside the firewall and is accessed via the Internet should be reviewed by an outside security firm.

■ **Reliable, available**

All applications will be designed for reliability and maximum availability. The business depends on the availability of tools and information. To assure this availability, it must be designed in from the beginning rather than added afterward. Measures such as tracking unit tests, acceptance tests, and production defects will ensure availability and reliability.

■ **Efficiency**

A key requirement is speed of operation handling high volumes of transactions. Systems must be designed for efficiency and not create a bottleneck.

■ **Standard**

Systems development and operational environments will strive for consistency. The variety of development tools, programming languages, and supporting systems must be minimized or standardized on the smallest number of alternatives to reduce total cost of ownership. The development tools and programming languages used will be upgraded periodically to maintain consistency and support from the vendor.

- **Worldwide**

  As the business expands internationally, we should consider having common business applications that support the entire business. It is much easier to standardize business processes and applications at the beginning of global growth rather than later in the process. A global strategy will also help handle the tremendous cost/price pressures, and distance themselves from competitors. Examples of global processes include ordering anywhere in the world, shipping anywhere in the world, and having consistent prices, products, and quality around the world. Common applications will provide the power to streamline, consolidate, maximize the capabilities of local uniqueness, and implement standard business processes and procedures to help unify worldwide operations and access.

- **Business application portfolio**

  The company's business application portfolio for the future will be heavily dependent on the vendor module selected and implemented for the core applications. As mentioned above, as many of the modules as possible should come from the same core vendor. We need to manage the business application portfolio as the business grows and needs change. For example, today customer relationship management (CRM) functionality may not be critical because the company has a relatively low number of customers. However, this may change in the future.

Once the business application principles have been identified, outline the specific direction for the business applications and plans on how to get there. Review the current business application situation and the business application weaknesses that were documented in the second phase of the planning effort. Review the application principles to identify the gap. Finally, list the specific areas that must change to achieve the business application direction. At this point, this list may not consist of specific projects but groups of projects. For example, you may identify the need to standardize on a common global ERP system, which may later decompose to several separate projects.

At this point, you may have several options to evaluate relative to the application direction. It is important to do a thorough job of investigating the options because many times when the cost estimates start accumulating for the project, management will want to go back to review the options again. You will save time if you do a thorough job of option evaluation at the beginning. At this level, your options are high-level and generic. For example, rather than identifying a particular software application package, one option is to implement new packaged software, whether it be package x, y, or z. Consider the option of continuing on the current path, or doing nothing. Identify options for each area of major change or investment. Exhibit 6.34 is an example of how one company identified its options for business application systems.

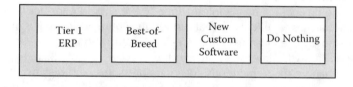

Figure 6.11   Options considered

▼

Exhibit 6.34   Option Introduction

1. Option Analysis

A number of options were evaluated to develop the application recommendation. Figure 6.11 shows the various options considered with supporting detail to follow.

    a. Tier 1 ERP: Select and implement a tier 1 integrated vendor-supplied ERP software package (i.e., Oracle, SAP).

    b. Best-of-breed: Select and implement a series of niche software packages including a tier 2 ERP system, warehouse management system, and transportation management system.

    c. New custom system: Develop a new state-of-the-art custom system, or new generation of the current systems.

    d. Status quo or do nothing: Keep the current systems and continue to enhance the systems over time to meet the changing business needs.

Each option is outlined in detail below, including a description, advantages, disadvantages, cost, and resource estimates.

▲

Next, analyze the various high-level options. This includes assembling the following information for each option:

Cost estimate: Be extremely careful to not underestimate costs at this point in the process. Include all costs, not just the vendor software costs. Once you provide managers with these high-level numbers, it can be amazing how good their memory is if you come back with higher costs than the original estimates. It is always easier to start high and find ways to reduce project costs rather than starting too low. Whatever numbers you provide at this stage, be sure that management understands that the numbers are very preliminary, and you need to do a significant amount of work to formulate actual budgetary numbers. Include all various costs, such as:

- Hardware and servers: Several additional servers and hardware components may be required. Will your query or data warehouse application reside on a separate machine than your transaction processing? Will you require a test or development server in addition to the production machine? Will you have additional disk or backup (for example, mirroring) requirements? Will you have to design an architecture for high availability? Will you need additional hardware peripherals for things like bar coding, RFID, and other functionality? Will new printers be necessary?
- Software: How many total users will be accessing the software? In addition to the core software application package, will you require other software for specific requirements? Will you need to buy additional licenses for existing software to port to a new hardware environment? Is additional database software required? Are any additional support software packages required?
- Maintenance costs: Typically, the first year of maintenance must be paid up-front. What level of support will be required? Maintenance and support fees are typically 18% to 22% of the net software and hardware costs.
- Tax: Many individuals forget to add the cost of tax in their estimates. This could be substantial.
- Consulting or contracting: Consulting may be necessary for conversion programming, consulting in the new business application package, network or technical consulting, business process reengineering consulting, project management, and so forth. A rule of thumb is that consulting costs can be half to two times the software purchase cost.
- Travel and expenses: Will costs be incurred due to out-of-town consultants, training classes, implementation assistance, etc.? Will travel be necessary to obtain input from worldwide users or locations? Will you have to train other users in various locations that will be utilizing the software? If consultants must travel, the consulting costs may increase by 15%–25%.
- Training: Include training of the users and the IS group in the new software. Does the IS group require additional technical training due to new platforms?
- Network costs: Are any network enhancements necessary to support the new application software?
- PC costs: Are any PC hardware or software upgrades necessary to support the new application software?
- Outsourcing costs: Will a service bureau operate the hardware and software?

Time: What is the total amount of time you need for the project and when is the latest you must begin the project? Time is also like the cost area; do not underestimate the time required to finish the project. It often takes longer than you think, and again management has an excellent memory for the first number you provided. Try to provide a fixed time upon project approval (e.g., the project will be completed 18 months after approval).

Resources: How many business resources and how many IS resources are necessary? Will the resources be part-time or full-time? One word of caution on part-time resources: To do a large project effectively, you need some commitment of full-time resources. With part-time resources, production and day-to-day issues always take precedence, and you often get fewer resources than you anticipated.

Benchmark information: Why should management believe your time and cost estimates? Can you give them examples of other companies, or what consultants or research organizations are saying that similar projects cost?

Advantages: List the high-level advantages this option would have for the company.

Disadvantages: List the high-level disadvantages this option would have for the company.

Ensure that all the advantages and disadvantages are documented. Examples to consider include:

- Access to information
- Functional depth and breadth of requirements addressed
- Integration
- Customer impact
- Ability to handle growth
- Ability to handle type of growth (i.e., global, acquisitions, new customers, new products)
- Best practice business processes
- Sarbanes–Oxley controls
- Risk
- Resources
- Supportability
- Extensibility
- Cost of ownership
- Value
- Risk of change
- Implementation scope
- Initial costs
- Vendor dependence

Figure 6.12   Information needs

After documenting the various options, discuss the options with the IS steering committee. Agree on an appropriate course of action and document the decision.

Information Architecture

In large global companies with various divisions and locations, the question is often raised as to what information resides at each site, what information is necessary at a corporate level, and what information must be shared across sites. This issue is very important to resolve in the strategic planning process. IS expenditures at a local or site level may not be necessary, or would not be approved if the direction is different at a corporate level. Although there are common corporate information needs, there are often different information needs at the site level or information that must be shared by the remote sites. Agree upon the information architecture in advance, even though it is possible to bring together the corporate information in a data warehouse. The locations and corporate must decide who is responsible for what information. Figure 6.12 depicts the different information needs that exist.

As information needs migrate toward the center (for example, the global or company group level), the cost and complexity of providing the IS solution are higher, and the degree of flexibility is reduced. This is because consistent systems and processes must be in place to transfer and collect the worldwide or group information in addition to the site information. Therefore, unless there is a business need to migrate the information to the center of the circle, it is best that it remain close to the site level. Even though an information need would be at the global or group level, the actual transaction-based system needs to exist at the site or geographic area. The global or group solution would typically be a data warehouse for reporting purposes.

It can be helpful to develop a grid with the information needs developed earlier and identify what portion the IS group is responsible for obtaining. This means that the information is needed at the particular level or site, to report the data or to update it. There may or may not be a separate IS organization or separate IS business applications at each of the sites. In the event there are multiple systems and organizations, typically the lowest level that is responsible for updating the information is the owner of the information and systems to maintain the information. See the example in Exhibit 6.35. The *Y* denotes that that business group has a requirement for the information.

The IS group and the business can further clarify the table with the use of the CRUD (creating, replacing, updating, deleting) criteria. The CRUD criteria would identify which entity is responsible for the information. Note whether the organization only requires the information for reporting purposes. This table can then become the basis of the future system development. There are tremendous business ramifications and questions within each of the information needs; closely review and discuss this list with management.

Even if the company is not a complex global or multidivisional organization, it is important to design the business application direction so that it provides the key information metrics or indicators that measure the organization's well-being. Review the information needs or business measures identified in the previous chapter. For the measures not currently available or difficult to get from the current applications, identify areas to address these needs in the business application direction.

Develop the E-Business Direction

An important aspect to address in both the application direction as well as the technical infrastructure direction is the e-business direction. To be effective, e-business applications must be designed from the external requirements of the organization, not internally. Review the information assembled in the first phase of planning. During the first phase, you identified the customers and all the stakeholders, their requirements, and their process of doing business with the company. You also identified the company vision and mission, and the value proposition. Next, identify the following to outline the e-business direction:

■ E-business strategy: How does the company want to utilize the Web? How can the company use Web technology to strengthen or enhance the value proposition?

Exhibit 6.35 Information Architecture

Information Need	Sales Site	System Eng Site	Manufacturing Site	Geographic Area	Global	Process Group
Marketing:						
Customer information	Y	Y		Y	Y	Y
Pricing and discounts	Y	Y		Y	Y	
Quote	Y	Y		Y	Y	
Forecasting	Y	Y	Y	Y	Y	
Technical reference	Y	Y		Y	Y	Y
Agreements, contracts, TC	Y	Y		Y	Y	Y
Sales goals, credits	Y			Y		
Pursuit information	Y			Y	Y	Y
Competitor	Y			Y	Y	Y
Training course	Y	Y		Y		
Sales tools (bulletin board)	Y	Y		Y	Y	Y
Order:						
Order information	Y	Y	Y	Y	Y	Y
Project information	Y	Y	Y	Y	Y	Y
Bookings	Y			Y	Y	

Information Need	Sales Site	System Eng Site	Manufacturing Site	Geographic Area	Global	Process Group
Backlog			Y	Y	Y	
Item and model level	Y	Y	Y	Y	Y	
CAD design information		Y	Y	Y	Y	
Configurator	Y	Y		Y	Y	
Sales	Y			Y	Y	Y
Distributions requirements plan	Y		Y		Y	
Shipping	Y		Y			
Invoicing				Y	Y	Y
Order status	Y	Y	Y			
Project history	Y	Y		Y	Y	
Service level	Y	Y	Y	Y	Y	
Table of denial	Y					
Project engineering:						
Project P&L	Y	Y	Y	Y	Y	
Resource availability		Y		Y	Y	
Project scheduling		Y		Y		
Resource skills		Y		Y	Y	

Quality:						
Internal failure	Y		Y			
Shipment and warranty	Y		Y	Y	Y	
Quality procedures	Y	Y	Y	Y	Y	
Hold information	Y	Y	Y			
Field failure information			Y	Y	Y	
Field service:						
Call tracking	Y			Y	Y	Y
Installed base information	Y	Y	Y	Y	Y	Y
Diagnostic	Y	Y		Y	Y	Y
R&D and technology:						
Bug and enhancement		Y	Y	Y	Y	
Manufacturing:						
Bill-of-material			Y			
Engineering change			Y			
CAD			Y			
Inventory and cycle count			Y			
Manufacturing item			Y			
Master scheduling			Y			

Information Need	Sales Site	System Eng Site	Manufacturing Site	Geographic Area	Global	Process Group
Material requirements planning			Y			
Manufacturing order			Y			
Purchasing			Y	Y	Y	Y
Vendor information			Y	Y	Y	Y
Capacity planning			Y			
Manufacturing routing and hours			Y			
Financial:						
Product cost			Y	Y		
Budgeting		Y	Y	Y		Y
Functional P&L	Y	Y	Y	Y	Y	Y
Balance statement				Y	Y	Y
General ledger		Y	Y	Y	Y	
Accounts payable		Y	Y	Y		
Fixed assets		Y	Y	Y		
Accounts receivable				Y	Y	Y
Credit	Y			Y	Y	Y
Sales tax				Y		
Foreign currency				Y	Y	

Human Resources:

Employee, position	Y		Y		
Payroll		Y	Y	Y	
Employee hours			Y	Y	Y
Benefit information		Y	Y		
Salary planning	Y		Y		
Applicant tracking			Y		
Employee training, skills	Y	Y	Y		

- E-business opportunities: For each stakeholder, identify the specific e-business opportunities by reviewing each step of the process and how the company wants to add value. Identify specific ways Web technology could be used. E-business opportunities would also have been identified in the business interviews in the first phase of the planning. Identify whether opportunities are informational, service related, transactional, interactive, or collaborative.
- Group the various e-business opportunities into phases.

Review the business application situation and direction. Identify the impact that e-business may have on the application environment. For example, as shown in Figure 6.13, each application area can be identified and prioritized that must be e-enabled.

Develop the Technical Infrastructure Direction

For a complex environment with many different components working together, it is necessary to have a common computing architecture. As the IS environment is expanded in the future, the additions must conform to the computing architecture to ensure that all components will continue to function together. Update this architecture on an ongoing basis with technology advances and changes. Start with the business operating vision in building the computing architecture rather than just focusing on technology itself. Have a business requirement or problem to solve before deploying technology. Looking at the IS mission and objectives developed earlier, determine what technical requirements are necessary to meet the business objectives.

It may be useful to separate the detailed technical architecture plan into a stand-alone document. This will provide the details necessary for the technical group, and this level of detail may not be necessary for business management. The following are the components of a separate technical architecture plan developed at one company:

- Executive summary: Provides summary information on the technical architecture plan. This section should also be included in the IS strategic plan for all business management.
- Architecture overview: Describes specific architectural principles, as well as identifying main system anchor points. Anchor points are technology or tools in which the company has a significant amount of money invested, and that will not change in the near future.

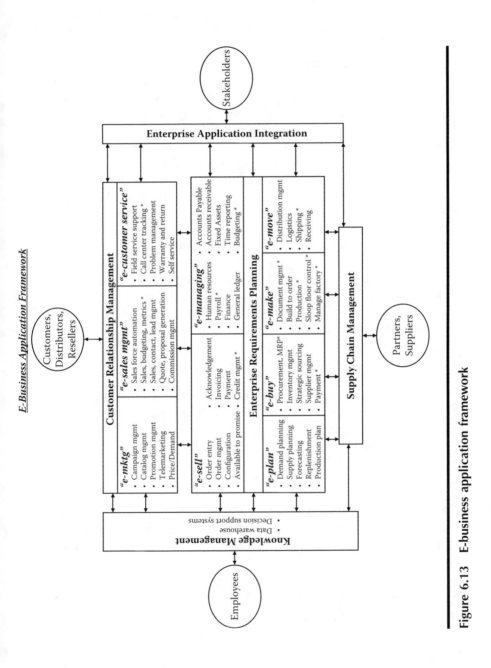

Figure 6.13   E-business application framework

■ Client architecture: Presents an examination of the hardware and software components that comprise the client architecture (PC, workstation). Details any assumptions made in the client architecture design, along with an analysis of implicit risks and concerns associated with its deployment and use.

■ Workgroup server architecture: Presents an examination of the hardware and software components that comprise the workgroup server architecture. Details any assumptions made in the workgroup server architecture design, along with an analysis of implicit risks and concerns associated with its deployment and use.

■ Enterprise server architecture: Presents an examination of the hardware and software components that comprise the enterprise server architecture. Details any assumptions made in the enterprise server architecture design, along with an analysis of implicit risks and concerns associated with its deployment and use.

■ LAN architecture: Presents an examination of the hardware and software components that comprise the LAN architecture. Details any assumptions made in the LAN architecture design, along with an analysis of implicit risks and concerns.

■ WAN architecture: Presents an examination of the hardware and software components that comprise the WAN architecture. Details any assumptions made in the WAN architecture design, along with an analysis of implicit risks and concerns.

■ Other enabling technologies: Provides a detailed look at the architecture associated with other add-on technologies.

■ Performance: Describes the physical placement of data and applications within the system, along with an analysis of its impact on performance. Outlines performance criteria and service-level expectations.

■ System management integration: Outlines the hardware and software necessary to manage the entire environment.

As with the business application direction, it is helpful to begin with identifying the guiding principles relative to the technical architecture. Exhibit 6.36 shows an example of technical infrastructure principles.

------------------------------▼------------------------------

Exhibit 6.36   Technical Infrastructure Direction

Technical Infrastructure Direction
The following principles will be the basis for the technical infrastructure direction:

- Standardize: The number of differing infrastructure components will be minimized. Whenever possible or reasonable, we will eliminate redundant components. Clearly defined standards will direct subsequent architecture choices. We will adhere to an approved software/hardware list. A standards-based architecture increases the ability to adapt to changes. Global standards will standardize on what to buy, but not from whom as countries can get better deals than shipping across borders.
- Mainstream technology use: *Mainstream* is defined to exclude advanced technologies not yet in general use and we will not have trailing-edge technology. Systems and infrastructure components will be kept relatively current so they are maintained and supported by the vendor, are current with the industry, and interface with other modern components. Obsolete hardware and technologies with no future will be sunset, rotated, and replaced. We will minimize risk through the use of proven technology.
- Scalability: Infrastructure components will be designed to be able to grow as the business grows. We will proactively manage and project capacity and will err on the side of over capacity rather than under capacity.
- Availability: The infrastructure will be designed for minimum downtime. Single points of failure will be eliminated or reduced after evaluating the cost of redundancy and the cost/risk of the outage. Systems and resources will be designed for 24/7 availability.
- Security: The technical infrastructure will be designed for a secure environment to ensure our business systems and data are protected. Reliable, robust, and scalable authentication methods must be deployed for all access, internal or external.
- Automation: Management of the infrastructure will be automated whenever possible to provide reliability and availability, and to reduce the long-term cost of ownership.
- Integration: Different components of the architecture will be integrated so that they function together transparently.
- Simplification, maintainability, and manageability: Products will be selected that are simple to install, administer, and support.
- Total cost of ownership: We will select products that minimize total cost of ownership. This includes purchase costs, implementation costs, training costs, maintenance costs, and support costs.

─────────────────────────────▲─────────────────────────────

Next, identify what must be done to accomplish the technical infrastructure principles. Review the current environment and the weaknesses. Identify the general areas that must be addressed to fill the gap. One area may include several individual projects. An example is provided in Exhibit 6.37.

▼

Exhibit 6.37   Technical Infrastructure Plan

Technical Infrastructure Plan (How Will We Get There?)

1. Disaster recovery and business continuance: As the business continues to increase its reliance on the systems, a disaster recovery plan is becoming even more critical than ever. Risk management has taken on a new light with the cyber attacks, viruses, 9/11, thefts, terrorism, risks due to war and weather, and other volatile global or political risks. With the move to a more centralized environment, protections are necessary.

   Today, the company does not have a disaster recovery plan or a business continuance plan, which is a significant risk to the business. The company must complete a risk assessment, identify mission and time critical data and systems, develop an appropriate disaster recovery strategy and plan that balances cost and risk, and develop an appropriate business continuance strategy and plan. The business continuance plan consists of the complete business operations and business processes that must take place in the event of a disaster. Finally, the plans must be implemented and tested.

2. Security: There are many security trends and technology that offer the company additional protection. Some areas of consideration include:
   - Anti-virus software: Viruses and worms are becoming more of a threat to companies than ever before. It is critical that the company stay up-to-date in anti-virus software and detection methods. New viral containment methods will also be deployed (i.e., personal firewalls).
   - ZENworks rollout: We will further the implementation of ZENworks to push virus scanning to the desktop to reduce the maintenance effort.
   - Single sign-on.
   - Firewalls.
   - DMZ.
   - Security policy.

3. Desktop rotation: Desktops must be continually kept up-to-date and modernized on a regular basis, in both software as well as hardware. Allowing PCs to get out-of-date will result in incompatibilities with basic computing provided in packaged software packages, communicating with outside entities, and performing basic functions such as printing and e-mail. Out-of-date and inconsistent desktops will also increase the support costs, total cost of ownership, and IS maintenance efforts.

   Today, we have approximately xxxx PCs and xxx laptops. We should rotate PCs on a four-year rotation, and every two years for laptops based on industry studies such as MHTA and Gartner Group.

4. Network: There are several network trends that offer us new technology to consider in the future. Some improvements could include:
   - Voice-over-IP (VoIP): An analysis must be completed to identify how and when we should convert to this technology. VoIP offers many advantages, such as a local dial plan throughout all sites, phone portability, and costs.

- Wireless: We have begun implementing wireless technology, and can expand its use. Wireless devices such as PDAs and downloading information to tools such as a Blackberry, mobile scanning devices, and other devices may prove to be valuable tools. Security issues and options, privacy issues, and interference are critical issues to address in the wireless direction.
- Phone switches.
- Voicemail system.
- Wiring.
- Load balancing using content switches.
- Upgrades: New network software provides improved reliability, manageability, and reduces costs. New network hardware components are smaller, faster, cheaper, and more powerful.
5. Server: Just as with desktops, we must continually improve the server environment to handle increased capacity needs due to business changes or new applications as well as taking advantage of advances in technology. The following are server enhancements that may be considered in the future:
   - Event management tools.
   - Capacity planning tools.
   - Consolidation.
   - Linux: We will continue to evaluate this technology and determine appropriate plans.
   - Blade servers: These are cluster-based systems that can be configured to include load-balancing and failover, and that can be hot-pluggable. This reduces the number of servers required, reduces costs, and improves availability and recoverability.
   - Clustering.
   - Fault tolerance.
   - Hyperthreading.
   - Grid computing.
   - Autonomic computing.

▲

Identify the various technologies and tools in the client, network, server, middleware, and application development environments. Identify technologies as follows:

- Strategic, full use: These technologies are strategic to the company and are in full use.
- Niche: These are departmental or specific use tools.
- Research: These technologies are in research and may become strategic once proven and tested. They can only be deployed for specific areas.
- Obsolete, sunset, transitional: These technologies may be in use, but the company is trying to phase out their use. They would be

provided with minimal IS support, but not development or upgrades.
- Unsupported: These are old technologies that are not supported and should not be in use.

Figure 6.14 shows an example of a plan for a technical infrastructure environment with a few of the products provided as examples. The categories and components should be reviewed and updated on an annual basis to reflect changes in technology.

Develop the Organizational Direction

Service architecture is the blueprint that specifies which IS processes and what kinds of people are required to support the business systems and computing architecture. The people side of the equation and direction cannot be overlooked; without the proper skilled people, a company cannot reach even the best-planned direction.

The service architecture includes:

- Processes: Major functions of the management IS organization
- People: Hiring, development, and compensation practices
- Organization: Internal structure of the management IS organization
- Culture: Values held within the management IS organization
- Technology: Characteristics of implemented technology
- Metrics: Methods of providing and ensuring quality

One company summarized the service architecture direction in Exhibit 6.38.

---------------------------▼---------------------------

Exhibit 6.38   Service Architecture

People

Business Area Experts

- Specialization by business processes
- Specialized knowledge of business systems that support those business processes
- General knowledge of technology

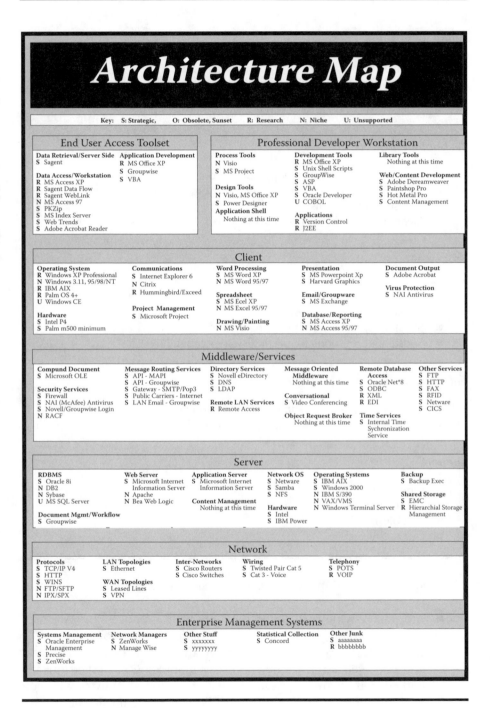

Architecture Map

Key: S: Strategic,   O: Obsolete, Sunset   R: Research   N: Niche   U: Unsupported

End User Access Toolset

Data Retrieval/Server Side
S Sagent

Data Access/Workstation
R MS Access XP
R Sagent Data Flow
R Sagent WebLink
N MS Access 97
S PKZip
S MS Index Server
S Web Trends
S Adobe Acrobat Reader

Application Development
R MS Office XP
S Groupwise
S VBA

Professional Developer Workstation

Process Tools
N Visio
S MS Project

Design Tools
N Visio, MS Office XP
S Power Designer

Application Shell
Nothing at this time

Development Tools
R MS Office XP
S Unix Shell Scripts
S GroupWise
S ASP
S VBA
S Oracle Developer
U COBOL

Applications
R Version Control
R J2EE

Library Tools
Nothing at this time

Web/Content Development
S Adobe Dereamweaver
S Paintshop Pro
S Hot Metal Pro
S Content Management

Client

Operating System
R Windows XP Professional
N Windows 3.11, 95/98/NT
R IBM AIX
R Palm OS 4+
U Windows CE

Hardware
S Intel P4
S Palm m500 minimum

Communications
S Internet Explorer 6
N Citrix
R Hummingbird/Exceed

Project Management
S Microsoft Project

Word Processing
S MS Word XP
N MS Word 95/97

Spreadsheet
S MS Ecel XP
N MS Excel 95/97

Drawing/Painting
N MS Visio

Presentation
S MS Powerpoint Xp
S Harvard Graphics

Email/Groupware
S MS Exchange

Database/Reporting
S MS Access XP
N MS Access 95/97

Document Output
S Adobe Acrobat

Virus Protection
S NAI Antivirus

Middleware/Services

Compund Document
S Microsoft OLE

Security Services
S Firewall
S NAI (McAfee) Antivirus
S Novell/Groupwise Login
N RACF

Message Routing Services
S API - MAPI
S API - Groupwise
S Gateway - SMTP/Pop3
S Public Carriers - Internet
S LAN Email - Groupwise

Directory Services
S Novell eDirectory
S DNS
S LDAP

Remote LAN Services
R Remote Access

Message Oriented Middleware
Nothing at this time

Conversational
S Video Conferencing

Object Request Broker
Nothing at this time

Remote Database Access
S Oracle Net*8
S ODBC
R XML
R EDI

Time Services
S Internal Time Sychronization Service

Other Services
S FTP
S HTTP
S FAX
S RFID
S Netware
S CICS

Server

RDBMS
S Oracle 8i
N DB2
N Sybase
U MS SQL Server

Document Mgmt/Workflow
S Groupwise

Web Server
S Microsoft Internet Information Server
N Apache
N Bea Web Logic

Application Server
S Microsoft Internet Information Server

Content Management
Nothing at this time

Network OS
S Netware
S Samba
S NFS

Hardware
S Intel
S IBM Power

Operating Systems
S IBM AIX
S Windows 2000
N IBM S/390
N VAX/VMS
N Windows Terminal Server

Backup
S Backup Exec

Shared Storage
S EMC
R Hierarchial Storage Management

Network

Protocols
S TCP/IP V4
S HTTP
S WINS
N FTP/SFTP
N IPX/SPX

LAN Topologies
S Ethernet

WAN Topologies
S Leased Lines
S VPN

Inter-Networks
S Cisco Routers
S Cisco Switches

Wiring
S Twisted Pair Cat 5
S Cat 3 - Voice

Telephony
S POTS
R VOIP

Enterprise Management Systems

Systems Management
S Oracle Enterprise Management
S Precise
S ZenWorks

Network Managers
S ZenWorks
N Manage Wise

Other Stuff
S xxxxxxx
S yyyyyyyy

Statistical Collection
S Concord

Other Junk
S aaaaaaaa
R bbbbbbbb

Figure 6.14   Architecture map

Application Experts

- Specialization by type of business system
- Specialized knowledge of business systems capabilities, operations, and supporting tools
- General knowledge of technology and business processes

Technology Experts

- Specialization by technology component
- Specialized knowledge of technology component capabilities, operations, and supporting tools
- General knowledge of business systems and business processes

Processes

Projects

- Deployment of new systems
- Substantial additions to existing system capabilities
- Substantial revisions to existing system capabilities

Enhancements

- Minor revisions to existing system capabilities
- Minor additions to existing system capabilities

Support

- Operations
- Maintenance
- Troubleshooting
- Consulting

▲

Some of the questions to consider in the service architecture include:

- Are you providing all the IS functions that are necessary? Are user areas providing support that the IS organization should?
- Are the IS processes efficient? Have the processes been mapped and reviewed for efficiency? Do user inquiries get handled quickly and efficiently? Are users satisfied with the support? Why or why not?
- Are you hiring people with the skill set you require in the future? Are you providing the proper development for employees? Can employees cross into other areas of IS and obtain cross training?

- Where and how should the company utilize outsourcing?
- What has been the turnover within the IS group? What have been some of the reasons for leaving?
- Are compensation policies aligned with market demands? Have you had significant turnover due to salaries?
- Is the organization structured efficiently? Do you have the functions that you will need in the future? Do job descriptions and titles accurately depict the functions that are needed today as well as in the future?
- Are the values reflected through daily decisions?
- Does the organization understand the direction?
- How do you measure IS efficiency and effectiveness?

Begin the service architecture by determining the organization direction. As was done with the business applications and technical infrastructure, develop organizational principles. An example of organizational principles is provided in Exhibit 6.39.

▼

Exhibit 6.39   Organizational Direction

IS Organizational Direction

- Worldwide leverage: Whenever possible, we will leverage IS resources globally. Although local resources will be assigned to meet global needs, overall costs will be reduced by leveraging resources. Redundant development groups and efforts will be eliminated.
- Minimize risk: Responsibilities will have a primary person as well as a secondary person identified to ensure proper backup and reduce overall risk. The IS group will invest in cross training to provide depth of knowledge and support. The overall IS staffing level will be planned in accordance with business needs.
- Consultants and outsourcing: If IS does not have the proper skill set or requires additional short-term assistance, consultants will be utilized as necessary. However, consultants will not be used for mission-critical ongoing activities without proper backup of knowledge internally. We will focus resources on areas of core competency and outsource nonstrategic areas that others can do better and less expensively. We will leverage application vendor staff of experts to support and maintain the applications.
- Simplify: The IS organizational structure will be kept simple with a minimum number of levels. Responsibilities will be clearly identified and defined by organization group and individual. The business users will understand where within IS to go for assistance.

- Employee Development: We will provide the necessary training so that personnel have up-to-date and necessary skills to maintain the systems. Internet programs, mentorship, and career paths will be used to provide employees with development and fulfillment.
- Empowerment: Whenever possible tools will be provided to business users to enable them to service themselves. Tools will also be provided to IS individuals for optimum efficiency and effectiveness.
- Staffing level: We will staff the IS function to a level that makes sense for the business. Costs and risks will be balanced to ensure the business needs are met. The IS priorities will be aligned with the business priorities.
- Business partner: The role of IS will be to partner with the business. IS will not be an "order taker," nor will IS dictate business decisions. Rather, IS will work with the business to proactively identify opportunities to best utilize technology to assist the business. To that end, the IS group will be staffed with business analysts that understand the business and can participate in business process reengineering efforts.
- Culture: IS will be a continuation of the company culture, valuing the employee, teamwork, communication, and productivity. We will promote a culture of fun while continuing to deliver quality service and support.

▬▬▬▬▬▬▬▬▬▬▬▬▬▬▬▬▲▬▬▬▬▬▬▬▬▬▬▬▬▬▬▬▬

A key organizational principle to address is outsourcing. At some point in time, management typically asks the question whether IS should be outsourced. Address this through the planning process. Identify whether outsourcing is a fit given the strategies and goals. Although total outsourcing may not be a good option, outsourcing certain aspects is typically sound management practice. It is important to identify which areas of IS are critical and should remain internal versus those functions that could be accomplished by an external party given a better cost of ownership proposition.

After identifying the organization principles, identify the tasks or projects that must be done to accomplish the principles. This may involve an organizational change. Changes in the role of IS, strategies, maturity, and technology may impact the organization and jobs responsibilities. For example, when client/server technologies were first introduced, many IS organizations were organized in the areas of network, PC, and business applications. They quickly found that the new client/server technology required skills that crossed all these areas to be effective. Many companies addressed this with additional growth opportunities and rewards for breadth of knowledge. Some companies implemented a "pay for skill" program. Job descriptions were also not indicative of the new technology and roles. Flexible and broad job descriptions were necessary so they would not require updating as the technology changed. Rather than having different titles for each function of IS (PC, network, business application),

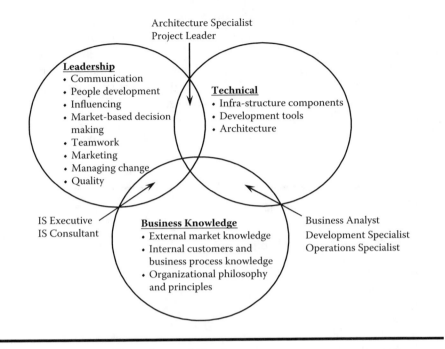

Figure 6.15   Future IS employee skill set

some companies chose generic titles and job descriptions to be used across all the functions. The jobs also encompassed several salary grades to accommodate the growth that was necessary. This also provided a technical career path that extended as high as the management ranks.

Through this process, your company may find it necessary to change job descriptions, titles, salary grades, and organizational structure. Although necessary, major changes such as these should be thoroughly considered before implementing as they can cause severe havoc in an IS organization, even if implemented carefully.

One company identified the new IS skill set that would be required for the future. It is a skill set that balances technical, leadership, and business knowledge skills that lead to greater resource optimization and well-rounded IS workers. In addition to investing in skills enhancement and staff retention, the company found it necessary to create new roles and responsibilities for both technical and business liaisons. The required skill sets are summarized in Figure 6.15.

Some companies find it necessary to review each open IS job and identify the specific skills desired, from both a personality side as well as the technical side. The desired skills can be prioritized (H: high, M: medium and L: low). A high priority means that an individual (no matter how good) would not be hired unless he or she had this skill. This can become a checklist and rating sheet for each individual interviewed. The list can also be used to provide a candidate with a checklist of what you are looking for and to ask that individual to rate his or her skills in each area. The list should be developed by the managers and individuals interviewing individuals for positions. It can be amazing to discover that each interviewer is looking for slightly different skill sets and individuals. Formulate interview questions to directly correlate to your desired criteria. An example is provided in Exhibit 6.40. Further define each adjective in a glossary.

▼

Exhibit 6.40   Skill Set Criteria

Senior IS Support Analyst (Application)

- H-Team player
- H-Independent
- H-Flexible
- M-Decision maker
- M-Leadership
- M-Dedication
- M-Career focus
- L-Company fit
- L-Visionary
- H-Analyst skills
- M-AS/400 skills
- M-Financial systems
- M-Multiplatform skills
- M-Years experience
- M-Specific vendor experience
- M-Desktop experience
- L-Education

Senior IS Support Analyst (Network)

- H-Communication
- H-Team player
- H-Independent
- H-Flexible
- H-Decision maker
- H-Visionary
- M-Dedication
- M-Career focus
- L-Company fit
- M-C++ experience

- L-Object orientation
- L-Education
- L-Experience
- H-Network architecture/design
- H-Network monitoring
- H-Server monitoring
- H-Capacity planning
- H-Security design
- H-Network performance tuning
- H-WAN experience
- M-Desktop experience
- M-UNIX experience

IS Support Architect (DBA)

- H-Team player
- H-Independent
- H-Flexible
- H-Decision maker
- H-Visionary
- H-Communication
- M-Leadership
- M-Dedication
- L-Career focus
- L-Company fit
- L-Education
- L-Experience
- H-Oracle experience
- H-Database security experience
- H-Backup/disaster recovery experience
- M-Worldwide replication
- M-Data warehouse, query tools
- M-UNIX experience
- M-NT experience
- M-Database performance tuning
- M-C++ experience
- L-Database design

Senior IS Support Analyst (Scientific)

- H-Team player
- H-Independent
- H-Flexible
- H-Dedication
- M-Decision maker
- M-Leadership

- M-Career focus
- L-Company fit
- L-Visionary
- L-Education
- H-DEC VAX VMS skills
- H-Years experience
- H-PC programming
- M-Analyst skills
- M-Statistical analysis
- M-Multiplatform experience
- M-UNIX experience
- M-Desktop experience
- M-Sybase/Oracle experience

IS Manager

- H-Communication
- H-Leadership
- H-Worker, set example
- H-Quick learner
- H-Decision maker
- H-Visionary
- M-Career focus
- M-Company fit
- M-Dedication
- H-Management experience
- H-Cross-platform experience
- H-Network management
- H-Data communication experience
- H-Desktop management
- H-Experience
- M-AS/400 management
- M-Technical background, programming
- M-Education

Senior IS Support Analyst (PC)

- H-People person
- H-Open-minded
- H-Creative
- H-Conviction
- H-Team player
- M-Company fit
- M-Database experience
- M-Microsoft certification
- M-Multi-platform experience

- M-Experience
- L-Education
- L-UNIX experience
- L-Oracle experience
- L-Notes experience
- H-Microsoft Office knowledge
- H-PC hardware knowledge
- H-PC programming, application development
- H-Cross-platform connectivity
- H-Middle-ware experience
- M-Network experience

▲

Also, review the skills of the existing resources and identify any training that will be necessary for each individual.

If you are significantly changing the organization or shuffling responsibilities, it can help to add clarity by providing a matrix with a column for each individual or group. For each individual, identify a list of that person's primary objectives as well as his or her secondary objectives. Each area of support should be identified under someone's name. It would be advisable to have items listed under more than one name to provide backup and depth of coverage. An example of this matrix is provided in Exhibit 6.41.

▼

Exhibit 6.41   Responsibility Matrix

Responsibility	*Person 1*	*Person 2*	*Person 3*	*Person 4*
Strategic planning	P			
Prioritizing projects	P			
Prioritizing requests		P		P
Ensure business alignment	P			
Communicating with business	P			
Communicating with IS	P			
Manage finances, budget	P			
Staffing, hiring	P			
Develop staff, career planning	P			
Performance management	P			

Responsibility	Person 1	Person 2	Person 3	Person 4
Salary reviews	P			
Vendor, contract management	P			
Policies, procedures, processes	P			
Personnel management	P			
Manage application group		P		
Business analysis		S	P	
Project management		S	P	
Financial systems				
Manufacturing systems				
Engineering systems				
Programming				
Lotus Notes				
Visual Basic				
Manage infrastructure group				P
DBA support				
WAN/network support				
LAN/server support				
AS/400				
Switches, hubs				
Firewall				
Novell administration				
Manage disk space, utilization				
Internet support				
Remote connectivity				
Backup support				
Phone support				
Security				
PC hardware support				

Responsibility	Person 1	Person 2	Person 3	Person 4
PC software support				
Install new PCs				
Palm support				
Printer support				
User training				
User calls, help desk				
Manage software licenses				
Track PC inventory				
Acquire PCs				

Develop IS Process Direction

Begin by identifying the principles for the IS process direction. An example of process principles is provided in Exhibit 6.42.

Exhibit 6.42   Process Direction

IS Process Direction

- Efficient and Effective: IS processes will be designed for overall efficiency and effectiveness.
- Automation: IS processes will be automated when possible to minimize cost and resource requirements. Industry-standard, up-to-date, but proven systems and technology will be used as necessary. An IS process will be improved before adding automation rather than automating a poor process. The IS process will be modified to fit software rather than modifying the software.
- Simplify: IS processes will be designed to eliminate waste and to simplify the overall process.
- Responsive: IS processes will be designed to be responsive to the needs of customers.
- Best practices: Whenever possible, the company will utilize best practices throughout the IS processes.
- Controlled, consistent, and repeatable: IS processes will be designed to be controlled, consistent, and repeatable. This will ensure that IS projects can be delivered on time and on budget, and meet the requirements.

■ Measured: Key metrics will be developed to measure the overall success and progress of IS and IS processes. A balanced scorecard will identify the IS metrics that are important to the business.

■ Continuous improvement: IS processes will be continuously improved.

▲

Next, review each IS process and identify it as high, medium, or low priority to the organization. For each process, assign a person within the IS group to be responsible for the process, as shown in Exhibit 6.43.

▼

Exhibit 6.43 Process Priority and Owner

	Improvement Priority	Process Owner
Manage systems:		
Capacity and storage management	Medium	Infrastructure manager
Performance and availability management	Medium	Infrastructure manager
Change management	High	Infrastructure manager
Backup and disaster recovery management	High	Infrastructure manager
Problem management	High	Infrastructure manager
Installation and configuration management		Infrastructure manager
Schedule management	Low	Infrastructure manager
Software distribution management	Medium	Infrastructure manager
Manage systems development:		
Understand requirements		Applications manager
Design solutions		Applications manager
Construct and integrate solutions		Applications manager
Test solutions		Applications manager
Customer acceptance		Applications manager

	Improvement Priority	Process Owner
Manage business relationships:		
Understand business needs		Applications manager
Market IS offerings		VP of IS
Service-level management	Low	VP of IS
Customer satisfaction management		VP of IS
Manage resources:		
Facilities management	Low	Infrastructure manager
Financial management	Medium	VP of IS
Vendor management	Low	VP of IS
IS strategic planning	Medium	VP of IS
Security management	High	Infrastructure manager
Inventory and asset management	High	Infrastructure manager
Human resources management	High	VP of IS

▲

Next, identify the specific projects that must be accomplished in the areas of processes. This could include general items to instill a process improvement culture within IS, specific process improvements, or tools that must be implemented.

As IS technology is moving out to the business, the IS organization may find that it has less control of the environment than in the past. Yet, it is even more critical for all the pieces to function together than it was in the past. Therefore, it is useful to establish certain guidelines, or policies and responsibilities, within which the business can operate while not jeopardizing the larger picture by conflicting with other objectives or tools in the environment.

Some of these items may be previously established in a corporate policies and procedures manual, in which case you can just reference the documents. Having policies and procedures well documented can save hours of frustration for both users and IS personnel. Be sure to update this information on a frequent basis and have convenient access of the information to all users. Identify any policies and procedures that require updating or development. The following are some examples of questions that should be addressed in policies and procedures:

1. What is the standard PC hardware that users can acquire that IS supports? What is the process for hardware acquisition? What requires the approval of the IS organization?
2. What is the standard PC software that the users can acquire that is supported by the IS organization? What software is available on the network? What is the process for software acquisition? What requires the approval of the IS organization?
3. Who is responsible for budgeting acquisition and depreciation of PCs? To whom does the PC belong? (For example, can IS redeploy or move PCs to match the business need?)
4. Who is responsible for ensuring optimum pricing on PC hardware and software (e.g., is it purchasing's or the IS organization's responsibility?)
5. Who is responsible for budgeting PC software, standard desktop software, as well as special software that is necessary? How do you ensure software license compliance?
6. How does the company manage PC retirement, and who is responsible? What methods do you utilize for PC disposal?
7. What standards does the company follow for user-developed PC applications? When does a PC business application become the support responsibility of the IS organization? What methods of backup and documentation are necessary? What are the policy and responsibilities for other user department tools that may be used, such as intranet, Internet, customer bulletin boards, EDI, and Lotus Notes applications?
8. What is the company policy regarding PC games and Internet access?
9. Who is responsible for organizing and funding PC training?
10. Who is responsible for ensuring a virus-free environment?
11. What is the responsibility of each remote site, and what is the responsibility of the central IS department?
12. What are the responsibilities of the users and IS for new business applications or projects?

Develop a Prioritization Process

IS projects must be aligned with the business objectives through the prioritization process. The following are common (although not recommended) prioritization processes:

Squeaky wheel: This is very common in IS organizations. IS works on projects from whichever group is screaming the loudest. This method can be very inefficient as priorities can change before completing projects in progress. It also does not ensure that projects with the most value to the business are addressed.

First in, first out (FIFO): Some IS organizations are essentially order takers, and complete projects in the order they are submitted. Again, this does not ensure that projects with the most value to the business are addressed.

Consensus: Consensus style typically involves the IS steering committee. They agree on what is the most important project and proceed. This process can be effective, but it can also be influenced by politics. An influential VP's favorite project can get pushed through the process rather than being selected through an objective review.

Return on investment (ROI): The ROI prioritization method attempts to add objectivity and business value into the selection criteria. However, the selection is only as accurate as the benefit numbers estimated. Often, a favorite project can be submitted with inflated benefits so that it is completed. Projects with benefits that are difficult to quantify, strategic efforts, and foundational projects may not be approved.

One company based the priority of projects on the following criteria:

■ User dissatisfaction with existing system as reported through surveys and interviews
■ Potential business benefits and alignment with the business goals
■ Number of areas that will receive benefits
■ Number of existing systems that are replaced

The IS steering committee should complete the prioritization process. Often, the prioritization can become an emotional and political event. With a solid process agreed to by the group before beginning, you can complete the prioritization process quickly and easily. This step of the planning process involves identifying and obtaining agreement on the prioritization process itself. Actually prioritizing projects will occur later in the process. However, it is helpful to discuss and agree on the process before discussing particular projects; that can get more emotional and a good processes helps tame the discussion. Use the prioritization process with projects in process that have obvious priorities to test and discuss each prioritization process.

It is possible to implement a prioritization process that is effective, efficient, and tolerable. After the prioritization process was completed in one company, an IS steering committee representative was asked what they thought of the process: "Of course I'm disappointed that my projects didn't come out on top, but I understand the process, why my projects didn't rank at the top, and agree that other projects are higher priority to the company." In another company, through the prioritization process, it was discovered that the IS group was working on projects in the wrong area of the company: manufacturing projects were being completed due to the involvement and pressure of the vice president of manufacturing. After going through a structured prioritization process, it was discovered that the marketing projects were more important to the strategic direction of the company.

Complete the prioritization only for projects above a certain level of effort or cost. This level should be set by the IS steering committee. The level should be high enough so the group is not evaluating every minor change, but low enough so the steering committee can direct the majority of time. The IS group can prioritize day-to-day individual requests and small projects with copies of the requests and priorities going to the IS steering committee for its information. However, projects must all be sponsored and represented by a member of the steering committee. The IS group presents only infrastructure projects.

Before beginning the prioritization process, the IS steering committee must have an understanding of the business purpose of each project. Ask each member of the committee to talk briefly about each project that has been requested from his or her area. The committee member can explain the purpose of the project and why it is important to the business.

Following are three processes to prioritize projects. Utilize whatever process best fits the environment, culture, and evolution of the IS steering committee. The processes are:

1. Prioritizing by business objective
2. Prioritizing by forced ranking
3. Prioritizing by business criteria

Prioritizing by Business Objective

1. List the business objectives.
2. Rank the importance of each business objective on a scale of 5–15, with 15 being the most important objective. If the company only has a few objectives, use 6–10 for mathematical purposes. The executive committee or the IS steering committee can help in this process.

3. List all the IS projects. If the list is too long, have the IS steering committee identify any low-priority projects that will not be prioritized and just list the projects to be prioritized.
4. Identify the impact (1–10) each will have on business objectives. With the IS steering committee, go through each project and discuss the impact the project will have on each business objective. Typically the sponsor of the project is the best able to score the project, but other members can challenge the rating. This is important to do in a group setting rather than an assignment because the entire group can gain appreciation for the importance of projects outside their area. Open debate and discussion should be encouraged, not avoided.
5. Multiply the impact times the business goal ranking and total the score for each project.
6. List projects in descending total score for a prioritized list of projects.
7. This mathematical model can only provide a starting point or recommended list. The IS steering committee can then review the list in total and make adjustments as needed. There may be other factors that affect the projects that were not identified in the business objectives, such as dates required or project dependencies.

Prioritizing by Forced Ranking

1. List all the IS projects. If the list is too long to prioritize the entire list, have the IS steering committee identify any low-priority projects that will not be prioritized and just list those projects to be prioritized.
2. Go through a forced ranking process by comparing the first project with the second, the first project with the third, fourth, and so on through the entire list. Then compare the second project with the third, fourth, fifth, and so on through the entire list. With each pair of projects, ask the IS steering committee members for a vote: if they could have only one project done of the two, which would they choose? The project with the most votes gets a mark. Do not spend time arguing, but rather ask for a vote, note the majority, and move on to the next project. Remind the steering committee members that it is their job to objectively determine projects with the most impact, rather than just voting for their own efforts.
3. Add up all the marks for each project. List the projects in descending order based on the marks for a prioritized list. Again, review the list in totality; this mathematical model only provides a starting point or recommended list.

Prioritizing by Business Performance Impact Criteria

This process is very similar to the prioritization process identified earlier for business processes:

1. Identify basic opportunities to impact performance, such as:
   - Impact to external customers or entities (e.g., customers, subsidiaries, buying groups, government agencies, ISO, SOX)
   - Impact on quality of service or product
   - Reduction of business costs
   - Impact on internal customers
   - Impact of the speed of the process
2. Rank the importance of the performance impact to the company using a scale of 7–10. This number will become the project multiplier.
3. List all the IS projects.
4. With the IS steering committee, agree on the impact the project will have on each of the performance impacts. Rate that impact on a scale of 0–10, with 10 having the highest impact.
5. Multiply the project multiplier times the rating for a score. Add up the total points for a project score.

List the projects in descending score order for a prioritized list of projects. Again, review the list in total because this mathematical model is only a starting guide.

Review and Confirm the IS Plan

This is a critical review point in the planning process. It is helpful to have the general direction of the business applications, technical infrastructure, organization, and processes discussed and approved before detailed prioritization, cost estimates, and project plans are developed. Review the plan for each area and the prioritization process with the IS steering committee.

Identifying IS Projects

Once the general plan is approved, next identify specific projects. Although you can identify projects in the areas of business applications, infrastructure, organization, and process, they should all end up on one list because they often utilize common resources. Review the plan and direction, and identify the projects. You may combine several projects together, or split large projects.

It may be helpful to develop project portfolio descriptions for each project. This could be a two-page overview that includes the following information for a project:

- Project title
- Project description
- Business sponsor
- Department requesting
- Business benefits
- External benefits (i.e., customers, stakeholders)
- Estimated business value (business continuance, medium business value, high business value)
- Estimated IS hours (small, medium, large, extra large)
- Estimated risk (high, medium, low)
- Estimated implementation cost (high, medium, low)
- Business implementation effort (high, medium, low)
- Recurring cost
- Project time frame
- Dependent projects
- Notes on project
- Priority

An example of a project profile is shown in Exhibit 6.44.

▼

Exhibit 6.44   Project Profile

Business Continuance and Disaster Recovery

Project Summary

Project Description: September 11 and increased terror threats have affected many businesses and provided new emphasis on business continuity and disaster recovery, particularly in government entities. With increased reliance on hardware and software, all businesses are evaluating their ability to recover and length of time to recover. Many companies are requiring automatic failover and continuous availability for critical applications.

Today, the County does not have a disaster recovery plan or a business continuance plan. This is a significant risk to the County. The Data Center has begun assembling phone numbers, contact information, and system documentation in the event of a disaster, but it is far from a full disaster recovery plan. No formal efforts have been made at the County to develop a business continuance plan.

The County will need to go through the following tasks to address this critical issue:

- Complete a risk assessment. Each disaster type has a different probability and carries a different impact on operations and recovery cost. The County must determine the desired recovery time after analyzing the risk.
- Identify mission- and time-critical data. The County must have a complete inventory of its data and applications and identify whether they are mission critical, critical, or noncritical.
- Develop an appropriate disaster recovery strategy and plan.
- Develop an appropriate business continuance strategy and plan. This will consist of the complete business operations and business processes that must take place in the event of a disaster. The plan will be developed through a partnership with IS, the business, and Corporate Audit.
- Implement and test the plans.
- Maintain the plans.
- Formalize and document the backup and disaster recovery process.

Business Benefits:

- Reduced risk (risk in loss of information, damaged reputation, loss in productivity, loss of revenue or financial performance, loss in services to citizens)

Estimated Business Value:

✔ Business Continuance ____ Medium Business Value ____High Business Value

Estimated IS Hours:

____ Small (< 200 hours)   ✔ Large (501–1200 hours)
____ Medium (200–500 hours)   ____ Extra Large (Greater than 1200)

Estimated Risk:	High	Medium	✔Low

Estimated Cost:	High	✔Medium	Low
	>$1M	$500K-$1M	<$500K

Recurring Cost:	$xxxx

Proposed Project Time Frame:	Q2 2006–Q3 2007

Dependent Projects:	None

Estimate IS Costs

For each project, estimate the costs. Depending on the company culture and the maturity of the planning process, this cost estimation can vary in detail and rigor. Some companies merely assign high, medium, or low cost ranges. Cultures that are more cost conscious must plan the costs in detail because funds cannot be increased after the budget is established. Complete costs should be identified, such as:

- Hardware costs
- Software costs (include all components of this, such as first-year maintenance cost, tax, all various modules, database)
- Internal IS resource costs
- Internal business resource costs
- External consulting costs
- Custom programming and implementation costs
- IS training
- User training
- IS and business documentation
- Travel costs
- Business process reengineering costs
- Miscellaneous expenses

Identify Business Benefits

Just as with costs, different companies go to a different level of detail in identifying the business benefits. It could be a simple estimate of high, medium, or low range, or it could be all the exact business benefits quantified. Keep in mind that actual benefits should be reviewed after project implementation in the postaudit process to ensure that the projected benefits are realized. Some benefits may be quantifiable, and some may not be easily quantified. Examples of areas of benefits include:

- IS operational savings
- Resource efficiencies
- Inventory reduction
- Opportunity cost of constrained growth
- Customer satisfaction
- Freight and postage costs
- Claims
- Risk reduction
- Cash flow
- Sales increase

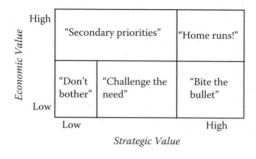

Figure 6.16   Strategic grid

Prioritize IS Projects

Next prioritize the projects with the assistance of the IS steering committee using the prioritization method determined earlier. One company summarized the application priorities by taking all the groups of information needs that were necessary to meet the business objectives and ranked them on a grid of economic value and strategic value. This grid identified those areas that were definite "home runs" for the company; those with high economic value and high strategic value as opposed to those that were applications they should not bother with because they had a low economic value and a low strategic value. The grid is shown in Figure 6.16.

After the prioritization process is complete, then balance against project resources available to determine how far down the list projects can be accomplished during the next year. Be sure to reserve resources for day-to-day support and maintenance activity. Allocate only the percent of resources able to be allocated to projects. List the projects in priority order with the estimated hours. From the work done earlier identifying resources and backlog, you have the number of project hours that you can accommodate with the current resources. Draw a line where the resources are depleted for the year. Consider skill type and availability required for the projects. The IS steering committee can then review the projects below the line. If the projects are critical to be completed this year, the committee has the choice of adding additional resources, either full-time or contract, to accommodate the business need.

Review and Confirm the IS Projects and Prioritization

Present this information to all the various planning groups, including the IS steering committee, IS organization, and finally, the executive committee.

Conclusion

Congratulations! You are now able to complete the direction sections of the IS strategic plan document and have accomplished the following:

- Developed the IS vision, mission, goals, and strategies
- Determined how to measure the success of IS
- Developed the principles and direction for the business applications, technical infrastructure, organization, and IS processes
- Developed a prioritization process, identified IS projects, and prioritized them after identification of costs and benefits

Notes for My IS Strategic Planning Project

_____

_____

_____

_____

_____

_____

_____

_____

_____

_____

_____

_____

_____

_____

_____

_____

_____

_____

_____

_____

_____

Chapter 7

The Recommendation Phase

*People are afraid of the future, of the unknown. If a man faces
up to it, and takes the dare of the future, he can have some
control over his destiny. That's an exciting idea to me. Better
than waiting with everybody else to see what's going to happen.*

— John H. Glenn Jr. (B. 1921)
American astronaut, U.S. Senator

Now that the IS direction is clear, it is important to document the detailed
roadmap for how to get from where you are today to where you want
to be. As shown in Figure 7.1, the fourth phase of the planning process
is the recommendation phase. In this phase, you will document the
detailed road map and steps to achieving the stated direction. A solid
road map ensures that the plan becomes actionable rather than a book
on the shelf. As shown in Figure 7.2, the recommendation phase has the
following components:

- Develop a road map
- Develop a business case
- Communicate the plan

Each of these components is discussed in more detail in this chapter.

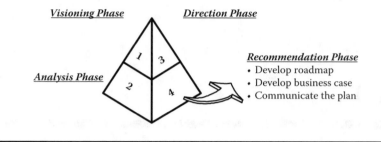

Visioning Phase Direction Phase

Analysis Phase

1 3

2 4

Recommendation Phase
• Develop roadmap
• Develop business case
• Communicate the plan

Figure 7.1 The recommendation phase

Develop a Road Map

Document a Detailed Road Map

In the previous phase, all the IS projects were identified and prioritized, costs were identified, and an implementation time frame was planned. Next, you need to organize the projects together on a timeline, or road map. A partial road map example is shown in Figure 7.3. You may also want to outline the various phases of a large project, as shown in the example in Figure 7.4.

Summarize Costs

Costs were estimated in the previous phases, but the estimates may have been high-level ones. Fine-tune the estimates for the immediate projects planned following your company-specific financial planning requirements. Establish the budget and communicate the monthly financial impact, accounts, and impact to capital and expense budgets. Table 7.1 shows an example of how one company illustrated the impact to the annual forecasted budget.

As mentioned earlier, be sure to include all costs, such as the following:

■ Hardware costs
■ Software costs (include all components of this, such as first year maintenance cost, tax, all various modules, databases)
■ Internal IS resource costs
■ Internal business resource costs
■ External consulting costs
■ Custom programming and implementation costs
■ IS training

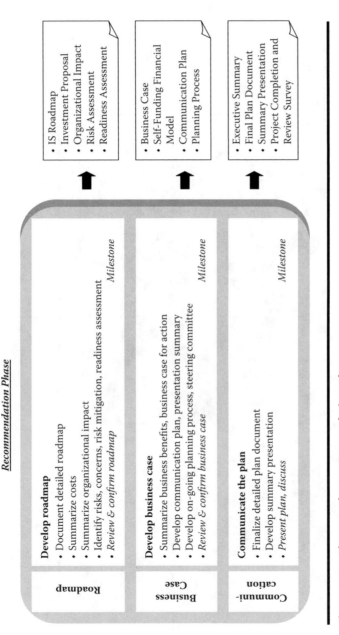

Figure 7.2 Phase 4, the recommendation phase

Project	2005				2006				2007				Business Value	Risk	Cost	IS Hours
	Q1	Q2	Q3	Q4	Q1	Q2	Q3	Q4	Q1	Q2	Q3	Q4				
Business Continuance and Disaster Recovery													Business Continuance	Low	Medium	Large
Data Storage and Reporting													Medium	Medium	Medium	Medium
Desktop Rotation													Business Continuance	Low	Medium	Medium
Document Management													High	Medium	Medium	Medium
E-Government													High	High	High	Extra Large
Enterprise Event Management and Service Desk System													High	Medium	Medium	Medium
Network Improvements													Business Continuance	Medium	Medium	Medium
Security Improvements													Business Continuance	Low	Low	Medium
Server Rotation and Server Improvements													Business Continuance	Medium	Low	Medium
Systems Development Process Improvement													Medium	Low	Low	Medium
Wireless													Medium	Medium	Medium	Medium

Figure 7.3   Road map

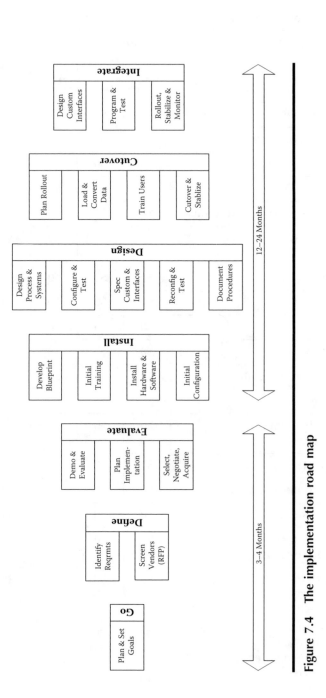

Figure 7.4 The implementation road map

Table 7.1 Budget Impact

Proposed IS Budget					
	2003	2004	2005	2006	2007
	Dec 03	Dec 02	Dec 01	Mar 01	Mar 00
Wages and benefits	$0	$0	$0	$0	$0
Contract and consultants	$0	$0	$0	$0	$0
Training, dues, subscriptions	$0	$0	$0	$0	$0
Supplies	$0	$0	$0	$0	$0
Computer hardware/software/misc.	$0	$0	$0	$0	$0
Computer software, licenses, maintenance	$0	$0	$0	$0	$0
Telephone	$0	$0	$0	$0	$0
Travel	$0	$0	$0	$0	$0
Miscellaneous	$0	$0	$0	$0	$0
Lease equipment	$0	$0	$0	$0	$0
Depreciation from capital	$0	$0	$0	$0	$0
Total IT Direct	**$0**	**$0**	**$0**	**$0**	**$0**
Division A US computer depreciation	$0	$0	$0	$0	$0
Amsterdam ITS expenses	$0	$0	$0	$0	$0
Europe computer depreciation	$0	$0	$0	$0	$0
Division B computer depreciation	$0	$0	$0	$0	$0
Division C shop computer depreciation (estimated)	$0	$0	$0	$0	$0
Total IT Costs	**$0**	**$0**	**$0**	**$0**	**$0**

- Personnel xx%
- xx% increase from 2003
- IS costs as a % of sales: x.x%
- IS spending/employee: $x,xxx
- Hidden IS costs
- $xxxK capital

- User training
- IS and business documentation
- Travel costs
- Business process reengineering costs
- Miscellaneous expenses

Summarize Organization Impact

Review the organizational plan and develop detailed action items. Consider:

- Individual performance discussions that need to occur
- Promotions that need to occur
- Organizational structure changes
- Personnel changes that may be necessary
- Resources that may need to be added
- Consulting resources that may be necessary to augment the staff
- Communication required for organization changes
- Impact to career paths
- Impact to salary structures
- Job descriptions that require updating
- Bonus plan or rewards program development
- Training that is necessary

It is important to take your time when dealing with organizational and people changes. Make sure any changes are well planned and executed with caution. It is important to understand and be sensitive to the change management issues that occur during the implementation of a new strategic direction. Many times, a strategic plan can indicate an entirely new direction that can have a significant impact on people and their roles and responsibilities. The CIO must understand the change process, communicate the right messages in a timely manner, and understand the impediments to change and plan how to overcome them. Consider the changes to the organization, culture, and individuals. Cultural changes often take a long time to apply and can be difficult to implement. Changes resulting from a new strategic plan can be dramatic and traumatic for some individuals. Do not make assumptions that individuals understand or agree with the new strategic direction and their role in the direction. Communication must occur often, on a regular basis, and must be consistent.

During the implementation of a new strategic direction, individuals may go through various stages, such as the initial realization of the new direction and the impact of the direction on them. They may begin to overcome anxiety and resistance as additional clarity is provided, particularly as their role is further defined. Next, they accept their new roles and responsibilities and see the benefits of the changes and new direction. Finally, they become supportive of the changes and personally committed to the success. It is important that the CIO recognize the stages and help individuals through the change process. As mentioned earlier, the way to do this is with communication that is continuous, complete, enthusiastic, simple, and honest. If the strategic plan is not communicated properly or completely, individuals typically fill the gaps with speculation and rumors. Regular status updates with open discussions of issues, concerns, and problems are critical throughout the process of implementing a new direction.

Identify Risks, Concerns, Risk Mitigation, and Readiness Assessment

The implementation plan should also address a plan for risk management. When completing an IS strategic plan, a large project is often highlighted as a critical need for the organization. Although completing a project may be very important for an organization, the company must be ready to execute the project. It is far better to not begin a project if the organization is not ready than to begin the project and fail. Any large effort, particularly one that involves major change, has a chance for failure. Identify reasons why the project could fail and what you plan to do to avoid each potential failure. The following are some reasons that projects fail:

Communication: How do you plan to keep the entire organization abreast of the project?

Inadequate project planning and control: How will you ensure all phases of the project are planned? What will be the method of ensuring control of the project? Who is responsible for planning? Who is responsible for controlling the project?

Unrealistic timetable: Have you received several opinions on the timetable for implementation? If the time frames are unrealistic at the beginning, they are bound to get worse!

Not prepared for extra work: Are both your user community and IS organization prepared for the level of resource commitment necessary?

Attempt to modify package: If you have identified benefits to be gained by implementing a standard vendor-supportable package, how will you ensure that modifications will be kept to an absolute minimum?

Too much reliance on vendor: What will be the role of internal resources and consultants? Who has ultimate responsibility for the project?

Unrealistic expectations: Can the project attain the objectives established?

Inadequate training: Is a training plan and costs included for both the IS organization as well as the user community?

Poorly defined requirements: Are the objectives of the project clear and understood by everyone?

Lack of management involvement: Do you have all the right players involved in the project?

Inadequate hardware configuration: Have you received benchmark information on the hardware sizing? Do you have contractual arrangements relative to the hardware sizing?

New technology: Is the technology proven? If not, how will you address the risk?

Package fit: Will there be a conference room pilot to confirm the software choice?

Skills: Will you train? Will you utilize consultants? What will be the role of the consultants?

Inadequate testing: What will be the testing phases? How will you assess readiness to implement?

Many areas of risk must be considered for large critical projects. Here are some areas of risk to consider:

Commitment: Consider commitment of the sponsor, user management, the user organization, and the relation to strategic business plans.

Project impact: Consider whether it is a new system, and the impact on computer operations, procedures, organization, policies, reports, and metrics.

Project size: Consider the total number of hours, calendar time, team size, number of sites impacted, interfaces to existing systems, organizations to coordinate, project budget, and number of end users.

Project definition: Consider the project scope definition, project scope breadth, the project deliverable definition, project deliverable complexity, benefits of the new system, complexity of requirements, user knowledge, business knowledge of the team, availability of documentation, and dependence on other projects.

Staffing: Consider the project manager experience, whether the team is full-time, the team experience, and the team location.

Structure: Consider the methodology used, change management procedures, quality management procedures, knowledge coordination procedures, the work project plan, the issue management process, and the decision management process.

Complexity: Consider the type of processing, response time requirements, availability requirements, technology mix, data complexity, and data quality.

Hardware and software: Consider the hardware requirements, hardware availability, knowledge of software, previous work with vendor, functional match to technical requirements, amount of IS involvement during software selection, and the vendor reputation.

Development: Consider the tools and techniques, language, and database.

A checklist can be a valuable tool to rate and communicate the risk. Examples of risk assessment checklists are shown in Exhibit 7.1 and Exhibit 7.2. After identifying the risks, prioritize the risks and develop a plan to mitigate each risk.

---------------------------------▼---------------------------------

Exhibit 7.1   Project Risk Assessment

Commitment

Factor	Question	Risk
Project sponsorship	The project sponsor is identified, enthusiastic, and has strong user influence.	1 2 3 4 5
Commitment of user management	The general attitude of managers is that they understand the value and support the project.	1 2 3 4 5
Commitment of user organizations	The general attitude of the user organizations is that they understand the value and support the project.	1 2 3 4 5
Relation to strategic plans	The new system is included in business plans, or added with approval.	1 2 3 4 5

Project Impact

Factor	Question	Risk
Replacement or new system	The project replaces an existing, primarily automated system rather than being a new system.	1 2 3 4 5

Factor	Question	Risk
Effect on computer operations	There is little change to the computer operations.	1 2 3 4 5
Procedural changes imposed by the new system	There is little change to the procedures required to support the new system.	1 2 3 4 5
Changes to organizational structure	No changes are planned to the organizational structure.	1 2 3 4 5
Policy changes	No policy changes are required to support the new system.	1 2 3 4 5
Effect on highly visible reports and metrics	Implementation of this project will not have a direct effect on business metrics.	1 2 3 4 5

Project Size

Factor	Question	Risk
Person hours	The total number of estimated hours for the project is less than 3,000.	1 2 3 4 5
Calendar time	The project is estimated for completion is less than 4 months calendar time.	1 2 3 4 5
Team size	The estimated team size, at its peak, will be 4 or fewer members.	1 2 3 4 5
Sites	Only one physical location will use the production system.	1 2 3 4 5
Interfaces to existing systems	There are no existing systems with which the new system must interface.	1 2 3 4 5
Organizations to coordinate	Only one user organization is involved with the system.	1 2 3 4 5
Project budget	The total project budget (external dollars) is less than $10K.	1 2 3 4 5
Number of end users	The number of end users is expected to be less than 20.	1 2 3 4 5

Project Definition

Factor	Question	Risk
Project scope definition	The project scope is well defined.	1 2 3 4 5
Project scope breadth	The project scope is straightforward with only one function or process.	1 2 3 4 5
Project deliverable definition	The project deliverables are well defined.	1 2 3 4 5
Project deliverable complexity	The project deliverables are straightforward, typical of other project deliverables.	1 2 3 4 5
Benefits of new system	The benefits of the new system are well defined or quantified or of strategic importance.	1 2 3 4 5
Complexity of requirements	The requirements of the system are straightforward and understandable.	1 2 3 4 5
User knowledge	Personnel responsible for providing application knowledge on the project are knowledgeable in both user and IS areas.	1 2 3 4 5
Business knowledge of project team	All project team members are highly knowledgeable about or experienced in the business area.	1 2 3 4 5
Availability of documentation	The status of the documentation of existing systems and procedures in the user areas is complete and current.	1 2 3 4 5
Dependence on other projects	There are no other development efforts on which this system is dependent.	1 2 3 4 5
Dependence of other systems on this project	There are no other systems development projects that are dependent on this project.	1 2 3 4 5

Staffing

Factor	Question	Risk
Project manager experience	The experience level of project managers is high; they have three or more prior projects of similar scope.	1 2 3 4 5
Full-time project manager	The project manager manages this project on a full-time basis.	1 2 3 4 5
Full-time project team	The project team is assigned to the project full-time.	1 2 3 4 5
Experience as a team	The team members have all worked together in the past.	1 2 3 4 5
Team's experience with application	The team members have implemented this application system more than once in the past.	1 2 3 4 5
Team location	The members of the team are physically located together.	1 2 3 4 5

Structure

Factor	Question	Risk
Methodology use	The methodology and other standards to be used on the project are fully documented and have been used before.	1 2 3 4 5
Change management procedures	The change management procedures for the project are well defined and accepted.	1 2 3 4 5
Quality management procedures	The quality management procedures for the project are well defined and accepted.	1 2 3 4 5
Knowledge coordination procedures	The knowledge coordination procedures for this project are well defined and accepted.	1 2 3 4 5

Factor	Question	Risk
Work project plan	The work project plan is documented.	1 2 3 4 5
Issue management process	An issue management repository and process exist.	1 2 3 4 5
Decision management process	A formal decisions management process exists.	1 2 3 4 5

Complexity

Factor	Question	Risk
Type of processing	The system requires only batch processing or simple online query and updating.	1 2 3 4 5
Response time as critical requirement	The system requirements for online response time are not challenging.	1 2 3 4 5
Requirements for system availability	The system availability (unplanned downtime) is not challenging.	1 2 3 4 5
Technology mix	Type of technologies the system requires (e.g., DBMS, networking, servers) is existing or simple architecture.	1 2 3 4 5
Data complexity	The level of complexity of the data used by the new system (measured by the number of entities and the relationships between them) is not complex.	1 2 3 4 5
Data quality	The quality of data for the conversion process is simple to convert or of good quality.	1 2 3 4 5

Hardware and Software

Factor	Question	Risk
New or nonstandard hardware or system software	There are no requirements for new hardware or system software.	1 2 3 4 5
Factor	*Question*	*Risk*
Availability of hardware for development and testing	Hardware is guaranteed available for development and testing.	1 2 3 4 5
Knowledge of package	The team has previous knowledge of the package to be installed.	1 2 3 4 5
IS prior work with vendor	IT has worked with the vendor of the package several times.	1 2 3 4 5
Functional match to system requirements	The package matches the system requirements very well and minimal or no customization will be required.	1 2 3 4 5
IS involvement in package selection	IS was heavily involved during the selection.	1 2 3 4 5
Vendor reputation	The vendor reputation is very good.	1 2 3 4 5

Development

Factor	Question	Risk
Tools and techniques	The development tools and techniques used by the project team will be very familiar to them.	1 2 3 4 5
Language	The project requires no new languages.	1 2 3 4 5
DBMS	The project will use a database that is well established in the organization.	1 2 3 4 5

▲

▼

Exhibit 7.2   Project Readiness Assessment

	Strongly Disagree				Strongly Agree

Organization:

■ Does user management want the project?	1	2	3	4	5
■ Do you have the support of upper management?	1	2	3	4	5

Project Team:

■ Is a project leader/manager assigned?	1	2	3	4	5
■ Has a project sponsor been identified?	1	2	3	4	5
■ Have enough resources been assigned to the project?	1	2	3	4	5
■ Do project team members have the necessary authority?	1	2	3	4	5
■ Are users deciding the business issues?	1	2	3	4	5
■ Are IS individuals deciding the technical issues?	1	2	3	4	5
■ Does everyone understand the business issues?	1	2	3	4	5
■ Do team members have sufficient knowledge?	1	2	3	4	5
■ Have team members been trained?	1	2	3	4	5
■ Is the project manager actively involved and understand the details of the project?	1	2	3	4	5

Project Plan:

■ Is there a formal project plan?	1	2	3	4	5
■ Is there a detailed project schedule?	1	2	3	4	5
■ Do individuals understand their roles and responsibilities?	1	2	3	4	5
■ Are the requirements, goals, objectives and vision clear?	1	2	3	4	5
■ Is it clear how success will be measured?	1	2	3	4	5
■ Are task estimates realistic? Do they account for vacation, sick, and nonproject time?	1	2	3	4	5
■ Are there short-term deliverables?	1	2	3	4	5
■ Are tasks structured so you can tell when they are done?	1	2	3	4	5
■ Is one person responsible for each task?	1	2	3	4	5
■ Are team members clear about what tasks are assigned and when they are due?	1	2	3	4	5
■ Is the budget for the project adequate?	1	2	3	4	5
■ Are expectations realistic?	1	2	3	4	5

Project:

■ Does the project utilize a methodology?	1	2	3	4	5
■ Is communication within the project team regular, thorough, and accurate?	1	2	3	4	5

- Is communication outside the project team good?   1   2   3   4   5
- Is the team environment honest, respectful, open, positive, and encouraging of new ideas?   1   2   3   4   5
- Are decisions made in a timely manner?   1   2   3   4   5
- Are there regular reports to management on the status of the project?   1   2   3   4   5
- Is there a methodology to track changes and problems?   1   2   3   4   5
- Are meetings structured and worthwhile?   1   2   3   4   5
- Are there control mechanisms?   1   2   3   4   5
- Has documentation been completed?   1   2   3   4   5
- Are there weekly progress reports by all team members? 1   2   3   4   5
- Are hours tracked by task and variances reported?   1   2   3   4   5
- Is the technology proven?   1   2   3   4   5

The risk assessment may help identify any areas that must change before a large project begins or identify specific actions that must be taken to mitigate the risks. Next, summarize the overall readiness to implement. Exhibit 7.3 provides an example of recommendations resulting from one company assessing its readiness.

Exhibit 7.3   Readiness Assessment

Implementation Readiness

- The company should not start the project unless everyone is ready to commit and assign the resources to make it successful. **The project must be the top priority!**
- Active, continual, and visible **executive support** is critical to success. The project will have difficult times, and it is this executive support and belief that will pull it through to completion.
- To be successful, **key people must be assigned**; those that you can least afford to lose. This is not a project for amateurs.
- **Less is more**. Having fewer people committed full time to the project is more effective than having many people each committed part time. Those key business individuals who are committed to the project on a full-time basis must have all of their duties back-filled by others. A part-time team moves much slower and wastes time making decisions by committee rather than analyzing, deciding, testing, validating with peers, and moving on to the next issue.
- **Emphasize the goals** and key outcomes the company hopes to achieve with the new system. This will help avoid re-creating the old system within the new software package. Sometimes you need to change policy to achieve the goal, so **empower the team** to challenge the rules where it makes sense to do so.

- A sold, well-thought-through **plan** is critical before beginning the effort. Have small and manageable project milestones. Clearly define project goals, objectives, and business direction. Before starting the effort, the company should clearly define the expectations and parameters.
- **Leadership**, management, and ongoing governance and control of the project is critical. Use structured project management processes: requirements analysis, scripted demonstrations, due diligence, rigorous project management, and change management. Testing must be thorough and disciplined to make sure it fits the business.
- Be sure to **select software** that fits the business today as well as the needs tomorrow.
- Plan on **using the software as standard** as possible. Customizations significantly increase the overall cost of ownership. This could be a critical failure point for the company, as they are very used to customizing and molding software for their specific needs. If this culture does not change, the project implementation could be a disaster if they go into it with the attitude of customizing. Customized software is not easy to upgrade to new releases, taking advantage of technology advances in the market. In addition, the overall cost of ownership is higher with a customized package rather than letting the vendor modify it and spread the costs over all their customers.
- The project will require **changing business processes**. The company must be ready to do that. The company will require business process improvement training.
- **Do not underestimate** the effort in terms of resources, costs, and impact to the organization.
- Communication and training are critical **change management** elements.
- View the project as a key **business project**, not an IT effort. Choose a project sponsor from the business. Make sure it is the business that establishes the goals and vision for the project.
- Use help from **experienced resources** to reduce time and risk to the company. The staff should be supplemented by expert consultants during the implementation.
- Plan to do **ongoing continuous improvement** effort after implementation. It is not done when the project goes live.
- Identify and implement in **phases** to reduce risk and improve manageability. However, the solution must be planned in total rather than piecemeal. In other words, plan for the whole; execute in pieces. A planned, measured execution will improve the likelihood of success and reduce the cost and risk.
- **Select democratically, implement autocratically.** A consensus-based selection helps achieve buy-in and mitigate the risk that someone might undermine the solution. Because the selection involves one big decision, it is reasonable to choose by committee. However, an implementation is made up of thousands of detailed decisions that build on each other. It would take years to make these decisions by committee. Rather, one or two respected individuals should design and configure the software with regular input and guidance from the broader user community.

▲

Review and Confirm Road Map

This is a great milestone to review the roadmap with the IS steering committee and the IS organization. It is far better to catch items that may have been underestimated or forgotten before the project is in progress, so ask both groups for items that have been missed.

Develop a Business Case

Summarize Business Benefits and a Business Case for Action

Before presenting the final recommendations to executive management for approval, you often need a return on investment (ROI) analysis. This could also be a net present value or internal rate of return depending on the requirements at your company. Executive management typically needs to know how much it will cost and how much benefit it will have to the business before making an investment decision. Depending on your company culture, this step may or may not be significant. It is extremely helpful if the business groups complete this economic analysis as they need to sign up for and deliver the anticipated savings. Exhibit 7.4 shows one example of an ROI analysis for a company, and Figure 7.5 shows an ROI calculation format.

──────────────────────────── ▼ ────────────────────────────

Exhibit 7.4   ROI Analysis

The business recognizes that improving our IS is a critical action and key enabler for our future business direction. We recognize that improving IS is the number two overall divisional business priority during the next year. Although we will outline benefits of implementing a new system in more detail in the Appropriations Request, this section will outline an overview of the key benefits.

The ROI for the implementation of the new system is xx%. This ROI is based on a capital request of $xK and implementation costs of $xK. The expected benefits for this program have been segregated into four categories: sales impact, direct material savings, manufacturing resource improvements, and asset management. The detailed ROI forms and schedules are included in the appendix.

Sales Impact:
A conservative estimate of the sales impact from implementing a new system is x% of market share (for example, with the system, we expect worldwide market share to be xx% in FY 2006; without the system, we expect worldwide market

share to drop to *xx*%). The dollar impact of this improvement is $xxK in operating profit five years after implementation.

One of the reasons for this market share improvement is better customer interfaces. Customers are currently demanding greater access to our system, which we will be able to provide with the new system. Additionally, the new system will allow us to more accurately process orders, update orders for changes, and provide more timely information on order status. We will provide improved responsiveness to customer needs with immediate information, which we do not have today. Ship complete logic, available to promise, customer credit card processing, and customer bar coding are just a few examples of customer requests that we are unable to meet today. These benefits are critical to ensure that we protect the market share we currently have.

The new system will also allow us to improve lead times, improve service levels, and reduce the time to market on new products and line extensions. Time-to-market will decrease through concurrent engineering, preferred vendor and parts lists, commonality of product design across multiple products, and a seamless integration between our engineering systems and business systems. These are key attributes that a system will need to provide for the division to grow its market share.

Direct Material Savings:

Direct material savings will come from two areas: yield improvements and reduced purchase costs. The model assumption is that yields, with the new system, will improve from *xx.x*% in FY 2004 to *xx.x*% in FY 2006. However, without the system, yields will improve only slightly, from *xx*% to *xx*%. These yield improvements are made possible by improved feedback within the shop control system that will allow for more timely response to process problems.

We will improve purchase costs because the system will provide our suppliers with better access to our forecasts and specs, as well as improved supplier management, common parts, and common designs. With worldwide purchasing information available, we will be able to leverage global procurement and planning strategies. We will also realize cost savings through a streamlined interface to our suppliers with electronic document transfer. The ROI model assumes that with the system we will be able to reach our net inflation goal of *x*%; however, without the system we assume that net inflation will be *x*%.

Together, these material cost reductions will generate material cost savings of $*xxxx*K in FY 2006 (*x*% of sales).

Manufacturing Resource Improvements:

The new system will not only allow us to do what we currently do more efficiently, but it will also allow us to grow the business without added resources as quickly as would be needed without the system. Depending on the function, the new system will provide an opportunity for efficiency gains of *x*% to *xx*% over our current headcount, as outlined in the efficiency comparison. Additionally, the new system will allow the division to continue to leverage headcount additions, estimated to be *xx*% of sales (same as the past 5 years), whereas, without the new system, the next 5 years' high expected sales growth will cause that leverage factor to drop (headcount growth expected to be xx% of sales in FY 2006).

These labor savings will come mostly from the areas of contracts, purchasing, planning, marketing, and accounting. This labor will be reduced through reengineering efforts of the business processes, including decreased rework of product and processes, and eliminating non-value-added tasks.

We expect the value of these savings to be $xxxxK in FY 2006.

Asset Management:
Improvements made in the front end of the booking process will yield corresponding improvements in days sales outstanding (DSO). Additionally, the EDI and credit card capabilities of the new system will also yield improvements in DSO. The model assumes that domestic DSO will improve by 2 days.

We will also improve inventory turns. Through reduced internal lead times, yield improvements, improved forecasting, and reduced safety stock, the model assumes that domestic turns will improve by xx%.

Finally, the model assumes that there will be a small improvement in capital utilization, and better utilization of capital assets will reduce the amount of new assets that we need to purchase. The model includes a 1% improvement in asset utilization. These three operating capital improvements — improved DSO, higher inventory turns, and better capital utilization — provide a $xxxK improvement in incremental operating cash flows in FY 2006.

This system will affect practically all areas of the business. As a result, the impact of these expected benefits are spread evenly among the above factors. A sensitively analysis of these benefits is outlined below:

	ROI
■ As presented	53%
■ Assume no market share improvement	38%
■ Assume no purchase costs reduction	44%
■ Assume no material yield improvement	49%
■ Assume no labor efficiency gains	44%
■ Assume no labor efficiency gains nor any additional leverage	40%
■ Assume no DSO improvements	49%
■ Assume no ITO improvements	50%
■ Assume no capital utilization	51%

Additional benefits not included in the ROI calculation are:

- ■ Supports quality initiatives:
  - – ISO 9000. ISO certification requirements will be easier and less expensive to implement.
  - – Reduce process variability. Our product will be consistent on a worldwide basis.
  - – Regulation compliance. This includes compliance to U.S. and worldwide government regulations such as hazardous material and licensing.

■ IS opportunity costs. There are many IS projects that have been requested that we would not need to complete as a result of implementing this system. These projects with approximate IS effort are as follows. Detailed project descriptions are listed in the appendix:

– Customer credit card	6 months, 2 people
– Shipment bar coding	6 months, 2 people
– Purchasing credit card	6 months, 2 people
– Purchasing EDI	6 months, 2 people
– Order link and sales link interface	3 months, 2 people
– Order link file transfer	6 months, 1 person
– General ledger release	4 months, 2 people
– Accounts receivable release	5 months, 2 people
– Focus solution and replacement	3 months, 1 person
– Available to promise	6 months, 2 people
– HR payroll	6 months, 3 people
– Configurator	9 months, 3 people
– Expand online system availability	9 months, 4 people
– Print improvement	2 months, 2 people
– Shop floor control	6 months, 2 people
– Link engineering, business systems	2 months, 2 people
– Worldwide forecasting system	6 months, 2 people
– Field failure returns	6 months, 2 people
– Bar coding in manufacturing	6 months, 2 people
– Project management	6 months, 2 people
– Invoicing and adjustments	8 months, 3 people
– Purchasing system	8 months, 3 people
– MRO purchasing	4 months, 1 person
– Final assembly system	8 months, 4 people
– Worldwide key measures	4 months, 2 people

▲

If the plan involves a large project and investment, it may be helpful to develop a business case for action. A case for action is a compelling, clear, believable, and concise argument for why the organization would invest the resources to implement the project. It typically is not lengthy, one to three pages, and the audience is executive management. The case for action states the need for dramatic improvements. It does not scold or assign blame for the current situation, but frames the need for improvements. It identifies the vision of how things will look and function after the project is completed. The case for action identifies why the project must be completed and supports the argument with facts and data. For example, the business need may be due to survival, growth, or security reasons. The statements should generate passion and persuade people that there is no other alternative. The argument is personalized so that every individual feels responsibility for changing the situation. The fear of not changing must be greater than the fear of changing.

SUMMARY	
Project:	ERP
Annual return on investment (ROI)	–
Payback period (years)	3+
Net present value (NPV)	0
Average yearly cost of ownership	0

ANNUAL BENEFITS	Pre-start	Year 1	Year 2	Year 3
Direct	0	0	0	0
Indirect	0	0	0	0
Total per period	0	0	0	0

DEPRECIATED ASSETS	Pre-start	Year 1	Year 2	Year 3
Software	0	0	0	0
Hardware	0	0	0	0
Total per period	0	0	0	0

DEPRECIATION SCHEDULE	Pre-start	Year 1	Year 2	Year 3
Software	0	0	0	0
Hardware	0	0	0	0
Total per period	0	0	0	0

EXPENSED COSTS	Pre-start	Year 1	Year 2	Year 3
Software	0	0	0	0
Hardware	0	0	0	0
Consulting	0	0	0	0
Personnel	0	0	0	0
Training	0	0	0	0
Other	0	0	0	0
Total per period	0	0	0	0

Error! - without pre-start costs ROI cannot be calculated correctly.

FINANCIAL ANALYSIS	Results	Year 1	Year 2	Year 3
Net cash flow before taxes		0	0	0
Net cash flow after taxes		0	0	0
Annual ROI - direct and indirect benefits				-
Annual ROI - direct benefits only				#DIV/0!
Net present value (NPV)				0
Payback (years)	3+			
Average annual cost of ownership		0	0	0
3-year cumulative ROI	#DIV/0!			
3-year IRR	#NUM!			

Figure 7.5   ROI calculation

Components to include in the case for action include:

Environment: What is happening in the business environment or what has changed to cause concern?

Problem: What is the source of the concerns?

Demands: What are the customer expectations?

Diagnosis: Why are the current systems and processes not able to meet the demands?

Cost of Inaction: What is the consequence of staying status quo?

Objective: What are the guiding goals that will indicate success?

The following are some areas to consider for business benefits:

- Resource efficiencies
- Overtime
- Inventory (finished goods, WIP, and raw material)
- Inventory accuracy
- Direct material savings
- Yield improvements
- Purchase costs
- Asset management
- Days sales outstanding
- Lead time
- Safety stock
- Yield improvements
- Capital utilization
- Freight and postage costs
- Copying and filing costs
- Exception based processing
- Customer satisfaction
- Customer claims
- Storage costs
- Sales impact of more competitive prices
- Sales
- Returns
- Direct material savings
- Opportunity cost of constrained growth
- Business risk
- Sarbanes–Oxley (SOX) and other compliance
- Decision making
- Support costs
- Operational costs

Table 7.2 shows an example of a summary of business benefits.

Table 7.2   Business Benefits Summary

Business Benefits	
Gap	*Business Opportunity*
1. Revenue management	Eliminates about *xxx* staff hours and *xxx* errors per month
2. Kits	Eliminates over *xxx* staff hours per month
3. Customers and orders	Eliminates over *xxx* staff hours per month and 58 filing cabinets
4. Subscription billing	Eliminates over *xxx* hours per month
5. Accounting and financial reporting	Eliminate *xxx* staff hours per month
6. Knowledgebase	Reduces support reporting ramp-up time by *xx*% and eliminates support staff growth requirements by 4 FTEs while improving quality and consistency
7. Sales management	Enables sales management consistent forecasting and team-based selling communication

Business Benefit Summary:
- Opportunity cost of constrained growth $xxK
- Resource efficiencies $xxK
- Reduced overtime $xxK
- Exception-based processing $xxK
- Inventory reduction $xxK
- Sales impact of competitive prices $xxK
- Direct material savings $xxK
- Management decision-making leverage $xxK
- Consolidation requirements $xxK

Develop a Communication Plan and Presentation Summary

The new strategic direction may be a significant change for both the IS organization as well as the company in general. Think about how the plan should be communicated and rolled out to the organization. If many individuals have been involved with the planning throughout the process, the communication plan may not be as important as if they had not been involved. Consider the following:

- Who in the organization should hear about the IS strategic plan?
- Who are the various stakeholders of IS?
- What will be their interest in the plan?

■ What sections and pieces of the plan are important for each of them to hear?
■ How important is their buy-in and support?
■ How should they hear about the plan?
■ Who should provide the information?
■ Should it be through a presentation, the detailed plan document, or both?
■ When should they hear the information?
■ What should be the order of groups to hear the plan?
■ Who must approve the plan?

Document the communication plan. The rollout and communication of the IS strategic plan is an important step and should be carefully considered and orchestrated, particularly in a large political organization.

Develop an Ongoing Planning Process and Steering Committee

Governance was discussed in the second chapter of this book. If an IS steering committee has not been formed previously, form one now for the ongoing updating and governance of the strategic plan. Discuss with the group how the plan will be kept up to date. At a minimum, plan an annual process to review and update the plan.

The strategic plan document is a great place to document the governance process to be used on an ongoing basis to update the plan and ensure execution in accordance with the plan. Document the following in the plan document:

■ Provide an overview of the IS steering committee. Outline its purpose, the members, and their specific roles and responsibilities.
■ Provide an overview of the executive committee or executive management as they pertain to IS. Outline their purpose, the members, and their specific roles and responsibilities.
■ Identify the role of IS. Does the organization want IS to be a partner, leading the organization, or in the backseat as an order taker?
■ Identify the specific decision making authority of the IS steering committee, executive committee, the CIO, IS management, and other key groups or individuals.
■ Identify the prioritization process that will be used to evaluate and prioritize projects and efforts.
■ Identify the process that will be used for anyone in the business to request a new project or request of IS.

Summary Initiatives Chart

	Priority	Estimated Benefits	Est. Impl. Costs	Impl. Timeframe
Business Applications				
• Estimating & Configurator Tools	●	●	○	●
• ERP & Process Harmonization	●	●	○	●
• Project Portfolio Management	●	●	○	●●
People & IS Processes				
• IS Governance & Metrics	●	●	●	●●●
• Organizational Transformation	●	●	◐	●●●
Infrastructure				
• Network upgrade	◐	●	◐	●●●●
• Web enablement	◐	●	◐	●●●●

Legend:

Priority	Estimated Benefits	Est. Impl. Costs	Impl. Timeframe
● High	● >$5 M	● >$5 M	• Quick Hit
◐ Medium	◐ $2–5 M	◐ $2–5 M	•• Short (6/97)
○ Low	○ <$2 M	○ <$2 M	••• Med. (12/97)
			•••• Long (1998)

Figure 7.6   Initiatives summary

Review and Confirm the Business Case

Review the business case, risk assessment, readiness recommendations, and communication plan with the IS steering committee. Make any modifications or adjustments that may be necessary. Figure 7.6 shows a summary of key initiatives.

Communicate the Plan

Finalize the Detailed Plan Document

You are now able to update the IS strategic plan document in its entirety. When you started the planning process, you had identified in the purpose and scope the specific questions that you wanted to answer in the planning process. Review the list of questions to ensure that all the questions have been addressed through the process.

Finally, complete the executive summary at the beginning of the plan document. This is a succinct summary (1 to 3 pages) of what must change (the vision), why (the need — survival, growth, security, etc.), how much it will cost, and how long it will take. Use portions of the business case and other sections in the plan document. Exhibit 7.5 and Exhibit 7.6 show two examples of the executive summaries.

──────────────────────────────▼──────────────────────────────

Exhibit 7.5   Executive Summary, Example 1

Executive Summary

Through the strategic IS planning efforts, our company was able to:

- Understand our current environment, organizational structure, level of investment and expenditures, project backlog, and environment outside of this location
- Review our competitors' use of IS
- Understand current and emerging technology in the marketplace
- Understand our business objectives and how the company wants to function in the future
- Understand what our customers are requesting from an IS perspective
- Objectively evaluate the strengths and weaknesses of our current systems
- Formulate improved interim strategies for managing resources and project requests

Although there are several aspects of our current IS environment that can be built upon to take us into the future (such as in the areas of PC, network, and product computing environments), it became evident that the existing business application systems are not adequate and will not propel us into the future without major overhaul or replacement. These systems do not meet the business requirements outlined in our business operating vision, nor do the systems meet our external customer requirements. Our old, custom, patched systems simply cannot keep pace with the changing business needs. Additionally, the base architecture of our current systems is not sufficient to build on for the future as indicated by the significant gap between our current system and our desired computing architecture resulting from the business requirements.

The following is a summary of reasons, as identified by business management, that lead us to conclude that a new business system solution is necessary:

- **Access to information:** It is very cumbersome to obtain information from our current systems. As a result, information needed to help manage the business is not readily available. Requests for special reports and information are difficult to respond to in a timely fashion. With the proper architecture in place, tools are now available on the market that will allow users to readily obtain the information themselves.
- **Business process reengineering:** Processes throughout the business are laden with inefficiencies, manual workarounds, and duplicate efforts due

to the inefficiencies in our systems. The current systems restrict our ability to eliminate manual workarounds and inefficiencies.

- **Inability of custom systems to keep pace:** Not only do we not have the capability to meet our future business goals, our systems do not meet our current business goals and requirements. It is very expensive and time consuming to modify and maintain the systems to meet the changing business requirements, as shown by our nine-year backlog of projects. We are too small an organization to maintain custom systems, and much larger organizations are finding custom software inflexible and too expensive to maintain.

- **Changing business requirements:** When the current systems were selected and implemented in 1986, the company was in the process manufacturing business. Our business has grown considerably and we now manufacture and market large discrete products. Future business changes are also inevitable, and the current systems do not provide sufficient flexibility to handle these changing requirements.

- **External customer requirements:** Our customers are requesting electronic capabilities such as electronic data interchange, bar-coding, credit card processing, subscription services, and information regarding contract compliance and cost per reportable test. Additionally, customers would like to see electronic communication, including drawings, literature, access to technical information, and product information. Today we are unable to provide these capabilities and, as a result, the company is finding itself at a competitive disadvantage in the marketplace. Providing secure customer access is essential to our expanded customer focus; our current systems close the window to important information necessary for business decisions.

- **Competition:** Our competitors provide capabilities to our customers that we are unable to provide today and are gaining a competitive advantage by making their systems more responsive to the management of the worldwide business.

- **Ability to manage the business on a worldwide basis:** Our current systems are not "open" technology, which means that it is difficult to interface with other systems to obtain worldwide information needed to help manage the business. Our current systems meet only some of our domestic manufacturing requirements, and do not have the capabilities to integrate worldwide information, process international orders, deal with international regulatory issues, and handle foreign currencies and foreign languages.

The following are the various options we have available for our current business application systems:

1. **Continue on our current path.** This involves continuously making incremental improvements to the current custom systems to address the business needs as has been done in the past. The total cost of this option is $xM, with an xx-month completion. This option would provide us with no progress toward meeting our strategic direction, business requirements, operating vision, or desired computing architecture.

2. **Upgrade our current system.** This involves implementing the new release of our current software. The total cost of this option is $xxM, with an xx-month completion. We would need to carry over the majority (70%) of our current modifications to the new release, so that we would essentially be in the same "custom" situation we are today. This option would be a short-term solution, with no progress toward meeting our strategic direction, business requirements, operating vision, or desired computing architecture.

3. **Implement a new system.** This option involves reviewing, selecting, and implementing an entirely new software (and potentially hardware) environment for our business application systems. It is estimated at $xxM over an xx-month time frame. This option would address our strategic direction; allow us to reengineer our business processes to eliminate waste throughout the business; provide improved abilities to access information; and allow us to meet our business operating vision, meet our business requirements, and establish our desired computing architecture.

The recommendation of the IS steering committee is to implement new business application systems. Developments within the past couple of years within the IS industry have made **now** an opportune time to pursue new business application systems. Changes in technology towards open and client/server systems make improvements in the above areas possible. Additional enhancements and investments are also necessary in the network area to build on what we currently have, because our infrastructure has not kept pace with the growth of the company.

To be successful, this project must be a priority for the company and will require a significant effort and commitment from all areas of the business as well as upper management. Not only is it an expensive project for the company, but it will utilize critical resources in the company and these critical resources will be unable to address other business issues. However, we feel the benefits to the company are also significant and worth the effort considering the other options available.

The purpose of this document is to communicate the results of the planning process and the logic used to reach our conclusions and recommendations.

▲

▼

Exhibit 7.6   Executive Summary, Example 2

Executive Summary

Introduction
The purpose of this document is to provide an assessment and outline a plan for our business application environment and outline recommendations to address the

business needs. Appendix A outlines the purpose, objectives, scope, and process used to obtain this information and recommendations.

In the past, our custom systems have served the company's needs well and the system has been modified over the years to meet the changing business needs. The system has met the needs and is still running today largely due the heroic day-to-day efforts of key personnel in IS and the business rather than through systematic repeatable processes.

Analysis

This plan reviewed our current business situation, including an understanding of customers, vendors, the general industry and competition, and each functional area. The business direction was documented, as well as business strengths, weaknesses, opportunities, and threats. Key business requirements were identified, as well as transaction volumes and key business indicators. Business process improvements were also identified. Finally, all the business factors were analyzed to determine the impact on the IS environment and direction. The business has several major requirements on the IS systems, such as:

- Business systems must be able to handle the new line of business; this is a growing and key profitable area for our future.
- Systems must be scalable and designed to handle our aggressive business growth, transaction volume, and growth by acquisition with multiple divisions, companies, facilities, and locations.
- To ensure profitable growth, business processes and applications must be improved and utilize industry best practices.
- Systems must be open and designed to connect to the customers and vendors through supply chain management.
- Systems must provide flexibility to meet customer needs; this has been a competitive advantage for us in the past.
- Improved access to information and business metrics will provide management the tools to improve business performance and manage growth.

Our current business application environment was documented, as well as the outstanding projects, the IS organization, and IS processes that support the application area. This assessment also reviewed the industry, including benchmark statistics, IS trends, warehouse, distribution, and manufacturing industry trends, and some competitor information was gathered. Finally, a complete assessment of our business application environment (including the applications, organization, and processes) was developed, including strengths, weaknesses, opportunities, and threats. Major shortcomings or weaknesses were identified relative to the business applications, such as:

- Not designed for the current business
- Lacking functionality
- Information access

- Data integrity
- Size and volume limitations
- Visibility to costs and profits
- Out of date architecture
- Risk
- Not flexible, requires programming
- Customized, not using best practices
- Customer-facing systems
- Interfacing of data rather than integration
- Ease of use
- Standard ERP functionality missing
- Ability to handle international order processes
- Fragile, brittle
- Not real-time
- Tools lacking
- Cost of ownership relative to functionality

Recommendation

After reviewing the future business plans, business requirements, and process improvement opportunities, it is recommended that we **replace the current legacy systems by the selection and implementation of an industry-standard Tier 1 integrated ERP vendor package**.

This implementation is necessary to be able to handle the company growth and growth by acquisition, and to support our competitive advantage of flexibility to customer needs. Industry best practices must be used to improve business processes to ensure profitable growth. The core infrastructure of the applications needs to be replaced rather than continuing to patch improvements. The current systems have such a significant gap of breadth and depth of functionality compared to the business needs, it is simply not feasible or cost effective to build on the current systems when there are packages that offer most of the missing features.

The payback for replacing the legacy systems is large and immediate. The current systems cost $x per year more than the estimates for a new tier 1 ERP system. A few specific resource efficiencies save an annual $xM and the inventory and freight impact adds another $xM to the bottom line. In addition, this is just the tip of the iceberg. There are numerous other intangible benefits including reducing the potential Sarbanes–Oxley exposure and reducing the risk of lost sales if the current system were to crash during the peak third-quarter season.

This project should be implemented in phases and is estimated to take a total of 18–24 months. A major project such as this can be a challenge for any organization. Several key components for success were identified, such as making the project a top business priority, ensuring executive support, assigning key business people, developing a solid plan, and ensuring rigorous leadership, governance, and control. With proper leadership, it is possible and probable for us to be successful in this critical effort, because it will provide the framework to meet the business needs of the future.

▲

Table 7.3   Presentation Agenda

Agenda

- Introduction
- Business impact
- IS situation assessment
- Future IS direction
- Implementation plan
- Summary

Distribute the plan document in draft form to the IS group and the IS steering committee and ask for input and changes. Hold another meeting with the IS steering committee to confirm that the committee agrees with the recommendation and plan. Also, ask for members' support by asking each of them to talk to their corresponding member of executive management and voice their support for the recommendation. It can also be helpful to ask the group for suggestions on how to present or obtain the support of the executive management group. Ask volunteers to help make the business case; it is significantly stronger if the business makes the recommendation rather than solely the IS group.

Develop the Summary Presentation

The best plan in the world is worthless without the ability to sell the plan to executive management and the entire organization. Often, changes in IS result in millions of dollars of investment for an organization. Management must see a solid and thorough process for determining the direction. Management must also understand the level of effort, investment required, and the risks to the organization.

If you have followed the process outlined in this book, by now you have increased communication and support of IS activities throughout the organization. Now it is time to obtain executive management approval before spending additional time getting into the details of the direction.

The presentation to executive management should be no longer than two hours. An example of an agenda is shown in Table 7.3. Looking at the table of contents of the detailed plan document, plan to have approximately one slide summarizing each section of the plan document.

As you can see from the timing of the agenda, the presentation needs to move rapidly to keep the interest of executive management. Whenever possible, use pictures or summary charts throughout the presentation. Table 7.4 is an example that summarizes the assessment, direction, and plan.

Table 7.4 Summary

Assessment *Where we are today*	Direction *Where we want to be*	Plan *How we will get there*
■ Different systems that address the same requirements ■ Current systems that do not completely fulfill existing business requirements	■ A portfolio of common integrated systems that satisfy business requirements for all geographies	■ Transitioning to common systems, primarily relying on commercially available application packages, supplemented by new development or existing systems
■ Different technical environments that support similar systems ■ A technical environment that does not have the necessary attributes or the capacity to support future mission-critical systems	■ A technical environment that is compatible with commercially available application packages, supportable throughout the world, and based on scalable and interoperable components	■ Identifying technology components that are compatible with commercially available application packages ■ Acquiring or upgrading components as necessary to support the implementation of those packages
■ Business systems solutions and services that are based on functional instead of enterprise needs and priorities	■ A partnership with business process owners in using accepted methods to deliver business systems solutions and services in accordance with enterprise needs and priorities	■ Developing and implementing processes that apply enterprise needs and priorities to the evaluation and prioritization of requests for business systems solutions and services

Present the Plan and Discuss It

Distribute a copy of the plan document to executive management to review several weeks before the scheduled presentation. Because it is a long document, attach a cover memo indicating why it is important for managers to read the document and identify a few key sections that are particularly important for them to read if they are unable to read the entire document. Also, mention that the recommendation and proposed plan is a joint decision by IS and the IS steering committee, and the managers can contact their appropriate member if they have any specific questions. This way you are enlisting the IS steering committee to be your salespeople. In the memo, indicate a date and time for an overview presentation once they have had an opportunity to review the information.

Have at least one member from the business who is on the IS steering committee for support at the presentation, if not giving a portion of the presentation. Begin the presentation by letting everyone know the purpose of the presentation and why the group should listen to the presentation. Next, explain the agenda of the presentation. Early in the presentation, recognize the IS steering committee, stress that the recommendation is from the whole group of business representatives that executive management appointed rather than the recommendation coming from the IS organization. Review the process the group used to arrive at a recommendation, explaining where you are in the process.

After the presentation, lead a short discussion to find out whether the group agrees with the plan and recommended direction. At this point, management has gained confidence in the process and recommendation, but may be struggling with the size of the investment necessary. Stand firm to the recommendation and refer back to the detail and solid foundation that have been carefully outlined. Call upon experts in management to support the business case as to why the recommendation is important for the company. You may need to alter the speed of the spending, determine creative ways of funding the investment, or have self-funding phases, but stand firm that the direction chosen is the direction in which the company must head.

Conclusion

You have successfully completed the fourth phase of the planning process. You now have an IS direction that is specific and aligned with the business direction. In this phase of the planning process, you have accomplished the following:

- Developed a detailed road map of all the IS projects, each with costs and benefits
- Identified the impact to the organization
- Identified the various risks and formulated a risk management approach
- Developed the business case for action and business benefits
- Planned the communication and plan roll-out

- Developed and documented a governance process to ensure ongoing updates to the plan
- Finalized the detail plan document
- Summarized the IS plan in a presentation to executive management

Notes for My IS Strategic Planning Project

_____

_____

_____

_____

_____

_____

_____

_____

_____

_____

_____

_____

_____

_____

_____

_____

_____

_____

_____

_____

_____

_____

_____

Chapter 8

Next Steps

Even if you're on the right track, you'll get run over if you just sit there.

— Will Rogers (1875–1935)
American actor, humorist

After completion of the IS strategic plan, there are four very important ongoing activities:

- Marketing
- Executing
- Managing
- Measuring

Each of these is outlined in detail in this chapter.

Marketing

An important role of a CIO is the continual marketing of IS to the rest of the organization. Many times, members of the IS group do a poor job of marketing; they work hard and diligently, but their work goes unnoticed and unappreciated. However, this can be their own fault as IS employees may not take the time to communicate their activities and impact to the organization in terms the business can appreciate.

You are never done with the strategic planning process and selling the recommendation. Constantly and continually communicate, communicate, and then communicate some more. Everyone in the organization must be aware of the IS direction and plan. Continue building relationships with all levels of management and nurturing personal alliances throughout the business. Communicate frequently to the IS organization about the plan and progress toward the goals. Do not set the plan away, but keep it alive. Take the strategic plan on a road show and present summaries to various departments, divisions, and locations. Explain where IS is today, where it is headed, and how success will be measured. As you progress on the plan, provide summaries of what has been done and the progress relative to the plan. The following are specific communication opportunities:

Status reports: Develop and widely distribute monthly and annual IS status reports. Status reports should be high-level, business-oriented, and easy to understand, and not technical gibberish. Organize the report by business project or business area so business users can quickly find their area of interest. Reference the road map and projects in the IS strategic plan, and report the progress of the plan.

Intranet: Post the IS strategic plan on the company intranet. Have hot keys by section so individuals can go to the area of interest. Publicize that the plan is available for all interested parties. Many individuals participated in the interviews and development of the plan; make sure they see the results.

IS newsletter: A monthly newsletter is an excellent method to report progress of the plan. Run fun contests. For example, the first one to e-mail three of the IS strategies gets a free lunch.

Key metrics: Through the planning process, key metrics were identified. Publish each metric and the result on a regular basis. Post the metrics on the wall for all to see and strive for improvement.

Surveys: Continue to distribute surveys on a regular basis. This will provide continual feedback to ensure you are proceeding as planned.

IS steering committee: For proper governance, it is absolutely necessary to hold regular monthly steering committee meetings. A portion of every meeting should be devoted to discussing progress of the plan.

IS executive committee: On a quarterly basis, hold a meeting with executive management to report progress of the plan.

IS organization meetings: On a monthly basis (quarterly for large IS departments), have meetings with the IS group. Talk about the plan and progress toward the goals.

Vendors: Now that the plan is complete, you have terrific documentation of the company and where it is headed, the current IS environment, and IS plans for the future. Use this document frequently to communicate your situation. It can be a valuable tool to hand to a vendor and say, "This is where we are headed; tell me how you can help us get there."

New IS employees: Again, use the document that has been assembled to give new IS employees a complete orientation of the current situation and direction. It will significantly accelerate their orientation process with complete information about both the business and IS.

Executing

After having a solid plan in place, execution is everything. The plan may have identified a large project or an area of the business applications that require new software, or a new ERP system. This section examines key steps in the process.

Project Plan

Start by developing the project plan. What is included in the project plan? The following are some of the components to include:

Project mission: What is the purpose of the project? What is the project trying to achieve? Exhibit 8.1 shows an example of a project mission for one company.

▼

Exhibit 8.1   Project Mission

The mission of our project is to strengthen the company's ability to meet worldwide customer expectations and company profitability goals by:

■ Reengineering global business processes to improve efficiency and lower costs
■ Providing common business operating systems with advanced computing architectures that will improve cooperation and communication between functional and geographical areas within the company
■ Providing high-quality, consistent, and timely information both locally and worldwide that will improve management decision-making capabilities

▲

Scope: State specifically what is in the scope of the project as well as any areas outside the scope of the project. For example, identify business applications, business processes, hardware environments, geographic locations, or divisions that will be included or excluded. Identify any known project phases.

Project goals: Identify specific expectations of the project. How will you know if the project is a success or not? What does management want the project team to accomplish? Project goals should be SMART: Specific, Measurable, Attainable, Realistic, and Track-able. Identify how the project fits in within the overall IS strategic plan.

Project team organization: List the names of all the business and IS participants. Identify the specific time commitment if it is a part-time role. Form a project steering committee for overall project responsibility and authority.

Roles and responsibilities: Identify the roles and responsibilities for each member or group of members who participate in the project. Exhibit 8.2 shows an example of roles and responsibilities for one project.

It is also helpful to include a matrix of each project participant, the business application he or she is responsible for, and which departments within the company he or she represents. This can ensure that no area will fall through the cracks during the project. Also, identify the role of consultants on the project.

──────────────────────── ▼ ────────────────────────

Exhibit 8.2 Roles and Responsibilities

The following are the specific roles and responsibilities for the various team members:

Project steering committee: 5% of time

- Provide communication to upper management of project status and issues.
- Ensure you meet project schedule and costs targets. Resolve resource constraints.
- Provide communication to project team of upper management requirements.
- Responsible for the decision and selection of package based on findings and recommendation of project team.
- Resolve interdepartmental or geographic conflicts that cannot be resolved by the business project leader.
- Meet on a monthly basis (via videoconferencing), or more frequently if necessary.
- Be involved with vendor negotiations as necessary.

Business project leader: 100% of time

- Main, key leader and voice of project.
- Decision maker for any conflicts that arise in functional or geographic areas.
- Communicate recommendation of team to project steering committee and worldwide management.
- Responsible for communication and coordination with other parts of the world.
- Prepares the formal request for funds.
- Responsible for project communication infrastructure and process.
- Responsible for determining and adhering to project schedule.
- Responsible for determining and adhering to project budget.
- Responsible for negotiating with vendors.
- Organize and lead regular team meetings.
- Management and selection of implementation consultants.
- Prepares management project status report

IS project leader: 80% of time, with other 20% going to regular IS activities

- Assist the business project leader in determining actions and schedules.
- Communicate recommendations of the team to the IS steering committee and worldwide management.
- Assist with communication and coordination with other parts of the world.
- Assist with preparation of the formal request for funds.
- Assist with establishment of project communication infrastructure and process.
- Communicate any technical impacts.
- Communicate hardware requirements.
- Communicate programming requirements.
- Lead the programming effort required.
- Determine and adhere to IS schedules.
- Assist with negotiations with vendors.
- Assist in organizing and leading regular team meetings.
- Leads or facilitates the project steering committee meetings.
- Management and selection of implementation consultants.
- Prepares management project status report.

Primary user representatives: 50 or 100% of time

- Responsible for communicating requirements and developing demo scripts
- Responsible for gathering input and communicating back to the organizations that they represent
- Responsible for reviewing packages and making recommendation
- Responsible for business process reengineering

- Responsible for worldwide harmonization of terms, fields, and measurements
- Responsible for establishing parameters in system to fit the business
- Responsible for establishing new processes and setup
- Responsible for testing system
- Responsible for training users
- Responsible for user documentation and procedures
- Responsible for ensuring accuracy of information (e.g., conversions)
- Responsible for providing input and adhering to project schedule and budget
- Responsible for providing written monthly status reports to the project leaders by the last day of each calendar month
- Responsible for leading subprojects as necessary

Primary IS representatives: 80% of time, with other 20% to IS activities

- Assist users with business process reengineering and the tasks outlined above for the primary user representative
- Responsible for developing technical requirements
- Responsible for determining hardware requirements
- Responsible for installing hardware
- Responsible for installing software
- Responsible for programming and testing of conversions
- Responsible for programming and testing of interfaces
- Responsible for providing input and adhering to project schedule and budget
- Responsible for technical documentation
- Responsible for providing written monthly status reports to the project leaders by the last day of each calendar month

Supplemental user resources: 10–50% of time

- Assist the full-time representatives with duties as outlined above

Supplemental IS resources: 10–50% of time

- Assist the full-time representatives with duties as outlined above

▲

Project communication: Communication is the number one reason why projects fail. You can never communicate enough. Identify in the project plan who is responsible for the main project communications and how it will occur. How will you update the average employee on the project? How will you update project members? How will you involve managers in the decisions? How often will the project steering committee meet, and who will run the meetings? What is

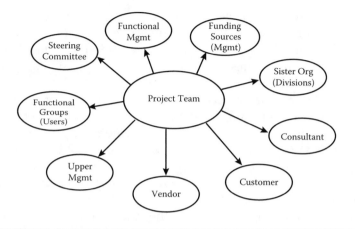

Figure 8.1   Communication

the format of monthly project status reports? How will project
meetings be run and documented? How will decisions be documented? Do not forget all the various people must be involved with
the communication, as shown in Figure 8.1.

Quality assurance compliance guidelines: What specific internal or
external guidelines or procedures must you adhere to during the
project life cycle? Are there ISO or SOX requirements?

Project schedule: Identify the high-level phases as well as the detailed
tasks in the project. Identify the person responsible, estimated hours,
and estimated time frame for completion.

Project budget: How will project expenses be tracked? How will team
members record time spent on the project? Who is responsible for
budgeting and assuming costs related to the project that occurs
within the business departments? What are the capital and expense
budgets for the project?

Training plan: What training classes are necessary for the participants
to be productive? Is any initial training necessary for the selection
team?

Project Kick-Off Meeting

Because a journey begins on common ground, it is important to establish
that common ground when beginning a new project through a project
kick-off meeting. Participants may be unclear about the specific objectives
of the project, or exactly what their role will be on the project. Ground
everyone with the same information and establish a clear vision of the
group direction so that each member of the group feels comfortable in

his or her new role. Obstacles are what we see when we take our eyes off the goal, so the project goals and objectives must be absolutely clear in everyone's mind. The information shared should include an understanding of the project mission, scope, goals, responsibilities, schedule, and initial tasks.

Everyone knows the project will be a lot of hard work; thus, initiate the project with enthusiasm, fun, and with a teamwork orientation. It is helpful to organize a day with teamwork challenges, project sweatshirts, brainteasers, competition, or anything you can think of to add some spirit to the project initiation. Perhaps have a contest to name the project. Begin the presentation by explaining why management selected these individuals to participate on the project.

It may be a new role for many of the team participants to function in a project role with members from other functional parts of the organization. Let the team know there will be some frustrating and unclear times, but as team participants, it is their role to help the team get back on track.

Request for Quote

Typically, large projects involve sending several vendors a request for quotation (RFQ). This can also be referred to as request for proposal (RFP), or request for information (RFI). No matter how thorough an RFQ is, use it only as initial scanning and qualification. Nothing will take the place of in-person vendor demonstrations to determine the true viability of a package in your environment. However, if you structure a quotation request well, you are able to narrow the field of packages to review. Send the RFQ to the top 10 (or fewer) vendors that meet the requirements.

What does a RFQ include? The RFQ must be as concise as possible; vendors do not want to wade through inches of paper before qualifying you as a potential customer. Fortunately, you have already done much of the work with various sections of the strategic plan. Exhibit 8.3 is an example of an RFQ format used by one company.

▼

Exhibit 8.3   RFQ Format

RFQ guidelines. This includes the following information:

- Who and where should RFQ responses be mailed?
- When are responses due back?
- To whom should the vendors direct any questions or inquiries?
- What should be the format of the response?

- What documents should the vendors include with their response? This list includes:
  - Signed confidentiality agreement (included in RFQ).
  - Responses to questions regarding company and software (RFQ section C-2).
  - Responses to company specific requirements (RFQ section C-3).
  - Any changes, updates, or notes to the vendor requirements (RFQ section C-4).
  - A copy of their contract along with any required license agreements so you can begin legal review.
  - A summary of the pricing with any tier, volume, or platform pricing indicated.
  - A copy of the training schedule.
  - A company brochure or annual report.
  - List of customers with names, addresses, and phone numbers for contact.
  - Implementation date, software version. You may need to sign a vendor confidentiality agreement for this information.
  - Include any online demonstration disks available.
- What is the next step for the vendor if the vendor makes the cut to the short list?
- Statement of confidentiality of RFQ information.

General Information

1. Company: This is a brief (1-page) description of your company. Include the following:
   - What business is the company in?
   - How old is the company? Include a short historic perspective.
   - How large is the company in terms of sales and employees? Is it public or privately owned?
   - Is this quotation for one division, one location, or the entire company? Provide information on parent, subsidiaries, and divisions.
2. Current environment: This is a short (1-page) description of your current IS environment. Include the following:
   - What hardware environments are you utilizing? Do you plan to change hardware environments?
   - What software is the company currently utilizing?
   - How many utilize the system you are replacing?
   - What network is in place? What locations are connected?
   - How many PCs do you have? What is the typical PC configuration?
3. Business requirements
   - Scope: This can be the scope section of the strategic plan.
   - Environmental requirements: This can be the environmental requirements section of the strategic plan.
   - Business direction: This is a summary of the business mission, objectives, and goals. Obtain approval from internal management before sending this information to an external company.

- ■ Information requirements: This can be the information needs section of the strategic plan.
- ■ External requirements: This can be the external requirements section of the strategic plan.

4. IS requirements: This is a summary of the computing architecture requirements of the strategic plan.
5. Project: This section is a summary of the project in progress, including when it started, how you got to this point, and where you plan to go.
6. Reason for change: What are the key motivating factors for the business to implement this project? What is the case for action?
7. Key issues: This can be a list of the key issues as identified with a vendor in the requirements definition step as outlined in Chapter 3. This is not an entire list of all the requirements, but rather the key requirements for your environment. Include the responses for those particular vendors that were in the database of the automated tool, if you used one. The vendor can correct, change, or modify the responses previously supplied.

Vendor response

1. Confidentiality agreement: This is an agreement ensuring that the responses to the RFQ are accurate, as well as keeping any information supplied confidential.
2. General company and package information. This includes general questions that are of interest to you about the vendor.

Please respond to the following questions:

Company:
    Company Name: _____
    Software Name: _____
    Date company formed: _____ Public/Private: _____
    Annual sales: _____
    Targeted markets or customers: _____

Employees:
    Number of employees worldwide: _____
    Number of employees in development: _____
    Number of employees in support: _____
    Number of employees in area: _____
    Number of employees in area with > 2 years experience: _____

Customers:
    Number of customers that have one module or more implemented in
       production: _____
    Number of customers that have full suite implemented in production: ____
    % of customers on annual maintenance: _____

% of customers on current release: _____
Average length of time for customers to implement modules: ____
Average length of time for customers to implement new release: _____
Is there an active user group in area? _____
List any customers in our business:

_____

Software:
 Handle process manufacturing: _____   Discrete: _____
 Repetitive: _____   Job shop: _____
 Make-to-stock: _____   Make-to-order: _____
 Language code written in: _____
 Year majority (>75%) of code written in: _____
 Databases supported: _____
 Hardware necessary: _____
 Operating system necessary: _____
 Date of last release: _____   Date of next release: _____
 Major rewrite planned: _____   When: _____ Why: _____
 Approximate cost (range) of various modules included in manufacturing,
  Distribution, and Finance for *xxx* total users, *xxx* active, including database
  and development tools needed: _____
 Developed with methodology: _____
 Development tools: _____
 Object oriented: _____
 Major areas of planned enhancements: _____

 _____
 _____

Training:
 Is public training offered in area: _____
 Cities public training offered: _____
 Average cost of training class: _____
 Number of days training needed for order entry person: _____
  Master scheduler: _____
  Information systems: ___

Support:
 Approximate cost of annual maintenance: _____
 24-hour support available: _____
 Cost for support: _____
 Product guarantee: _____
 Implementation support available for turnkey: _____
 Any automated conversion support or tools available from our current
  software: _____

3. Company-specific requirements: This is a list of the requirements specific to your company identified in the requirement's definition phase. These would be only the requirements not included in the generic requirements in the database of all vendor information. Because these requirements were not in the database, you will need to send the company-specific requirements to the vendor for response.

4. General requirements: Include a disk of the requirements identified with the responses for that particular vendor included from the outside company. Ask the vendor to review the responses provided to ensure accuracy and only provide updates if any discrepancies exist.

Appendix

■ Company brochures, annual report. Include any company literature that is helpful for the vendor to better understand your business.

───────────────────▲───────────────────

RFQ Response Review

After obtaining the responses from your RFQ, review all the information and assemble the answers to compare the vendors. Try to narrow down the vendors to two or three for a detailed review. It may be easiest to assemble a key criteria sheet to evaluate the vendors. An example is provided in Exhibit 8.4.

───────────────────▼───────────────────

Exhibit 8.4   RFP Response Review

	Vendor 1	Vendor 2	Vendor 3
Company:			
Name of company			
Name of software			
Date company formed			
Public/private			
Annual sales			
Targeted markets			
Employees:			
Number of worldwide			

	Vendor 1	Vendor 2	Vendor 3
Number in development			
Number in support			
Number in our town			
Number in our town > 2 yrs experience			
Customers:			
Number in production			
Number with full suite			
% on annual maintenance			
% on current release			
Implementation time			
Time to implement new release			
Active user group in area			
Customers in our industry			
Software:			
Make/engineer to order			
Discrete/make to stock			
Repetitive/job shop			
Integrated configurator			
Language of code			
Year code written			
Databases supported			
Relational database			
Windows interface			
Current release			
Date released			
Hardware needed			
Operating system			
Date of last release			
Date of next release			

	Vendor 1	Vendor 2	Vendor 3
Major rewrite planned			
Reason for rewrite			
CASE developed			
Methodology used			
Object oriented			
Planned enhancements			
Cost:			
Software			
Database, tools			
Hardware			
Training			
Consulting			
Bolt-ons			
Training:			
Public training in our area			
Cities training offered			
Average cost of class			
Number of days order entry			
Number of days master scheduler			
Number of days information systems			
Support:			
Cost of annual maintenance			
24 hours support available?			
Cost for support			
Does product have guarantee?			
Implementation support			
Local partner consultant			
Conversion support			

	Vendor 1	Vendor 2	Vendor 3
Requirement ratings:			
Industry rating			
Industry comments			
Other:			
Date received			
Quality of response			
Notes			
Contact name			
Contact number			
Comments			
Comments			
Group thoughts			

It may be helpful to utilize a structured decision-making process to select three vendors from the larger group of vendors. This can be done by using the following steps:

1. *Identify the criteria key to making the decision.* If it were your money and your company, how would you evaluate and select an option? This list should be high-level and no more than 15 criteria.
2. *Force-rank the key criteria.* Ask the group members if they had to choose between the first criteria and the second, which would they choose? First and third? First and fourth? Follow this for each combination. Count the votes for each criterion; the one with the most is the highest priority to the group.
3. *Weight the criteria.* Assign a weight using 8 through 10. The higher priority items would be a weight of 10, and the lower items would be an 8. This will become the multiplier.
4. *Rate the criteria against each option.* If you have ten vendors, rate all ten. Use a scale of 1 through 5. A 5 would indicate the vendor does an excellent job at meeting the criteria, 3 average, and 1 poor.
5. *Multiply the rating times the weight.* Total the scores for each vendor. The highest vendors would be the preferred options.

This method should be used as one indicator and the results should be reviewed and updated. An example is provided in Exhibit 8.5.

Exhibit 8.5   Evaluation Criteria

Priority	Requirement	Weight	Option 1 Rate	Option 1 Weight* Rate	Option 2 Rate	Option 2 Weight* Rate	Option 3 Rate	Option 3 Weight* Rate
1	Stable vendor for future	10	5	50	3	30	3	30
2	Meets business requirements	10	3	30	5	50	5	50
3	Technical architecture	10	3	30	3	30	5	50
4	User friendly	9	3	27	5	45	5	45
5	Flexible	9	3	27	5	45	5	45
6	Support reengineering processes	9	3	27	5	45	5	45
7	Vendor support	9	3	27	3	27	3	27
8	Cost	8	5	40	3	24	1	8
9	Resources	8	5	40	3	24	1	8
10	Time	8	3	24	3	24	3	24
	Total			322		344		332

Software Demonstrations

It can be very difficult to ascertain in a demonstration how the software will work in your environment. Software demonstrators are typically very good at showing you the best features without allowing you to see the deficiencies until it is in your own environment. To get the most out of the vendor demonstrations, direct and guide the demonstration for your particular requirements. A typical ERP demonstration will require 16 hours of demonstration, 2 to 4 hours of technology discussions, and 2 to 4 hours of post-demo follow-up. The following are items to prepare for the vendor review:

Script: Assemble a detailed script of what you want to see and how you want to see it. Demonstrations can be very time consuming, so focus on the areas that are critical to your business rather than areas that any software package can do. Develop the script by the various areas of the business that are evaluating the package. A script can be very generic or very detailed, and you can complete it at a level the team is comfortable with. The demo is your opportunity to test-drive the software for your particular business.

Data package: This is a package of your own company data for the vendor to use in the demonstration. Typically, this consists of the major information requirements of the system, such as customer, item, and bill of material information; order header; and line item information.

Key requirements: Assemble a short list of the key requirements the company requires from the vendor or in the new software package. These are differentiating items that are critical for your business upon which you would rate the vendors.

Rating methodology: Decide upon a ranking or rating methodology before viewing any vendors. Decide whether the team will rate each requirement on the script, or only the key requirements. Average all participants ranking, or give a weighted average with the most weight going to the expert in that functional area.

Demonstration guidelines: Prepare demonstration guidelines for both the vendor and the team participants. Several team members may not have experienced demos before, and should be prepared as to what to expect. Examples are provided in Exhibit 8.6 and Exhibit 8.7.

Demo agenda: Develop a high-level agenda of how you want the demo to flow. An example is shown in Exhibit 8.8.

Vendor introduction to company: Once you prepare for the demonstrations, have each vendor visit your company site to learn more about the business and processes. This typically takes a full day. An example of an agenda of items to cover in this day is shown in Exhibit 8.9.

▼

Exhibit 8.6   Vendor Demonstration Guidelines

- Demo the software version used on the *<name of platform>* hardware platform.
- Demo the current release that would be generally available if we signed the purchase agreement today. Do not show or discuss vaporware. If answering a question with future availability, make sure it is clearly stated as a future direction. When answering questions, answer it for the version software we are reviewing.
- Use the actual software; note canned screens or demonstration slides.
- Follow the script provided.
- Create the actual demo agenda after reviewing our proposed script and agenda, and adjust it accordingly considering how long the areas typically take to review in your software.
- If the software cannot do what we request, please just say so.
- Please make sure you have knowledgeable resources to answer the questions. If you do not know the answer, do not guess; take note and get back to us. We would rather hear that you do not know than get the wrong answer.
- If we do not ask about an area that you feel is a key differentiator, please tell us.
- Use the data provided.

▲

▼

Exhibit 8.7   Team Member Demonstration Guidelines

- Keep an open mind until you have seen all three vendors. Do not lock on or lock out a solution. The groups may prefer different packages, and we will need to work through the differences.
- If a key requirement is not met, do not shut the vendor out. Again, keep an open mind. If all other areas are great, perhaps we can meet the missing requirement with a bolt-on package or by rethinking the business requirement. Do not shut out the vendor because you will need to discuss the complete reasons that you liked or did not like the package.
- Do not tip your hand to the vendor and look totally discouraged or encouraged. You can show enthusiasm for the software.
- If a requirement is not met, take notes and move on. Do not take it out on the vendor. The software is not going to be perfect; do not expect it.
- Give the demo your complete attention. We need everyone to have a thorough understanding of each package to reach a decision.
- Please turn cell phones off. Do not leave the demo for phone calls or other business. Come on time and stay until the end. Stay attentive and focused.
- Take good notes of ratings, advantages, and disadvantages. Without good notes, the various vendor packages will begin to look the same. Stay organized from the beginning.

- Manage time and questions. Each application area will have an allocated amount of time. Watch your questions and the level of detail to make sure you make it through all your key points. Do not derail on a detailed topic. Take notes for follow-on questions to address in another session if necessary.
- Attend all the vendor demos. You will not be able to compare if you only see one of the packages. Each area can coordinate if additional participants are needed.
- Be flexible on following the script and data that was provided. Their package may require significant setup to show exactly what we want.
- As time allows, feel free to ask questions. This is your time to see the package and obtain answers. We need to make a decision based on what we see. If you need more information, please ask for it.

Exhibit 8.8   Demo Agenda

- Day 1:
  - Morning: Company overview, general software questions, system navigation, reporting, interfaces
  - Afternoon: Manufacturing
- Day 2:
  - Manufacturing
  - Distribution
  - Financial
  - Technical

Exhibit 8.9   Vendor Introduction

- Background
- Project
  - Mission
  - Scope
  - Team
  - Schedule
- Demo
  - Guidelines
  - Agenda
  - Script
- Business Overview
- Tour

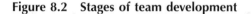

Figure 8.2   Stages of team development

Vendor Selection

After each demo, assemble a list of strengths and weaknesses in addition to the vendor rankings. Obtain input from all project participants. This is good to discuss in a group setting, because different areas can have different opinions that are helpful to discuss as a group. As a group, you can easily reach a consensus as to the recommended software with the process outlined.

Managing

Provide the leadership that is necessary in times of change. Change can be difficult for the organization, and it is important to help employees through the process. As shown in Figure 8.2, there are four stages of team development:

1. *Getting started:* In the first stage, getting started, the team is getting to know the task and team members, learning one another's skills and expectations, testing one another's commitment and attitude, beginning to define tasks and roles, and focusing on symptoms and problems not related to the task. Team members in this stage feel excited about being part of something new, anxious about the goals and what it takes to achieve them, suspicious about what is expected of them, and unsure about how their contributions will fit in with the team's mission and goals.

2. *Going in circles:* In the second stage, going in circles, the team may be setting unrealistic goals, relying on only one person's experience and ideas, resisting working together, not making much

progress, competing for control, or focusing on the task or goal, not on how to get it done. As a team member in this stage, you might feel frustrated that progress is not being made as fast as expected, angry that ideas are criticized or ignored, impatient with members who are slow or who do not pull their weight, or jealous of others who might have more rewarding or easier responsibilities.

3. *Getting on course:* In the third stage, the team may be having some difficulty, but is making progress toward reaching the goal. Team members are using one another's ideas, giving and receiving constructive feedback, setting and usually following team ground rules and norms, and valuing individual differences. As a team member in this stage, you feel respect for other members' needs and capabilities, relief that the team is making progress, a growing sense of trust because everyone is committed, and increasingly comfortable working together.

4. *Full speed ahead:* In the fourth stage, the team is making progress toward the goal with speed and efficiency, working together to diagnose and overcome obstacles, using feedback to make changes, and finding ways to continuously improve how the members work together. As a team member in this stage, you feel pride in your work, excited about being part of the team, enjoyment in working together and meeting goals, fully committed to the team, and secure in relying on other members.

As a team leader, strive to have your team in this fourth stage as much of the time as possible. However, teams typically go through the various stages several times during a project. A high-performance team is one in which the members meet their goals, trust one another, actively listen, and create realistic and challenging objectives. Work out conflicts in a healthy manner, use performance standards, give positive feedback, and create a positive, candid, and relaxed team environment. Define clear roles and goals, and make decisions through consensus. Complete a self-assessment rating at various stages in the project so that weak areas can be corrected before they adversely affect the project. An example of a team assessment survey is shown in Exhibit 8.10.

▼

Exhibit 8.10   Team Rating Example

Rating Our Project Team
Please complete this survey as honestly as possible so that we can see where our team is strong and where we need to improve it.

	No, not at all			Yes, very much so

1. **Purpose:** Team goals and objectives are clear.
   - My team has clear direction, goals, and objectives.   1   2   3   4   5
   - The project goals are consistent with company goals.   1   2   3   4   5
   - We have the support of upper management.   1   2   3   4   5
   - The project is popular and wanted.   1   2   3   4   5
   - Users and management agree on objectives.   1   2   3   4   5
2. **Process:** Using well-defined procedures for making decisions, solving problems, and accomplishing work assignments.
   - My team has well-defined procedures and uses them consistently.   1   2   3   4   5
   - Meetings start on time and are worthwhile.   1   2   3   4   5
   - I have an adequate budget (or ability to spend if needed).   1   2   3   4   5
3. **Communication:** Expressing oneself openly, honestly, and clearly with others.
   - My team's members always express themselves openly, honestly, and clearly.   1   2   3   4   5
   - We resolve conflicts in a healthy manner.   1   2   3   4   5
   - The team environment is positive, candid, and relaxed.   1   2   3   4   5
   - We encourage new ideas.   1   2   3   4   5
   - We make decisions timely with enough discussion and consensus.   1   2   3   4   5
4. **Involvement:** Using individual skills and talents to help the team succeed.
   - My team's members actively volunteer skills and ideas.   1   2   3   4   5
   - I am enthusiastic about this project.   1   2   3   4   5
   - I have adequate time to spend on the project.   1   2   3   4   5
   - I have adequate skills to complete this project.   1   2   3   4   5
   - I have sufficient authority to complete this project.   1   2   3   4   5
   - We have the right people involved.   1   2   3   4   5
   - The team is enthusiastic about the project.   1   2   3   4   5
   - I am able to get assistance from the right people when I need it.   1   2   3   4   5
   - Roles and responsibilities are clear.   1   2   3   4   5
5. **Commitment:** Willingness to accept responsibilities and perform them in a timely manner.
   - My team's members always fulfill their responsibilities.   1   2   3   4   5
   - I fully support the team's stated goals and direction.   1   2   3   4   5

6. **Trust:** Confidently relying on others to fulfill their
   individual responsibilities toward the team.
   - My team's members confidently rely on one
     another.   1 2 3 4 5
   - We have respect for one another.   1 2 3 4 5

Comments:
Issues, or things that are not going so well:

Things that are going well:

───────────────────────────▲───────────────────────────

Stress that it is the responsibility of all team members to help the team improve in areas in which they feel the team is weak. Often, team participants will blame the leader for a less-than-perfect environment rather than taking action themselves to improve the team. One company developed actions to take for each area of team improvement as shown in Exhibit 8.11.

───────────────────────────▼───────────────────────────

Exhibit 8.11   Team Improvement Areas

If the team needs improvement in purpose:

- Write a charter or mission statement. Keep it and the goals posted in a common team area.
- Relate short-term goals to your company's mission and long-term goals.
- Ensure that each team member has a clear and meaningful role.
- Revise roles and short-term goals as projects or tasks change.
- Question assignments that do not contribute to the long-term goals.
- Write clear and concise goals that everyone agrees with.

If the team needs improvement in process:

- Establish procedures for solving conflicts.
- Establish a set of steps for solving problems or carrying out new ideas.
- Provide training in problem-solving methodologies.
- Follow agendas during all meetings and publish minutes with action items.
- Use flip charts, blackboards, and schedules in meetings. Come prepared with copies of information for all members.
- Make procedural suggestions.
- Listen and respond with empathy.

When the team needs improvement in communication:

- Listen and respond with empathy.
- Maintain or enhance self-esteem.
- Explore ideas instead of judging them.
- Avoid jumping from topic to topic in discussions or meetings.
- Share information with everyone.
- Include all team members in decisions, updates, and problem solving.

When the team needs development in involvement:

- Encourage quiet team members to contribute.
- Ask for help and encourage involvement.
- Distribute action items evenly.
- Let everyone have a say before making a decision.
- Encourage and build on others' ideas and initiatives.
- Recognize others' ideas.
- Share information; avoid holding back facts and materials.

When the team needs development in commitment:

- Ask for help in solving problems.
- Respect others' ideas.
- Use others' unique, individual talents.
- Encourage the involvement of all team members.
- Meet deadlines and live up to agreements.
- Attend all scheduled meetings and events.
- Focus on team goals.
- Attend and start meetings on time.

When the team needs development in trust:

- Maintain each other's self-esteem.
- Support and praise each other.
- Keep sensitive information confidential.
- Stand up for each other.
- Avoid gossip or unfair criticism of others.
- Get the facts; do not deal with opinions.
- Appreciate each other's skills and differences.

▲

With the process utilized and information gathered and communicated throughout the planning effort, the recommendation now has the support of the entire organization. Congratulations! You have all the groundwork completed for a successful project implementation. You can now move on to the enjoyable task of implementing your new strategic direction.

Measuring

You cannot improve what you do not measure. Be sure to measure the progress toward the IS strategic plan. As part of the planning process, key metrics and a balanced scorecard were identified to measure the progress of IS. Metrics were selected that tied into the IS vision, mission, goals, and strategies, and the metrics were determined to be meaningful to the business. Report these metrics on a regular basis. Make the metric visible to business management as well as the IS organization.

Conclusion

During the subsequent years, go back and update or revise the IS strategic plan. Particularly if there are major business changes, redo portions of the plan. Long-range planning in today's fast-changing technology industry is at most a three-year window. Strategies for the IS organization to help business units meet or exceed their information management and sharing requirements need to be reviewed and redirected on a regular basis. Make annual updates to the plan. This allows the opportunity to make timely changes to technology and business process strategies and direction. An iterative strategic planning framework allows for flexibility and practicality in strategy formation, funding planning, resource allocation, and execution. Figure 8.3 shows the concept of continuous review and planning of strategies, funding, resource allocations, and execution.

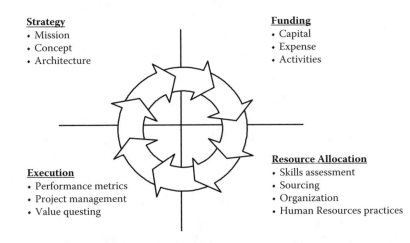

Strategy
• Mission
• Concept
• Architecture

Funding
• Capital
• Expense
• Activities

Execution
• Performance metrics
• Project management
• Value questing

Resource Allocation
• Skills assessment
• Sourcing
• Organization
• Human Resources practices

Figure 8.3   Iterative strategic planning framework

358 ■ *A Practical Guide to Information Systems Strategic Planning*

Although you do need to modify the plan with technology or business changes, you must also be careful to not change the direction too frequently. Once a strategy is stated and a plan is outlined, it is important to stick to the plan and not revise it constantly or unnecessarily. A strategy or plan is a long-term direction and must tolerate occasional losses in addition to the wins. Stay the course to solidify the direction and prove its success. The purpose of a strategy or plan is to determine how to do things over a period of time in the face of much change. With the process completed, you have a solid plan supported by the entire organization. It will be able to stand the test of time and prove to be a success. You have laid the framework and foundation to utilize technology for a competitive advantage in the market.

I would love to hear about your strategic planning successes and challenges. Feel free to e-mail me at acassidy@strategiccomputing.com!

We cannot solve our problems with the same thinking we used when we created them.

— Albert Einstein

Notes for My IS Strategic Planning Project

Index